UNDERAGE DRINKING

RESEARCH AND RECOMMENDATIONS

ALCOHOL AND DRUG ABUSE

Additional books in this series can be found on Nova's website under the Series tab.

Additional e-books in this series can be found on Nova's website under the eBooks tab.

CHILDREN'S ISSUES, LAWS AND PROGRAMS

Additional books in this series can be found on Nova's website under the Series tab.

Additional e-books in this series can be found on Nova's website under the eBooks tab.

ALCOHOL AND DRUG ABUSE

UNDERAGE DRINKING

RESEARCH AND RECOMMENDATIONS

ROGER D. HURLEY

snova
New York

Library of Congress Cataloging-in-Publication Data

ISBN: 978-1-53613-636-4

Published by Nova Science Publishers, Inc. † New York

CONTENTS

PREFACE*

This book was reprinted from a public document and records from the US Government. It is a collection of hearings that took place in Washington DC by the Committee on Education and the Workforce, U.S. House of Representatives on September 30th 2003.

This book examines how drinking in youth affects short and long-term thinking and memory skills as well as causes problems such as unwanted sex, health consequences such as accidents, injuries, or overdoses. This book also discusses the withdrawal effects, gender differences and the implications of drinking, such as altered brain development, and the higher likelihood of alcohol problems as an adult. It also explores the co-dependency that many teenage drinkers have with marijuana and provides suggestions on how to reduce the number of underage, teenage drinkers.

* This is an edited, reformatted and augmented version of a hearing on "Underage Drinking: Research and Recommendations," before the Subcommittee on Substance Abuse and Mental Health Services 108th Congress, first session, dated September 30, 2003.

Chapter 1

STATEMENTS

TUESDAY, SEPTEMBER 30, 2003

U.S. Senate, Subcommittee on Substance Abuse and Mental Health Services, of the Committee on Health, Education, Labor, and Pensions, Washington, DC.

The subcommittee met, pursuant to notice, at 10:12 a.m., in room SD-430, Dirksen Senate Office Building, Senator DeWine presiding.

Present: Senators DeWine and Dodd.

OPENING STATEMENT OF SENATOR DEWINE

Senator DeWine. Let me welcome all of you to the second hearing of the Subcommittee on Substance Abuse and Mental Health Services. I want to apologize for getting started a little late. As you know, the Senate was voting and we can't control the votes around here, at least I can't control the votes.

We are here today to discuss a very serious issue affecting the health and well-being of our Nation's young people, an issue that really has been ignored I think for too long, an issue that kills thousands of American teenagers. We are here today to talk about underage drinking and the devastating impact it is having on this country's young people.

We all know that underage drinking is a significant problem for youth in this country. We have really known this for as long time. We have known that underage drinking often contributes to the four leading causes of death among 15 to 20 year olds, that 69 percent of our young people who died in alcohol-related traffic fatalities in the year 2000 involved young drinking drivers; that in 1999, nearly 40 percent of people under age 21 who were victims of drownings, burns and falls tested positive for alcohol.

We have known that alcohol has been reported to be involved in 36 percent of homicides, 12 percent of male suicides, and eight percent of female suicides involving people under the age of 21. And we know that underage drinking accounts for 6V2 times more deaths among young people than illicit drug use. Let me repeat that: we know that underage drinking accounts for 6V2 times more deaths among young people than illicit drug use.

It should be of little surprise that the 2002 National Survey on Drug Use and Health, administered by the Substance Abuse and Mental Health Administration, found that 10.7 million young people, age 12 to 20, reported drinking alcohol within a 30-day period. Of these, over 7 million were binge drinkers, binge drinkers defined as those having five or more drinks on the same occasion at least once in the past 30 days. Furthermore, about three in ten of our Nation's high school seniors are not only drinking alcohol, but also are doing so to extreme excess. In fact, nearly one-third of 12th graders reported binge drinking.

How did we get where we are today? How did our Nation reach this point, a point where today 12 percent of eighth graders, 12 and 13 year olds, binge drink? Yes, 12 and 13 year olds.

Add to that the 22 percent of tenth graders, 14 and 15 year olds, who binge drink. These statistics are frightening. Too many American kids are drinking regularly, and they are drinking in quantities that can be of great harm to them and to society.

Another study reinforces this concern. Monitoring the Future, 1975-2002, conducted by the National Institute of Drug Abuse, found that experience with alcohol is "almost universal" among secondary school and college students, in spite of the fact that it is illegal for almost all of them to buy alcohol.

This study found that 47 percent of 8th graders, 67 percent of 10th graders, 78 percent of 12th graders, and 86 percent of college students have tried alcohol. The National Institute of Drug Abuse also reported that 95 percent of 12th graders perceive alcohol as readily available to them.

Again we ask, how did we get here? As a Nation, we clearly haven't done enough to address this problem. We haven't done enough to acknowledge how prevalent and widespread teenage drinking is in this country. We haven't done enough to admit that it is a problem with very real and very devastating consequences. We haven't done enough to help teach America's children about the dangers of underage drinking.

We talk about drugs and the dangers of drug use, as well we should. But the reality is that we, as a society, have become complacent about the problem of underage drinking. This simply has to change. Our culture has to change. What we tolerate has to change. What we accept has to change.

In reaction to the binge drinking and drug use problem on college campuses in particular, I have worked with my friend and colleague from Connecticut, Senator Lieberman, to write a bill that would provide grants to States to create or enhance collaborations with universities, campus communities, local businesses and nonprofit organizations to change the culture of abuse and underage use of alcohol that pervades so many of our Nation's colleges and universities. This would be an important step toward reducing underage drinking on our college campuses, but as these statistics have clearly shown, we need to do more and we need to do it as quickly as possible.

Kids are beginning to drink earlier and earlier, at younger and younger ages, and they are doing so in ways that could negatively affect their bodies, their minds, and certainly their futures.

Our hearing today will include an examination of the recently released study by the National Academy of Sciences. That study is entitled,

"Reducing Underage Drinking: A Collective Responsibility." We will examine this study and its recommendations. The purpose of this study was to develop cost-effective strategies for reducing and preventing underage drinking, as directed by Congress in the fiscal year 2002 Labor-HHS Appropriations bill.

In this report, we find 10 main areas of recommendations. Arguably, the most controversial of these recommendations is to raise the State and Federal excise tax on alcohol. I must say that that recommendation is not within the jurisdiction of this subcommittee and, therefore, I do not expect that we will spend a whole lot of time on this recommendation, at least today.

Instead, I would like to focus our time today on other recommendations contained in the report, such as the creation of an adult-oriented media campaign, improved limits on access to alcohol for potential underage drinkers, community interventions to prevent underage drinking, and the role of media and entertainment in fostering underage drinking.

Before we continue, I want to thank my friend and colleague from Connecticut, Senator Chris Dodd, for his dedication to combating the problem of underage drinking. He certainly is a tireless fighter for America's children and our young people. He cares about children. He cares about their well-being.

I am privileged, I must say, to have worked with Chris on many, many issues involving our young people, with the many pieces of legislation that we have worked together on to protect children and to promote their health and their welfare. I know that combating teenage drinking has been and continues to be very important to Senator Dodd, and I thank him for his interest in this area and for being with us today.

I would like to thank our guests at this time. First let me introduce Dr. Richard Bonnie from the University of Virginia School of Law. Dr. Bonnie is the chairman of the Institute of Medicine committee that created the NAS report and he has a wealth of expertise in the fields of mental health and drug law, public health law, and bioethics. He served as a member of the National Advisory Council on Drug Abuse from 1975 to 1980, and was elected to the Institute of Medicine in 1991.

Dr. Bonnie has previously chaired IOM committees on injury prevention and control, opportunities in dug abuse research, and has served as vice-chair of the IOM Committee on Preventing Nicotine Dependence in Youths and Children.

Second, let me introduce Patricia Kempthorne, the First Lady of Idaho. Mrs. Kempthorne has been tireless in the fight against underage drinking. She joins 33 other governor's spouses as a member of the Leadership to Keep Children Alcohol Free, a coalition of Federal agencies and public and private organizations dedicated to helping prevent alcohol use in children from the ages of 9 to 15. This is the only national effort to focus on this specific age group.

Third, let me introduce Mr. Jeffrey Becker, President of the Beer Institute. Mr. Becker was appointed President of the Beer Institute in 1999. He currently serves on the Board of Directors of the National Commission against Drunk Driving and the Techniques of Effective Alcohol Management Coalition. Before joining the Beer Institute, he was the National Director of the Techniques of Alcohol Management for the National Licensed Beverage Association.

Let me introduce also Wendy Hamilton, National President of Mothers against Drunk Driving. She began her career in activism after three separate drunk driving crashes occurred within her own family. In 1984, after having suffered through the death of her sister and 22 month old nephew at the hands of a drunk driver, she joined the local Indiana MADD chapter. In 1995, she joined the MADD National Board of Directors, where she served as a national vice president of victim issues, and then as national vice president of field issues.

Let me at this point invite Senator Dodd to introduce his witness.

Senator Dodd. Thank you very much, Mr. Chairman. We are pleased to have David DeAngelis with us from North Haven, CT, who has been a wonderful young advocate against teenage drinking. David, we're truly honored to have you here from North Haven as a representative of the younger people on the panel. I am delighted to have David with us and truly honored to have the entire panel.

I would ask to make opening comments at the appropriate time.

Senator DeWine. Good.

As you all have seen, we are also honored, in addition to Mrs. Kempthorne, to have other distinguished guests in the front row. Let me introduce them.

First is Mrs. Bush, the First Lady of Florida, who is with us today. In addition to Mrs. Bush, we have Vicky Cayetano, the past First Lady of Hawaii; Theresa Racicot, the past First Lady of Montana is here; Sherri Geringer, past First Lady of Wyoming; Mary Herman, past First Lady of Maine; Sharon Kitzhaber, former First Lady of Oregon; Michele Ridge, past First Lady of Pennsylvania; Martha Sundquist, past First Lady of Tennessee; and Sue Ann Thompson, past First Lady of Wisconsin. We welcome all of you and thank you very much for being here.

Senator Dodd. That's a potent group. [Laughter.]

Senator DeWine. It is a very potent group. We are delighted to have all of you. It is so impressive that each one of you would take your very, very valuable time to join us here today. If the panel gets stumped, we will turn to you and bring you up here for the tough questions, because I know you have all dealt with a lot of tough issues in your States. So if Senator Dodd or I get stumped, we will just turn to you, right, Chris?

Senator Dodd. Thank you, Mike. Absolutely.

Senator DeWine. Let me now turn to my colleague, Senator Dodd, for his opening statement.

Opening Statement of Senator Dodd

Senator Dodd. Thank you very much, Mr. Chairman.

I think you should know, Mr. Chairman, that David is missing a cross-country track meet today to be here with us.

Senator DeWine. He looks like a cross-country track star. [Laughter.]

Senator Dodd. Thank you very much, Mr. Chairman, for holding this hearing and for allowing me to come by. I'm not the ranking member of this subcommittee—Senator Kennedy is—but he very graciously allowed me to come in his place.

As Senator DeWine has already indicated, he and I have worked on numerous issues involving children. Having chaired the Subcommittee on Children and Families for many years and having been the ranking Democrat on the committee, working with Mike DeWine has been truly a pleasure on so many issues. I won't belabor the point here, but there have been numerous bills that have become law that Mike and I worked on together and it's truly an honor, a privilege and a pleasure to be with him again today on this subject matter, which is so vitally important.

Let me thank as well the First Ladies, former and present, for being here from your various States. It is tremendously important that you lend your support to this effort because so much of it needs to be done at the local and State level. I think the Federal Government can play a very important role, a cooperative role here, but ultimately, as we have all learned over the years, it's what happens on the ground locally that makes the difference.

Mrs. Kempthorne, it's a pleasure to have you here. We miss Dirk as a great pal and friend, so it's a pleasure to have you on the panel with us this morning.

Let me share a few opening thoughts, if I can, Mr. Chairman, and then we'll get to our panel of witnesses.

As I pointed out, today the subcommittee is examining the significant problems caused by the consumption of alcohol by our Nation's young people. The word "staggering" doesn't really do it justice, but the numbers are staggering in my view of what is going on across the country with is problem.

Alcohol is the most commonly used drug—and I'm preaching to the choir here; many of you here know this already—is the most commonly used drug among America's youth. More young people drink alcohol than smoke tobacco or use marijuana. In 1996, which is the last year we have any reliable numbers on in this area— which also tells you something about the problem, where we have to go back almost 7 years to get some decent national numbers— in 1996 underage drinking caused around 3,500 deaths, more than 2 million injuries, 1,200 infants were born with fetal alcohol syndrome, and more than 50,000 youths were treated for alcohol dependency. That was 7 years ago.

In 2002, 20 percent of 8th graders had drunk alcohol in the previous 30 days. Forty-nine percent of high school seniors are drinkers, and 29 percent report having had five or more drinks in a row in the past 2 weeks. The numbers, as I said at the outset, are staggering.

Earlier this month, the Institute of Medicine released a comprehensive study, "Reducing Underage Drinking: A Collective Responsibility," that many of our witnesses this morning will reference in their comments. The important report laid out the national problems presented by the consumption of alcohol by young people and established a multitiered national strategy to reduce the great toll caused by underage drinking. The IOM report estimates that the social costs associated with underage drinking are close to $53 billion annually, including $19 billion from automobile accidents and $29 billion from associated violent crime. Some people aren't impressed with the numbers of the cost, and those numbers ought to get people's attention.

While no one can argue with the tragic loss of life and the significant financial costs associated with underage drinking, too few of us think of the equally devastating loss of potential that occurs when our children begin to drink. Research indicates that children who begin drinking do so at only 12 years of age. We also know that children that begin drinking at such an early age develop a pre-disposition for alcohol dependence later in life.

Such early experimentation can have devastating consequences and derail a child's potential just as he or she is starting out on the path to adulthood. The consumption of alcohol by our children can literally rob them of their future.

As the IOM report makes perfectly clear, the problems presented by underage drinking are wide-reaching. Mr. Chairman, similarly, our responses to underage drinking must be equally far-reaching, in my view. I think that all of us here this morning would agree that the battle against underage drinking begins first and foremost with parents and their children.

However, as the IOM report makes perfectly clear, parental involvement makes up only one part of a needed national strategy to combat underage drinking. In fact, the IOM calls for "a deep shared commitment" among broad institutions and constituencies to combat underage drinking; restraint in the advertising of alcohol; a national media campaign to encourage adult involvement in efforts to prevent underage drinking; vigilance in preventing the sale of alcohol to minors; and most controversial, high excise taxes on alcohol.

While I believe that all of these suggestions have tremendous merit, I am most convinced that the effort to prevent underage drinking requires a greatly strengthened Federal commitment, as Government spending to prevent underage drinking pales in comparison to that devoted to drug and tobacco prevention efforts. I don't underestimate the importance of our commitment in those areas, but when you compare the numbers and compare the cost of life and the devastation that occurs, then I think people may get the point here. In fact, the Federal Government spent $1.8 billion in the year 2000 to discourage illegal drug use, and only $71 million to discourage youth drinking. Clearly, there needs to be a greater sense of balance considering the loss of life and the problems associated here.

So it is with great hope, Mr. Chairman, that I attend this morning's hearing with your leadership and your commitment to this issue. The toll that underage drinking extracts from our Nation each and every year is a terrible one, a toll far too great to continue or one to be ignored.

It is my hope that the discussion we have this morning will provide us with a starting point from where we, as policy makers, can make a difference. Public health advocates and representatives from the industry can begin with us to outline a national strategy to save our Nation's youth from the dangers of underage drinking.

I want to thank all of our witnesses today, as well as you did, Mr. Chairman, for being here to share their testimony with us. I look forward to hearing from them.

Senator DeWine. Senator Dodd, thank you very much.

Dr. Bonnie, why don't we start with you. What we will do is have a five-minute rule, if you could just kind of summarize your testimony. We have the written testimony from all of you. If you can summarize your testimony in five minutes, that will give us plenty of time to have questions.

STATEMENTS OF RICHARD J. BONNIE, DIRECTOR, UNIVERSITY OF VIRGINIA INSTITUTE OF LAW, PSYCHOLOGY AND PUBLIC POLICY; PATRICIA KEMPTHORNE, FIRST LADY OF IDAHO; JEFF G. BECKER, PRESIDENT, BEER INSTITUTE; WENDY J. HAMILTON, NATIONAL PRESIDENT, MOTHERS AGAINST DRUNK DRIVING; AND DAVID DEANGELIS, STUDENT, NORTH HAVEN HIGH SCHOOL, NORTH HAVEN, CT

Mr. Bonnie. Thank you, Mr. Chairman, and Senator Dodd.

As you mentioned, my name is Richard Bonnie and I'm the John Battle professor of law and Director of the Institute of Law, Psychiatry, and Public Policy at the University of Virginia. I did serve as chair of the Committee on Developing a Strategy to Reduce and Prevent Underage Drinking.

As the chair mentioned, the study was conducted at the request of the Congress, and we did conduct an intensive study that involved many components and many efforts to gather information.

The starting point for our report I want to emphasize is the current national policy that sets 21 as the minimum drinking age.

Alcohol use by young people is an endemic problem that is not likely to improve, in the committee's judgment, in the absence of significant new interventions. As Senator Dodd mentioned, many more of the Nation's youth drink than smoke cigarettes or use other drugs, and young people tend to drink more heavily than adults, exacerbating the dangers to themselves and to people around them.

As noted both by Senator DeWine and Senator Dodd, the prevalence, frequency and intensity of underage drinking is disturbingly high, and I won't go over the numbers that each of you has mentioned. The social cost of underage drinking is enormous and far exceeds the social cost of illegal drug use and other problem behaviors.

Now, although the public is generally aware of the problems associated with underage drinking, the Nation's social response has not been commensurate with the magnitude and seriousness of this problem. The disparity is evident not only in the fact, as Senator Dodd mentioned, that the Federal Government spends 25 times more on the prevention of illicit drug use by young people than on the prevention of underage drinking, but also in the lack of sustained and comprehensive grassroots efforts to address the problem in most communities.

Some people think that the key to reducing underage drinking lies in finding just the right messages to send to young people to instill negative beliefs and attitudes toward alcohol use. Others tend to focus on changing the marketing practices of the alcohol industry in order to reduce young people's exposure to messages designed to promote drinking. However, in the committee's view, the problem is much more complicated than either of these positions would suggest because alcohol use is deeply embedded in the economic and cultural fabric of life in the United States. Annual revenues of the alcohol industry amount to $116 billion.

The challenge then is how to reduce underage drinking in a context where adult drinking is widespread and commonly accepted and where billions of gallons of alcohol are in the stream of commerce. We believe that this will require a broad, multifaceted effort.

The primary goal of the recommended strategy is to create and sustain a broad and strong societal commitment to reduce underage drinking. All of us, acting in concert, including parents and other adults, alcohol producers, wholesalers and retail outlets, the entertainment media and community groups must take the necessary steps to reduce the availability of alcohol to underage drinkers, to reduce the attractiveness of alcohol to young people, and to reduce opportunities for youthful drinking. Underage drinking prevention is everybody's business.

The report emphasizes that adults must be the primary targets of this national campaign to reduce underage drinking. Most adults express concern about underage drinking and voice support for public policies to curb it. Yet, behind this concern lies a paradox. Youth often get their alcohol from adults, and many parents downplay the extent of the problem, or are unaware of their own kids drinking habits. Thirty percent of parents whose kids reported drinking heavily within the last 30 days think their kids do not at all.

The sad truth is that many adults facilitate and condone underage drinking. We need to change the behavior of well-meaning adults in communities all over the Nation, including people who are holding drinking parties for their kids in their homes, in violation of the law, thinking that they are doing the right thing.

As the centerpiece of the committee's adult-oriented strategy, our report calls on the Federal Government to fund and actively support the development of a national media campaign designed to create a broad societal commitment to reduce underage drinking, to decrease adult conduct that tends to facilitate underage drinking, and to encourage parents and other adults to take specific steps in their own households, neighborhoods and businesses to discourage underage drinking.

The comprehensive strategy we suggest also includes a multipronged plan for boosting compliance with the laws that prohibit selling or providing alcohol to young people under the legal drinking age of 21. Efforts to increase compliance need to focus both on retail outlets and on the social channels through which underage drinkers obtain their alcohol.

The committee also supports specific interventions and education programs that are aimed at young people, as long as these programs have been evaluated and found to be effective. That goes for publicly-supported programs as well as privately-supported ones.

Community leaders need to mobilize the energy, resources and attention of local organizations and businesses to develop and implement programs for preventing and reducing underage drinking. These efforts should be tailored to specific circumstances of the problem in their communities. The Federal Government, as well as public and private organizations, should encourage and help pay for relevant community initiatives that have been shown to work.

The alcohol industry also has a vitally important role to play in the strategy we have proposed. The committee acknowledges to industry's declared commitment to the goal of reducing underage drinking and its willingness to be part of the solution. We believe there is much common ground, and that opportunities for cooperation are now being overlooked.

Specifically, we urge the alcohol industry to join with public and private entities to create and fund an independent, nonprofit foundation that focuses solely on designing, evaluating, and implementing evidence-based programs for preventing and reducing underage drinking. Although the industry currently invests in programs that were set up with this goal, the results of these programs have rarely been scientifically evaluated, and the overall level of industry investment is modest in relation to the revenues that are generated by the underage market. We think it is reasonable to expect the industry to do more than it is now doing, and to join with others to form a genuine national partnership to reduce underage drinking.

We also urge greater self-restraint in alcohol advertising. We recognize, of course, that advertising is a particularly sensitive issue and that the industry has recently taken important steps forward.

The FTC recently announced that the beer and distilled spirits trade associations have joined the wine industry to increase the threshold to 70 percent for the minimum proportion of adults in the viewing audience. This is a step in the right direction, but the committee believes that the industry should continue to reduce underage exposure and should refrain from marketing practices that have particular appeal to young people, regardless of whether they are intentionally targeted at young audiences.

Companies and trade associations in the entertainment sector also have a responsibility to join in the collective effort to reduce underage drinking —

Senator DeWine. Could you please wrap it up?

Mr. Bonnie. — and exercise greater restraint in disseminating images and lyrics that promote or glorify alcohol use in venues with significant underage audiences.

The Federal Government should periodically monitor these practices and take a number of other steps that are mentioned in the report, and which I hope we will have a chance to discuss later.

Let me just mention, if I might, Senator, just a couple of points, again about the controversial feature of the recommendations that we made.

To help pay for the proposed public programs and to help reduce underage consumption, Congress and State legislatures should raise excise tax rates on alcohol, especially on beer, which is the alcoholic beverage that young people drink most often. Alcohol is much cheaper today, after adjusting for inflation, than it was 30 or 40 years ago. Fligher tax rates should be tied to the Consumer Price Index to keep pace with inflation. Research indicates that changes in these tax rates can decrease the prevalence and harmful effects of drinking among youths, who tend to have limited discretionary income and are especially sensitive to price.

In summary, we have proposed a comprehensive strategy that, taken as a whole, would foster as deep, unequivocal societal commitment to curtail underage drinking. As a national community, we need to focus our attention on this serious problem and accept a collective responsibility to address it. This is an admittedly difficult challenge, but the committee believes that our country can do more than it is now doing. The Nation needs to develop and implement effective ways to protect young people from the dangers of early drinking while respecting the interests of responsible adult consumers of alcohol. The committee's report attempts to strike the right balance.

Thank you for your interest and the opportunity to testify to the subcommittee.

[The prepared statement of Mr. Bonnie may be found in additional material.]

Senator DeWine. Mrs. Kempthorne. Mrs. Kempthorne. Thank you, Mr. Chairman, Senator Dodd. The Governor does send his best wishes to you, too.

As First Lady of Idaho, I thank you for this invitation to speak here today on behalf of 34 current governor spouses and 11 emeritus members of Leadership to Keep Children Alcohol Free. I would like to acknowledge again myself the commitment shown by our membership by being here today in support of this issue.

We are a nonpartisan group, devoted to increasing public awareness, engaging policy makers, and mobilizing action to stop childhood drinking. Our specific focus is the 9 to 15 year old age group. The Leadership to Keep Children Alcohol Free was established to make childhood drinking prevention a national health priority. We are here today to emphasize for the committee the immediate and far-reaching consequences of childhood drinking and also to offer our recommendations for action.

On a personal note, as an individual, as a parent, as a community encourager, a proponent for the health and well-being of our Nation's children, I would like to thank you and acknowledge the need for your leadership in addressing this issue.

During most of my childhood, my father worked for a distributor of wine and distilled spirits. It was very clear to me at the time that alcohol was not meant for me as a child. Growing up, I learned to respect alcohol as an adult beverage, but also saw some of the effects of the abuse of alcohol. Witnessing the hurt and confusion caused by the abuse of alcohol was instructive in helping me make choices about how much alcohol I consumed. I do not believe that message is clear in our society today.

So while it is unsettling to think that we have to consider elementary students when we think about drinking prevention, we do. The environment surrounding our children often contributes to their attitudes and expectations about alcohol. Making healthy life choices starts earlier than when we were children.

Frightening but true, 29 percent of students report they first drank alcohol—and that's more than a few sips—before the age of 13. By the 8th grade, more than 12 percent of 13 to 14 year olds surveyed reported having had five or more drinks in a row, or binge drinking, within the past 2 weeks. They are drinking with the goal of getting drunk.

Children are our top priority. We expend tremendous energy ensuring that they are vaccinated, use infant car seats, have access to educational opportunities and health care. Yet there is a serious disconnect when it comes to childhood drinking.

Research documents that more than 40 percent of the children who begin drinking before the age of 15 will develop alcohol abuse or dependence at some time in their lives. The adolescent brain is still a work in progress and, therefore, vulnerable. Science tells us that children who engage in heavy drinking before the age of 15 show noticeable changes in the brain, develop fewer learning strategies, and remember less than nondrinkers.

While parents certainly bear responsibility for their own children, families do not live in a vacuum. Our homes are not bunkers from reality. Parental guidance is constantly challenged by external influences. We are not here to place blame, but to address a serious public health issue that is affecting a significant number of our Nation's children. The responsibility for solving this problem rests with all of us, including individuals, communities, policy makers and the industry.

The National Academies of Science and the Institute of Medicine have identified opportunities for all of us to play a role in tackling the problem of childhood drinking. We are all stakeholders in the future of our Nation's children. We need to be motivated by what is in the best interests of our children. Cooperation and coalitions, not confrontations, will move us forward in our common interests of making sure the children of this Nation are healthy.

On behalf of the Leadership to Keep Children Alcohol Free, and speaking as a parent, I would respectfully offer four recommendations for action:

First, please do not let this be the only hearing on this critical public health issue. Let this ignite a series of hearings leading to significant deliberations and proposals.

Second, we request that the subcommittee ask the Surgeon General to issue an independent "Call to Action on Childhood Drinking."

Third, we request that national surveys begin collect data on alcohol use and attitudes, including brands, that include children as young as age 9.

Finally, since alcohol is the number one illegal drug when used by our youth, we urge the subcommittee to support increased funding for research, prevention and treatment. It is time to increase the Nation's investment on this issue and to bring it in line with what is spent on illicit drugs and tobacco.

Each of us can make a difference to ensure that our children have a strong foundation for life. Please recognize this is a serious problem. Our children are drinking alcohol at a younger and younger age, and that should be a concern for all of us.

Thank you very much.

[The prepared statement of Mrs. Kempthorne may be found in additional material.]

Senator DeWine. Mr. Becker.

Mr. Becker. Good morning, Mr. Chairman, and Senator Dodd. My name is Jeff Becker and I'm the President of the Beer Institute, the national trade association of America's brewers. I am pleased to be here to represent the almost 900,000 men and women employed by our industry.

Our industry has a long and proud tradition of giving back to the communities where we live and do business, and we share the commitment of the members of this subcommittee in addressing illegal underage drinking.

To that point, I want to specifically acknowledge the important role of community-based beer wholesalers. Beer wholesalers play a critical role by giving back to their communities through charitable contributions, implementing responsibility programs, and importantly, as employers. We share the same concern that all parents do about the safety of our children because we are parents, too. We do not want the business of young people below the legal purchase age.

Let me first address the facts on underage drinking. According to a recent study by the Department of Health and Human Services, 82 percent of today's adolescents do not drink. Other recent Government studies show that teen drinking has been on the decline. The Department of

Transportation reports a one-third reduction in fatalities among drivers 16 to 20 between 1990 and today.

While many factors explain this success, a critical reason is greater parental involvement. Brewers have long advocated and sponsored programs to help parents prevent underage drinking among teens and college-bound youth. By acknowledging the important decisions involved with underage drinking and encouraging their children to respect themselves and the law, parents have made an enormous difference.

To help parents, we have distributed free of charge more than five million copies of materials in five different languages, with useful information to explain why drinking is inappropriate for youth.

As stated in the Federal Trade Commission report earlier this month, retailers also play a vital role in stopping underage drinking by following their State laws and checking and verifying IDs. Brewers have helped here, too. Our members have sponsored seller and server training programs for over two decades. We have provided materials in English, Spanish, Korean and Vietnamese to teach retailers how to properly check and spot fake IDs.

In addition, brewers have sponsored programs on college campuses and have supported research and programs, collectively known as "social norms." These programs are a positive approach that reminds college students that the large majority of their peers make healthy and responsible decisions about drinking.

Since our industry's advertising activities have recently been the subject of congressional interest, I would like to briefly touch on some other developments that underscore brewers' commitment to marking and selling our products to adults.

Over the last 6 years, the Federal Trade Commission has conducted four comprehensive reviews of our industry's advertising practices. The 2003 FTC report unequivocally stated that beer industry members do not target youth. The FTC report also discussed a number of changes in our industry advertising code which was first adopted in 1943. The code has served as the foundation for our long history of responsible and vigorous self-regulation of advertising and marketing practices. In fact, we recently changed our code of advertising to incorporate some of the best practices of our member companies and to address several FTC recommendations.

I am pleased to inform you that our members have revised the standard for advertising placements in television, radio and magazines. The revised code now requires placement where the proportion of audience age 21 and older is expected to be 70 percent or higher, which reflects the percentage of adults in the U.S. population.

We do have some fundamental differences with the National Academy's recommendations and the process used to develop them. We believe the key to further progress in reducing underage drinking lies in family and community-based efforts. We are disappointed that the National Academy's panel ignored the clear direction of Congress to evaluate existing Federal, State, and nongovernmental programs. Unfortunately, the panel focused heavily on costly and experimental government solutions. The report does not provide the kind of guidance Congress sought to determine policy and funding priorities to further reduce illegal underage access and consumption.

The Academy did recommend to increase excise taxes, and even though that is not part of the discussion today, it should come as no surprise that the beer industry opposes such a measure. We oppose higher taxes because they are not an effective deterrent to underage drinking. The National Institute on Alcohol Abuse and Alcoholism's special report to Congress showed that their research indicates that teens are not affected by higher taxes. It also exposes methodological flaws in the research that the Academies use to support their recommendation.

In closing, I would first like to leave you with this fact. Brewers fully recognize that underage drinking is a problem that our society must tackle. We want to be a meaningful part of the solution to this issue, and by focusing our collective resources on proven, targeted and effective approaches, we can make a difference.

As a father of two children, I share the committee's concern just like every other parent out there, and I very much appreciate the opportunity to be with you today to discuss these important issues.

Thank you.

[The prepared statement of Mr. Becker may be found in additional material.]

Senator DeWine. Mrs. Hamilton.

Mrs. Hamilton. Thank you, Senator.

My name is Wendy Hamilton, National President of Mothers Against Drunk Driving. I am delighted to be here today to discuss this important issue.

MADD's mission is to stop drunk driving, support the victims of this violent crime, and prevent underage drinking. I would like to thank Chairman DeWine and Senator Dodd for holding this hearing and for their commitment to protecting America's youth. MADD looks forward to working with this committee, the Congress, and with prevention partners like the Centers for Science in the Public Interest, the Center for Alcohol Marketing and Youth, and the American Medical Association to save lives.

There are 10.1 million underage drinkers in this Nation. The proportion of high school seniors who drink and binge drink has not changed since 1993. There has been no progress in the last decade to reduce underage drinking.

A collective memory that we all share are images from a recent touch football game between suburban Chicago high school girls that turned into a brutal hazing incident, resulting in the hospitalization of five students. Younger girls were beaten and splattered with mud, paint and feces while 100 students and adult onlookers cheered while waving cups of beer. Sixteen and 17 year old girls were held upside down over a keg of beer while drinking from the tap. School officials cited alcohol as a major factor in the violence and police charged two parents with providing three kegs of beer to minors.

That incident could have occurred in almost any town in America. Today, teens have easy access to alcohol. Underage drinking laws are not well enforced, and parents and communities often look the other way, in many cases even providing the beer.

There is no such thing as responsible underage drinking. Young drivers make up seven percent of the driving population, yet constitute 13 percent of alcohol-involved drivers in fatal crashes. In the past year, youth drove

11 million times after drinking, and 40 percent of those who drove after drinking had passengers. Young drivers are putting themselves and others at risk.

Nearly 40 percent of youth under age 21 who died from drowning, burns and fatal falls tested positive for alcohol. Youth alcohol use is associated with violence and suicidal behavior. In addition to the human costs, this economic cost to society is staggering. Conservatively, underage drinking costs this Nation $53 billion each year. The NAS report provides a monumental opportunity to stem the Nation's number one youth drug problem, and my testimony will focus on areas that MADD believes will have the greatest impact on reducing youth alcohol use.

In 2000, this Nation spent $1.8 billion on preventing illicit drug use, which was 25 times the amount targeted at preventing underage alcohol use. The GAO found that seven percent of total funds available for alcohol and other drug use prevention had a specific focus on alcohol and targeted youth. NAS concludes that the multitude of agencies and initiatives involved suggest the need for an interagency body to provide national leadership and provide a single Federal voice on the issue of underage drinking.

Recommendations 12-1 through 12-6 demonstrate a clear need for better Government assistance and coordination, beginning with a Federal interagency coordinating committee, chaired by the Secretary of HHS. All of these recommendations included in my written testimony should be implemented by Congress.

Despite the fact that alcohol is the number one youth drug problem, underage drinking prevention messages are excluded from the ONDCP anti-drug media campaign. MADD strongly supports NAS Recommendation 6-1. The Federal Government should fund and actively support the development of an adult-focused national media campaign to reduce underage drinking.

Many adults do not recognize the prevalence of or the risks associated with underage drinking, and many adults even facilitate kids drinking by providing access to alcohol by not responding to their kids drinking and by not adequately monitoring young people's behavior.

Our youth are bombarded with irresponsible alcohol marketing messages, depicting drinking as cool, sexy, and glamorous. In 2001, the alcohol industry spent $5 billion on measured and unmeasured product advertising and promotion. MADD and the NAS believe stricter standards must be placed on all alcohol advertising to protect our children from constant exposure to alcohol messages.

MADD supports all of the NAS recommendations on alcohol advertising but, in particular, urges action on NAS Recommendations 7-4 and 12-6, as outlined in my written testimony.

Limiting youth access to alcohol is a proven way to decrease underage drinking. Sixty percent of 8th graders and 90 percent of 12th graders report that alcohol is fairly easy to obtain. MADD strongly supports Recommendation 9-3, that the Federal Government should require States to achieve designated rates of retailer compliance with youth access prohibitions as a condition of receiving grant block funding, similar to the Synar amendment's requirements for youth tobacco sales.

NAS also underscores the need for expanding youth and community interventions. MADD strongly supports Recommendation 11-2, which states that Federal funding should be available under a national program dedicated to community-level approaches.

MADD's youth programs are based on the latest scientific research and strive to empower children, teens and parents, with the knowledge to keep themselves and others safe from harm. It is imperative that evidence-based prevention efforts, such as MADD's Youth in Action and Protecting You/Protecting Me programs, as outlined in my written testimony, receive the needed support from the Federal Government.

Finally, research shows that increased beer prices lead to reductions in the levels and frequency of drinking and heavy drinking among youth and lower crash fatality rates among young drivers. MADD strongly supports Recommendation 12-7, which urges Congress and State legislatures to raise excise taxes to reduce underage consumption and raise additional revenues for prevention programs. Top priority should be given to raising beer taxes in particular.

It is time for this Nation to end our complacency about underage drinking and to take action to end this public health epidemic. More youth drink than use other illegal drugs, yet Federal investments to protect and prevent underage drinking pale in comparison with resources targeted at preventing illicit drugs.

MADD stands ready to work with Congress, the public health community and others, to pursue introduction of a comprehensive, science-based legislative package to reduce and prevent underage drinking. I urge this committee to use the NAS report as a road map to create a healthier future for our children.

Thank you.

Senator DeWine. Mrs. Hamilton, thank you very much.

[The prepared statement of Mrs. Hamilton may be found in additional material.]

Senator DeWine. Mr. DeAngelis.

Mr. DeAngelis. Good morning. My name is David DeAngelis and I'm a senior at North Haven High School in North Haven, CT. I would like to thank Senator Dodd, Chairman DeWine, and the subcommittee for inviting me to be here this morning. I am honored to have the opportunity to speak on this issue.

Three summers ago, three classmates and I attended the Connecticut MADD Power Camp. One speaker left a lasting impression on us. A drunk driver killed her teenage daughter and she felt compelled to speak to young people about the perils of drinking and driving. But the task grew increasingly difficult. On the way to our group, she prayed to her daughter for a sign to help her continue. A car passed. The license plate read "SAVE 1."

The four of us left the camp determined to address the problems of underage drinking in our community and started a newspaper column titled "SAVE 1." We decided to target adults, hoping to enlighten parents and encourage them to help their children make the right choices. After the other three students graduated, I continued to write the articles. I would like to submit some of them for the record.

Although I received positive feedback about the column, I sometimes get frustrated. Last spring, I gave a presentation to parents at my town's middle school and only 30 people showed up. Trying to remain motivated became a challenge.

Senator DeWine. We have that problem sometimes, too, with some of our audiences. [Laughter.] Not Senator Dodd, but I do. [Laughter.]

Mr. DeAngelis. That changed this summer, when I volunteered as a staffer at Power Camp, and I worked with students to develop a project for that town. I left the camp optimistic after watching them rally behind their idea to focus on passing a local ordinance against serving alcohol to minors at house parties.

So today I speak before you on the heels of the release of the NAS report on underage drinking. When I read the report, especially the committee's proposal for a national, adult-oriented media campaign, the words "adult-oriented" jumped out at me. Targeting adults is necessary to effectively address underage drinking. Parents often take on a "kids will be kids" attitude and think that drinking is part of growing up. Actually, young people try to emulate adults whose social life revolves around alcohol. Many parents not only condone the use of alcohol, but also provide liquor to their children and their children's friends.

Last May, a classmate of mine had an after-prom party where alcohol was included. To make sure the guests would be safe, his parents confiscated their car keys. This summer, what started as a few kids hanging out in a basement turned into a full-fledged party as more and more kids showed up with beer. The parents spent the entire evening upstairs, never checking on the group.

Then there are the times when parents are not home. Kids party, drink, and do stupid and dangerous things. One girl hosting a party jumped into her pool fully clothed after getting drunk. Three times. Another classmate celebrated his birthday by drinking at a friend's house and then falling down the stairs.

Underage drinking is not a problem confined to the town of North Haven. It happens everywhere. This past July, I was here in Washington for Boys Nation. Standing in the airport, I met some of the other delegates and casually asked what they like to do for fun. One promptly replied, "Drink" and began recounting stories that involved getting drunk with his friends.

A large number of high school students are affected by underage drinking, including those who have made the decision not to drink. These kids are often ostracized by students in the more popular drinking circles and fight daily pressures to join.

This initiative is extremely important. It will take a national movement to change the apathetic attitudes of parents. Blatant disregard for the drinking age simply cannot be tolerated. The youth of America are receiving the message that underage drinking is acceptable, not to mention the messages they receive from the media.

The alcohol industry spends over $1 billion each year on advertising, portraying drinking as a ticket to good times. Most disturbing is the fact that alcohol companies advertise during TV programs viewed predominantly by teenagers. On the radio, more beer commercials are heard by children than by adults. These ads are clever, entertaining, and humorous. I can still recite a radio commercial for Beck's Beer that I heard almost every day this summer.

When children are not getting bombarded with commercials, they are seeing images promoting drinking in the shows that they watch. Who else is watching MTV at 4:00 o'clock in the afternoon, or at 1:00 o'clock on a Saturday, when shows like Spring Break, Mardi Gras, or Fraternity Life are aired?

Connecticut has the highest rate of underage drinking. The average age that children begin drinking is 11 for boys and 13 for girls. The Connecticut Coalition to Stop Underage Drinking has been at work for the past 7 years addressing these issues, focusing much of its energy on the role of adults. It has also begun work on each of the local recommendations in the NAS report.

But they only scratch the surface of the problem. We, the entire Nation, need the Federal Government's guidance, direction and resources. Underage drinking is a national crisis which is only getting worse. The NAS recommendations are too valuable to ignore.

Thank you.

[The prepared statement of Mr. DeAngelis may be found in additional material.]

Senator DeWine. Very good testimony. Thank you very much, and thank you all.

Mrs. Kempthorne, I was interested in your written testimony where you talked about the European model. You said that is certainly not something we should emulate in the United States. It strikes me how many people that I come across, who kind of casually say, you know, the Europeans have got it right. You know, they sort of introduce their kids to alcohol at 14 or 15 and they don't seem to have the problems that we do in the United States.

Could you comment on that?

Mrs. Kempthorne. I can get you copies of the studies that really show that, when you look at testing in the United States and the European countries, looking at the amount of binge drinking that's being done, the United States is actually lower than most of them. We think that's because they drink as part of the family social life, that they don't binge drink later on. I think you will also find there are many countries out there that have already started similar types of programs, because they're seeing this issue really affecting them.

I know one thing, that in Idaho we had seven Balkan countries come to Idaho to learn about teaching underage drinking prevention from our school system because of the problems they were having just in the Balkan countries. So it's pervasive all over the world. It's definitely a problem. There is not proof that shows that the European perception of what the European social life is actually helping to curtail underage drinking, or actually the problem of alcoholism, which we talked about when they start at that age.

Senator DeWine. In fact, according to your testimony, it's just the opposite.

Mrs. Kempthorne. Absolutely.

Senator DeWine. You talk in your written testimony about the problem with alcoholism, and if I read it correctly, I think you also talked about the long-term damage to those who start drinking earlier than 15.

Mrs. Kempthorne. We know that 40 percent of those who start drinking earlier than 14 will most likely have an alcohol dependence or develop alcohol abuse in their lifetime, and that has been proven, yes.

Senator DeWine. So I guess it's like other forms of addiction, other problems like smoking cigarettes. If you can keep a kid from doing it until they reach a certain age, they're probably okay. You know, the longer you can stop the from starting, the better off we're going to be.

Mrs. Kempthorne. Yes. The research does show that starting to drink at 21 does reduce the possibility of becoming dependent on alcohol, and that's just what they've seen from the studies. It does prove that.

Senator DeWine. Thank you.

Mr. Becker, you heard Dr. Bonnie's comment—and let me read it from his written testimony. I want to get your reaction, if I could.

"Specifically, we urge the alcohol industry to join with private and public entities to create and fund an independent, nonprofit foundation that focuses solely on designing, evaluating, and implementing evidence-based programs for preventing and reducing underage drinking. Although the industry currently invests in programs that were set up with that stated goal, the results of these programs have rarely been scientifically evaluated." I'm putting emphasis on "scientifically," but I think that's the intent.

What would be wrong with doing that? Wouldn't that achieve your stated goal, and wouldn't that also kind of take you guys off the hot seat in the sense of you wouldn't be subject to criticism from someone saying gee, these programs aren't scientifically based, we don't know if they work. You know, you could create a nonprofit that was an independent nonprofit, and you could set it up and it would do exactly what Dr. Bonnie said, and you could adequately fund it. What would be wrong with that?

Mr. Becker. Well, Senator, I guess I would say several things about that. First of all, the industry has been and continues to be involved in a variety of independent organizations that receive both industry and government funding. Two of those you mentioned in your introduction of me—the National Commission Against Drunk Driving and the Techniques for Effective Alcohol Management Program. Those are but two of many other things that the industry is involved with, mostly at the community level.

I think our concern really is about how things are done at the community level. Our concern on national programs tends to be a lack of diversity of thought, that a "one size fits all" approach we know doesn't work in general, that community-based programs that take into account the unique circumstances of either that State or that community tend to be more effective.

We have had long running partnerships with a variety of different organizations. Frankly, there has been an unwillingness on the part of some organizations to even work with our industry. That has been a challenge, particularly over the last 10 years. This industry will work with anyone who is truly interested in solving underage drinking. As I mentioned in my testimony, I am a parent and I live in a community just south of here. I want to see underage drinking resolved as well. But I think there needs to be a little more groundwork done before this industry can commit to that type of a coalition, including, I think, encouraging some organizations to work with our industry.

Senator DeWine. Does anybody want to respond to that? Then I will have a comment. Dr. Bonnie, you're the one who sort of set this up.

Mr. Bonnie. Yes. Well, I'm actually very encouraged by what Mr. Becker just said. I think all of us can see that this tends to be a highly polarized issue and that the industry is concerned about those who take positions that don't seem to allow room for a genuine partnership.

As I said, I think there is a tremendous amount in the report that is very, very consistent with positions that the industry has taken, focusing on enforcing the underage access restrictions, focusing on community coalitions, focusing on effective youth-oriented programs, and concentrating on good parenting and other issues relating to adults. I think most of this report is very, very consistent with positions the industry has taken. There ought to be room for people who have this common agenda to sit around the table and think about how the cause can be furthered. So I appreciate Mr. Becker's response.

Senator DeWine. Let's get right down to it. The reality is that Mr. Becker's industry is never going to support anything that talks about raising taxes on their product. So that's a different issue and we can debate that.

But beyond that, if I listen to him and I listen to you, and listen to Mrs. Hamilton, and I listen to Mrs. Kempthorne and Mr. DeAngelis, or I listen to myself, Senator Dodd or any of us as parents, you know, what in the world do we have to disagree about?

We don't want our kids drinking underage, and we don't want kids getting in a car who have been drinking, and we don't want our kids dying. It seems to me that it shouldn't be this hard. To see this battle go back and forth between the industry—and it is a legal industry, and it's going to stay legal. We sort of resolved that issue when we went through Prohibition. So it is legal and it's going to stay legal.

Now, the question is, we ought to get the industry to spend as much as we can get them to spend on trying to deal with underage drinking, and we ought to move forward here, it seems to me.

Mr. Bonnie. I think so, too. I think it would be a mistake for the disagreement about the tax issues to obscure and impede the numerous opportunities that I think you just identified for collaboration. We can make this an inclusive effort, if we can just

Senator DeWine. It seems to me you sort of do what you do in arbitration, where each side picks a third party and you sort of move on. You're not going to appoint somebody and they appoint somebody. You probably get two people removed and then you end up and get this independent group.

We are not going to settle this today, but it just seems to me that we ought to move beyond this, and these types of squabbles are not very productive and they become for the public, frankly, a little irritating. For parents, they get a little irritating. We ought to move on and start saving some kids' lives here.

Frankly, Mr. Becker, it still is a problem. You may have made some progress, but it is still a problem. We still have kids dying out there. As Senator Dodd has pointed out, we are spending an awful lot of money dealing with drugs, as we should, in this country, but we are not spending enough money dealing with underage drinking. We ought to start spending more money on it, and we ought to start focusing more on it. We are just not doing enough. That is the reality. Whether or not in the climate we have today, with the budget problems, that we're going to convince anybody here to do it, I don't know. But we need to start doing it.

Let me turn it over to Senator Dodd and then I will come back for some more questions.

Senator Dodd. Thank you, Mr. Chairman. Let me thank all of you again for your testimony.

First of all, David, I'm very proud of you as your Senator.

Mr. DeAngelis. Thank you.

Senator Dodd. Tell us what might work. I mean, in spending time with young people, do you know of young people that have stopped drinking, who were drinking and stopped, and if so, what motivated them to stop? Or what do you think would work? What do you think helps? I mean, you have brought up the focus on adult issues, but give us some more specific examples of what might work.

Mr. DeAngelis. Well, I don't really know of any kids who have stopped drinking, but many of my friends have made a commitment not to drink. I think that just stems from their strong families lives, of having involved parents, parents who are there for all their activities, parents who know what their kids are doing. They have made it clear from an early age that drinking is illegal and that should be a good enough reason not to drink, besides all of the health factors and other things that can happen through underage drinking.

My parents have been extremely supportive of everything I have done. They have been with me every step of the way. I know there are other parents out there like that. I believe it is just a matter of reaching the other parents out there who just don't get it yet.

Senator Dodd. What sort of messages do you think would work? You talked about messages. Give me some idea of what those should be.

Mr. DeAngelis. There is a national campaign about talk to your kids about smoking marijuana, ads like that, sort of counteracting the messages that they are receiving now. Just talk to your kids, spend time with them. Be an involved parent. I think the more parents have a role in their kids' lives, the more—Kids want that. Kids want their parents to be with them and know that they really support them and that they love them.

Senator Dodd. I understand that an awful lot of people don't have the wonderful luxury of having two parents at home all the time. A lot of times it is a single mother raising more than one or two children. The pressures are tremendous, maybe holding down two or three jobs and trying to keep the family together economically. The pressures are really tremendous, particularly for single parents. There are just horrendous pressures on them.

Mr. DeAngelis. Absolutely. But even so, they are still with their kids at least some time during the day. Kids look up to their parents, and a lot of them, without realizing it, want to be like their parents. And even if there's just a single parent out there, they will listen to he or she.

Senator Dodd. You mentioned the Beck's Beer ad. What is that? Do you remember how it goes? [Laughter.]

Mr. DeAngelis. It started off talking about steaks, and when a steak is cooked all the way through, it is considered well done. But when a life is well done, it is completely and totally rare. Something along those lines. It is somehow related back to beer and how life is best enjoyed sharing steaks over beer. It was a nice summer ad.

Senator Dodd. I am concerned as well about this.

Mr. Becker, I appreciate some of the changes that have been made. But in just looking at some of these ads that have been on— tell me whether these are still on or not. Here is one that says Game Day. This is the one where Heineken's has a Nintendo game toy, with two Heineken beer bottles as a part of Game Day. That is obviously not aimed at adults, is it?

Mr. Becker. Well, sir, I happen to own a Play Station, so I might not be the best person—[Laughter.]

Senator Dodd. Mr. Becker, get serious with me.

Mr. Becker. No, I'm not trying to make light of it.

Senator Dodd. Well, that is light. That's silly. You're not going to try to convince me that's for an adult. Really, are you?

Mr. Becker. Well, sir, I would respectfully suggest that there are adults who do enjoy doing that, and I

Senator Dodd. Oh, please. Don't insult me now.

Mr. Becker. I'm not trying to insult you, sir. I am simply

Senator Dodd. That's is a child's toy, isn't it?

Mr. Becker. Well, I happen to own one, and so I guess I would personally suggest that I enjoy it, too.

Senator Dodd. Let me read you another ad and you tell me whether or not you think this is for an adult. How about the Bacardi ad, where the young lady in hip-huggers is sitting here watching—you probably can't see it here, but it's the ad that shows a young lady pouring Bacardi down here stomach here, and the young man licking it off her stomach. Who is that designed to appeal to?

Mr. Becker. Certainly not me, sir. [Laughter.]

Senator Dodd. Yeah. So you're somewhere between the Nintendo and this, right? [Laughter.]

Look, there have been all sorts of studies done here of the advertising campaigns. There's reams of it here. The ad we also saw last year of the two women in a wrestling match in a fountain. You know, what's going on here? I appreciate the modest changes that have occurred in the last year or so, but what's going on with the industry that is clearly—When I read down the list of programs where the bulk of the beer advertising has occurred, it has Buffy the Vampire Slayer, Dark Angel, Gilmore Girls, Survivor, X-Files, Mad TV, the Daley Show, and Insomniac Music Theater. These are all programs designed specifically for a very young audience. The bulk of beer advertising is occurring on those programs.

What is the thinking that's going on?

Mr. Becker. I would disagree with that, and I would base that disagreement on the 2003 Federal Trade Commission report that looked at where beer advertisements were placed. Their conclusion was according to the 50 percent or simple majority standard that was in our code prior to a few weeks ago, and there was virtually 99 percent compliance with that code.

As we said when we released our new code, we wanted to make sure it was clear about where our ads were being placed and to what audience. We raised that standard to 70 percent.

Senator Dodd. I went back to some of the earlier stuff that went on in the various magazines, with the percentages of the people underage. Under that new standard, obviously magazines like Vibe and Spin, where the percentages of youth readers was higher, there would be a ban in the advertising. Rolling Stone, Allure and so forth.

But you get to things like Sports Illustrated, it's 25 percent and you still advertise there. The difference is that you have over 6 million readers spending $39 million. Sometimes by reducing these numbers and having merely a percentage, you get sort of an illusion in terms of whether or not you're actually appealing to these underage kids in terms of their drinking habits.

Mr. Becker. I think there is really two issues there, Senator. One is that clearly the new advertising placement threshold will create a circumstance where ads won't appear in some places that they have over the last number of years. I would say, however, that our members have been advertising, just as a practice for the last few years, in the 70 percent range.

But I think the other thing to look at here is what is advertising and who does it influence. The Roper organization has done a poll now for over 10 years that has consistently shown that when young people are asked what their primary influences on drinking are— and I think we have acknowledged certainly the role that parents have today, the number one answer —

Senator Dodd. Fine. I agree with that, too. Don't misunderstand me. But an awful lot of this has to do with advertising. Come on. You guys spend millions and millions of dollars, not because you're VISTA or the Peace Corps. You do it because it makes good economic sense to do it.

Now, looking at a Coors ad on now, a very prominent musician, rock star, in a football stadium buying beers for all of his friends there, that's designed specifically for—you know, the only people who really know who that is, most of them are younger people.

Why do you do this? What is the point of advertising to appeal to that age group when, in fact, you know legally you can't sell to them? Why do you do it?

Mr. Becker. Well, the ads are only created to appeal to those people of legal purchase age and older. The fact that they are interesting —

Senator Dodd. Come on, be honest with me. You're appealing to try to develop loyalties to certain brands. That's what people do, don't they?

Mr. Becker. Certainly if it's for people who can legally purchase and consume the products. But we do not—and I think the FTC report underscored that quite clearly—we do not target our ads to young people and do not attempt to make them appealing to them. I think it's —

Senator Dodd. That "cat fight" ad was designed to appeal to an adult audience?

Mr. Becker. Yes, sir, it was. And I think that the controversy surrounding that ad, and others, has caused a circumstance where those companies have pulled those ads because of the controversy surrounding them. So I do think that our industry has been very responsive when consumers and others have raised those issues with us. That is one of the reasons why we think changing our code to ensure there is no misperception about where and who we're trying to advertise to is clearer for people.

Senator Dodd. Mrs. Hamilton, what is your reaction to all of this?

Mrs. Hamilton. Interesting. Twenty percent of the profits, up to 20 percent of the profits that the alcohol industry makes is on the sale of their beverages to underage drinkers. It is very important for us to remember that the bottom line of this is profits for their industry.

While I understand that parents need to play a role in this, parents don't have the information that they need. There is no evidence that shows that the prevention programs the industry has put forward are based on science, that it's effective in reducing underage drinking, when we see, in fact, that the numbers are status quo.

There is much more that needs to be done. They need to be more responsible in all parts of advertising, from the Internet to radio to newspaper. Young people have access to this. They are seeing it, they're acknowledging it, and they are drinking.

Senator Dodd. Talk to me a bit about the single parent issue. David talked about obviously a wonderful family and a lot of involvement. There are a lot of pressures obviously on other families, given their makeup and so forth, to be able to have that kind of time.

I wonder if any work has been done on that. Mrs. Kempthorne, you might respond to this as well. Sometimes we imagine sort of the traditional family, which is very different than what many of us grew up with today. How do we work with that family? Are there some unique and effective programs that have been more successful with today's family, the single parent family, with two parents working three or four jobs in some cases?

Mrs. Hamilton. Families are very different from 20 years ago, when I was raising mine, and there are more challenges that are facing them, being in the workforce. It is important for us to get the messages out, the real messages, the truth about how alcohol affects children.

I would also like to submit for the record Alcohol and the Brain, how drinking in youth affects thinking skills. I don't think parents have this kind of information.

Senator DeWine. That will be made a part of the record, as well as what Mr. DeAngelis had for the record. We will make that part of the record, too.

[The information may be found in additional material.]

Mrs. Hamilton. In addition, the elementary school program that MADD has been focused on in the last several years, Protecting You/Protecting Me, goes into elementary schools to teach children about alcohol's effects on the developing brain, where to sit in a car, when they're driving with someone, to make good decisions, and the skills that they need to make good decisions. That has been named a model program by the Federal Government.

There is much more work that needs to be done. We're working with the First Ladies Initiative on some programs. Education is key to parents.

They need to understand the consequences because, quite frankly, they don't. They still think this is a "right of passage" in this country.

Senator Dodd. Ms. Kempthorne, do you want to comment?

Mrs. Kempthorne. I agree with Mrs. Hamilton, and I also did want to say that the parents do need help. Parents are trying to get that message out. Being a parent of 20-somethings, I have just been through that and still finishing going through that, you give the message. You tell the kids that it's illegal, you tell the kids that they will want to do it because they have a genetic predisposition to it.

But that doesn't have half as much meaning as the new friend they met the other day who is going to have a six-pack of beer at their house, so why don't you come over. It's okay because their parents are there, but the kids are downstairs in the basement and they're upstairs.

I also agree with Mr. DeAngelis, that it is really each child making that decision. That's why we start as young as we do. We have got to teach them how to make these decisions before that friend hands them the beer when they're 12 years old and says, "Hey, it's no big deal. Nobody will ever know."

Other things are happening. In the schools now, they don't even want you to bring water or sodas because the kids are mixing alcohol with it. Many schools won't let them come in. We don't believe that as a parent. That can't be true. But it really is true. Our children find that there's a message out there that it's okay because parents really don't get it, you know. They really don't get it. I have heard these messages.

And it isn't just the advertising. It is media of all sorts. Our children have grown up getting messages from many more sources than us as parents. Sometimes it feels like we're the counterculture pushing against everything else that's telling them what is okay, and we say we want you to have a healthy, productive life, and yes, have fun, and what they see is how to have fun is to consume alcohol. It will at least make it happen a little quicker.

The other thing about single parents, we know now that most parents are in the workplace. I think it's over 80 percent of parents with children

18 or under are in the workplace. So yes, it's a challenge. Who's taking care of the children and who's giving them the message?

Senator Dodd. Just on a final note, as a father of a 2 year old, I'm just envisioning the problems coming down the road. A sister of mine has 15 grandchildren, and she was saying the other day something very smart. She said, you know, parents have a choice. Not all do, but they have a choice. They normally will say they'll stay out of the workforce, or one or the other will, when they're very, very young, and when they reach school age, 10 or 12, then I'll go back to work.

It's really just backwards.

Mrs. Kempthorne. Absolutely.

Senator Dodd. In many ways, children, as long as they're being loved and cared for and fed, and have done all the normal things when they're very young, they will make it okay. It's when they get around 10 or 12 that they really need you. Too often parents decide they're on their own and are really okay, but in fact the opposite is true.

We have this notion somehow that they really need you more when they're infants and less so when they reach the preteen years. I see you're nodding in agreement with that notion as well.

Mrs. Kempthorne. Absolutely. Experience.

Senator Dodd. Thank you.

Mr. DeAngelis. I would like to briefly add to that, if I may.

As far as the water bottles, I know of a classmate of mine where this is absolutely true. He showed up at the North Haven affair a couple of weeks ago with a water bottle filled with vodka, so it does happen. It is not something that is just a myth.

Senator Dodd. Thank you.

Senator DeWine. I just have a couple more questions.

Mr. Becker, you were talking with Senator Dodd about the code. I'm a little confused about the code. How is that enforced? That is your own code, is that right?

Mr. Becker. Yes, sir, it is.

Senator DeWine. How is that enforced?

Mr. Becker. The code is enforced when Senator DeWine. Do you all enforce that yourselves?

Mr. Becker. No, sir. It's a voluntary code. When we receive a complaint from an individual or an organization, we refer that complaint to that specific brewer. That brewer then responds to the complainant directly. That process has served us very well, and I think if you looked at that process and at not only the quick response that our members have but the response of the complainant, we believe that's been a very effective tool thus far.

Senator DeWine. So it is a code that each brewery says they're going to live up to, right?

Mr. Becker. At a minimum. The industry code, each company also does

Senator DeWine. Hopefully they will live up to it.

Mr. Becker. Correct.

Senator DeWine. So that's why the general counsel of the Beer Institute said that "It's not our job to enforce it."

Mr. Becker. It's not our job to enforce the code, but it is our job to oversee the code, to convey the complaints directly to the brewer

Senator DeWine. Because he said "the code is not going to work if we become the judge." That was a quote in the paper.

Mr. Becker. Well, I agree with him. As an association, we cannot be the subjective judge of the complaints. The company itself has to look at what it's doing and has to look at that complaint and decide

Senator DeWine. Each company decides how it interprets that and goes back and forth with the complainant then; is that how it works?

Mr. Becker. That's correct, Senator.

Senator DeWine. Let me get back to this. I don't want to belabor the point, but Mrs. Hamilton made a comment again talking about the scientific basis of some of the things that we're doing. I just want to make one more comment and then I will get off it.

It seems to me that you have been subject to criticism, that some of the things you have done have not had a scientific basis to them. I'm not judging today whether that is true or not true, but it seems to me you can certainly get rid of that criticism by setting up this independent group that Dr. Bonnie is talking about. It seems to me that is something you all should explore. I really think you ought to look at that.

Mr. Becker. Well, Senator, I guess I would take issue with the fact that our programs are not evaluated.

Senator DeWine. That's the point. I understand you would take issue with it, and I appreciate that. Again, I don't think we are going to get anywhere debating that today. You know, you take issue with it and some people criticize it. That is sort of my point.

My point is you get rid of that criticism by setting up an independent group, you fund it, you take credit for funding it, but it is independent. You get rid of the criticism and you let somebody else take the flak and the criticism. You say, "Look, we funded it, we made a good faith effort to do this. We have the same interest that MADD does; we have the same interest that every other parent does in this country. We want to stop underage drinking and we have put in a good faith effort and we're putting x-million dollars into this every single year. Get off our back." That's what I would do if I were you. I would get it out of my ballpark.

This is just a suggestion, just as a citizen. It's a little suggestion, that's all.

Mr. Becker. I appreciate that Senator.

Senator DeWine. And you won't be up here listening to us yell at you.

Mr. Becker. I certainly do appreciate that, Senator. But since you mentioned

Senator DeWine. How hard is that?

Mr. Becker. Since you mentioned "ballparks," I would like to briefly say that one example

Senator DeWine. You're not going to bring up how my Reds are doing this year, are you? [Laughter.]

Mr. Becker. No. Sadly, I really couldn't tell you how your Reds are doing. I know the Red Sox are better than they used to be.

I would say that the team coalition that we participated in, and a significant effort with major league baseball to train people in stadiums, has been evaluated and has been demonstrated to have made the fan experience more enjoyable. That is to say, they have had fewer problems. That is just one of the programs that has been evaluated, that the industry has been participating in. So to say we have not evaluated our programs is not correct.

Senator DeWine. OK. OK.

One of the suggestions that has been made, and one of the things I would like your comments on, is the idea that the Federal Government should fund and start putting some significant money into advertising that would deal with underage drinking. Dr. Bonnie, I believe that was one of your recommendations.

Mr. Bonnie. Yes.

Senator DeWine. Let me go quickly through the panel because we are about out of time. Why don't you kick that off, and then I will go to Mrs. Kempthorne and go right down the panel. Just real quickly make your comments on that.

Mr. Bonnie. If I could put that into a larger context, maybe picking up on some points that were made here

Senator DeWine. That would be good. You've got a minute, though, 1 minute.

Mr. Bonnie. I think Senator Dodd observed at some earlier point that this is really about the culture. I kind of sympathize in a certain respect with Mr. Becker here. He's been on the hot seat about this and the industry is obviously an important part of the culture.

But this is bigger than the industry. I think we need to keep that in mind. The report emphasizes this is a collective responsibility. We all have a role to play here. We do need to give parents the help that they have been seeking in trying to deal with this. We need to built coalitions at the grassroots level. I mean, this is much bigger than the industry. I think the media campaign that we recommended is the cornerstone of that effort, really, to galvanize the public engagement in this effort by recognizing the seriousness of the problem.

I should take note, by the way, that Judy Cushing, who was a member of our panel, is here. She is the head of the Oregon Partnership and that's what she does with her work. I think we just need to try to strengthen her hand and the hands of people like that.

In that context, I just want to make one comment on this advertising issue. Obviously, advertizing is a difficult policy problem. I think it's important for all of us that are trying to find how we're going to affect the messages that kids and parents and everyone receives, to acknowledge that there is a commercial difficulty that the industry has in terms of trying to get at the young adult audience, the audience that is in their early 20s. That's a legitimate interest that they have to advertise to that audience, and obviously, there is going to be the spill-over problem in terms of the messages getting to the younger kids. They have acknowledged that this is an issue that they have to try to deal with, and I think they are taking one step at a time and they need to continue. We need to keep the pressure on them to take one step at a time.

The Government role in this is to make sure that we monitor what is going on in terms of the brand usage of kids and the exposure of kids to these messages, so that the industry can be held accountable to the public by having that information made available. That was a core part of the recommendations as well. So I think that that needs to be emphasized. That's really the approach in dealing with the advertising issue.

Senator DeWine. When you came up with your recommendation about the anti-drinking advertising—if I may call it that—did you look at what States are doing? Do we have any experience level in what the States are doing, are any of the 50 States putting significant money into this? Is anybody doing this?

Mr. Bonnie. If you want to compare, for example, with the tobacco area, where I think we do have —

Senator DeWine. No, I don't. I want to look at it and see if anybody is doing it in regard to underage drinking with alcohol. Is anybody doing it, any State doing it significantly? Is anybody putting money —

Mr. Bonnie. Not at a substantial level, as far as I know.

Senator DeWine. Nobody is doing it with any significant amount of money?

Mr. Bonnie. Not a significant amount of money. But we need to pay attention to making sure that we've got evidence-based, for whatever is done—Again, the committee also emphasized that we have the evidence available for this, that we need a lot more research to be done on the messages that are going to work with kids, if we're talking about kid-oriented advertising.

Senator DeWine. Right. We have seen how difficult that is to do with drugs.

Mr. Bonnie. Exactly. And we have to be careful —

Senator DeWine. We have a trial-and-error with drugs and we have seen that we've spent a lot of money and sometimes it doesn't work, but sometimes it does. It's tough.

Mr. Bonnie. Let's do the research before we implement hundreds of millions of dollars in a campaign.

Senator DeWine. Mrs. Kempthorne, in regard to that type of advertising, do you have a reaction to that?

Mrs. Kempthorne. Yes. The part that confuses me is how on one side they spend so much money on advertising, and then you will see a quote that says advertising really doesn't change behavior. I don't understand why on the one side they do, but then they go against it and say they want to do advertising that promotes not drinking. I'm still confused on where that comes from.

From a State level, no, we have not put money into stopping underage drinking. But I do know in adolescent pregnancy prevention that the advertising we have done has made a significant difference, but we have targeted it specifically, sometimes to parents, sometimes to boys, sometimes to girls. It is a ten-year long plan to figure out how we do that, and we have seen a significant statistical drop.

The other thing that would be important as we look at their codes, what they consider fulfilling their code and what, as a parent, I may consider fulfilling their code, when I see those I don't think that's what I want my children to see. But I'm not even sure, as a 51 year old adult, that's what I want to see, either. So I would like to be more of a participant and a player. I don't know how they do their focus groups on what the advertising is, but we need to bring all the parties together to decide what is effective advertising.

Senator DeWine. Mr. Becker.

Mr. Becker. Well, Senator, to the specific issue, advertising can influence an adult consumer's decision to buy a brand. What it has not been demonstrated to do is to sell more beer than it ordinarily would. I think the evidence on that is very clear, and I would be happy to provide that for the committee.

To your specific question, however, on the adult media campaign, I will go back to what Dr. Bonnie said. I think the evidence suggests that campaigns that have been done can be counterproductive, or campaigns can send a message that may not change someone's behavior.

Our industry believes that today it is premature for us to express support for a media campaign because we don't have details, such as message, etc. Having said that, however, we are open to further discussion. I think as you have very well outlined, Mr. Chairman, we are all in this together. This industry has and will continue to support effective solutions to underage drinking.

Senator DeWine. Mrs. Hamilton.

Mrs. Hamilton. Senator, you asked at the beginning in your opening remarks how did we get here. I think more importantly is where we go from here, now that we have this incredible document that has been prepared by the NAS.

What we absolutely have to do is have an adult media campaign that is going to focus on adults, to tell them the consequences of what happens when young people are drinking and what happens when they provide alcohol. We need to have a central Federal agency that is coordinating these efforts.

Five years ago, when we started focusing on underage drinking, when we added the prevention of underage drinking to our mission, we couldn't find that research. We couldn't find those documents. We had to wade through everything. Communities need that information available through a web, through a central agency with their States, so they can get access to community programs that work, that are evidence-based. And we absolutely need enforcement on the 21 drinking age laws.

Senator DeWine. Mr. DeAngelis.

Mr. DeAngelis. Adults are essential to reducing the problem. That is why 2 years ago we started the column to target adults. Because at our 4 days at Power Camp, we tried to get at the root of the problem and we kept coming back to the roles of adults. We felt the best way we could reach them was through a column.

Advertising on a national level would reach so many more. TV is such a huge part of our culture, it will at least start to make an impression on our minds. Whether it affects their behavior from day one, probably not. But over a period of time, it can really make a difference.

Senator DeWine. The last question—and I will go right down the line.

Other than advertising, if there was one thing we could do nationwide, one thing, what would that be?

Mr. Bonnie. Other than the media campaign you mean?

Senator DeWine. Yes, other than advertising and media campaigns that we just discussed. What else, one thing?

Mr. Bonnie. I think I would say that the second priority in this—and I guess you have put aside the tax issue at the beginning. So among the other recommendations, I think we —

Senator DeWine. I'm not saying we shouldn't do that. That's not in the jurisdiction of this committee, but we can address that some other day.

Mr. Bonnie. There is a whole series of recommendations here about strengthening compliance with the underage drinking prohibition, and I think that is the next set of issues. That involves steps that are taken at the national level and involves steps that are taken at the State level, in terms of State level enforcement, and it involves empowering community coalitions to be able to put social pressures on the retailers.

This is not only about law enforcement. It's about education to promote compliance. So I would say that's the second main recommendation.

Senator DeWine. Good. Mrs. Kempthorne.

Mrs. Kempthorne. All politics is local, building community coalitions and really making it happen at the grassroots level.

Senator DeWine. Mr. Becker.

Mr. Becker. I would like to echo that sentiment, that community-based coalitions do work. I would also like to commend the students for coming up with this well thought out idea, that we really do need to help parents and adults with better information, to empower them to do a better job of parenting.

Senator DeWine. Ms. Hamilton.

Mrs. Hamilton. Enforcement of the 21 minimum drinking age law, just as Dr. Bonnie said, and Mrs. Kempthorne. It's critical.

Senator DeWine. Mr. DeAngelis.

Mr. DeAngelis. The same thing, compliance checks. When we go out and do compliance checks, we're not trying to trick the package store owners. We go in there and try to buy liquor, and see if they ask for and check IDs. It's very straightforward, and oftentimes they don't. You just need to keep plugging away with that, because they have to learn at some point.

Senator DeWine. Senator Dodd, your last comments.

Senator Dodd. Thanks, Mr. Chairman. I thank all of you again.

I just come back to the point that I think someone made earlier. The IOM, not an insignificant organization, the Institute of Medicine, estimates that the social cost of just underage drinking—we haven't talked about the medical cost of just drinking, but just underage drinking—is $53 billion a year, and $19 billion a year alone just in automobile accidents and health related costs, and $29 billion associated with violent crime. We need to keep those numbers in mind here. This is a staggering problem here. It's not small. In fact, the numbers go up and down a bit.

You can make a difference. I have always used the example of Mothers Against Drunk Driving. I think it began with one woman in the basement of her home, as I recall the history. I hope I'm right about that because I have used that story over and over again, about how one person who decided to make a difference has made a difference in many ways.

Certainly what we have done with smoking in this country today. When you think back just a few years ago, these committee rooms, we smoked as members of committees up here. If you got on an airplane, every place you went to there was smoking. And yet, because there was a determined effort recognizing the health costs to it, the advertising campaigns, all of the efforts made, we have made real headway on that issue. And there were tremendous voices against it, about choices and parental involvement and so forth. But by reducing the association with smoking as being something that was culturally acceptable, it made you more attractive, all of that was part of it. It was in the movie industry, on television, everywhere you went, it was all part of an effort to say this was okay, in a sense.

Now, I know that drinking is certainly very much a part of our culture. No one is recommending a constitutional amendment here to change this. But the idea somehow that we just sort of accept this because it's part of the embedded fabric of the country is something we've got to challenge, particularly when kids are involved.

So, Mr. Becker, my point with you is, I'm not picking on you particularly here, except that I know when you write these ads—you know, you spend a lot of money doing this. You mall test these things. You do focus groups. You don't just do an ad and put it out on television. People have tested it, who is it going to appeal to. You spend a lot of money putting those ads on television.

The question is, when you're sitting and making that decision about putting these ads on—you have one here that shows, obviously—I don't know how old this girl is. She doesn't look 21 to me. They're in the car, rear view mirror, the radio is on, necking, a nice finish. It's a Michelob ad. You know, maybe 21-5 and so forth. I'm not arguing someone isn't that.

But the appearance of that child in that situation, someone made a decision. They didn't pick someone looking a little older. They picked someone looking younger. Again, you're here, and obviously there are multifaceted aspects of this. I acknowledge that completely. But the fact of the matter is, millions of dollars are being spent to appeal to these kids. That's a fact, in my view.

So I'm trying to get the industry to be far more responsible about this, and I encourage you to consider what the chairman has offered here as a way of getting involved in this.

The reason these numbers got changed and you went up to 35 was because there was a tremendous reaction to those ads on television. That's why it happened. By your own admission, that's what occurred. People were outraged by what they saw on television. So the industry responded to consumer reaction. It wasn't a law passed here, and it wasn't a regulation adopted. It was the industry responding to what they saw as a very dangerous situation if they didn't change those ads.

So I'm encouraging you to do what the chairman has suggested. Get together with these people. Sit down and try and work this out. You don't want industry members promoting this stuff on television with these kinds of ads. I think it's going to hurt you terribly. I may be one voice up here right now. I guarantee you there will be a sense of collective outrage about this if you keep doing it. Then steps will be taken that go far beyond suggesting getting together to support a foundation. You mark my words, it will happen.

The smoking industry and tobacco industry never believed it would happen, and it did. I'm telling you, it will happen with this industry if you don't smarten up and stop this stuff.

Thank you, Mr. Chairman.

Senator DeWine. Let me thank all of you very much.

You know, politics is about choices. As parents, we worry about things. My wife, Fran, and I have eight children. The youngest is 11 and the oldest is 35. As parents, you worry about your kids. I think that with the mass culture we have today, and with the 24 hour news, sometimes we get off and worry about the wrong things. You sort of calculate what you should be worrying about.

I believe one of the things we have learned, if you just look at the statistics, what you learn is that many times we worry about the wrong things. One of the things that has come from this hearing is that, if you want to worry about something that really matters in society today, as parents, at least if you believe the statistics, you ought to worry about underage drinking. If that message can come from this hearing, it's the right message.

Getting back to the priority issue, politics and government, we do not put enough priority at the Federal level on underage drinking. We don't worry enough about it. We don't care enough about it, because the reality is that it's a major killer of our young people. We need to take from this hearing a new dedication to do something about it.

We do spend a lot of money today worrying about illicit drug use. I don't know anybody in this Congress who has spent more time on that than I have. I started worrying about that when I was a county prosecutor many, many years ago. And Senator Dodd is worried about it and has spent a lot of time on this. He and I worry about illegal drugs coming into this country, and I think both of us are going to continue to worry about that, as we should.

But if you look at how much money we have spent on that versus underage drinking, it pales in comparison. That doesn't mean we shouldn't worry about the drug problem, but it does mean we should start worrying a little bit more, a lot more, about underage drinking.

Senator Dodd recited the number of kids who are killed. Mrs. Hamilton recited the number of kids who are killed in cars because of drinking, the number of suicides that are possibly facilitated because somebody has been drinking, the accidental deaths that are caused because someone is drinking, the college campus deaths that occur because someone has been drinking, the binge deaths that occur. You can just go on and on and on. These are not accidents. They are preventable. So we need to take this information today and see what we can do about it.

Senator Dodd and I are going to be talking on this committee about what we can do from this testimony. So we appreciate it. We appreciate all of you coming in, the First Ladies and former First Ladies, we thank you for taking the time to be here today from all across the country. We appreciate it, and all the rest of our panelists.

Thank you very much.

[Additional material follows:]

Chapter 2

ADDITIONAL MATERIAL

PREPARED STATEMENT OF RICHARD J. BONNIE

Good morning, Mr. Chairman and Members of the Subcommittee. My name is Richard Bonnie. I am the John S. Battle Professor of Law and Director of the Institute of Law, Psychiatry and Public Policy at the University of Virginia. I served as chair of the Committee on Developing a Strategy to Reduce and Prevent Underage Drinking of the National Research Council and the Institute of Medicine. The National Research Council is the operating arm of the National Academy of Sciences, National Academy of Engineering and the Institute of Medicine, chartered by Congress in 1863 to advise the government on matters of science and technology.

The report of this committee was produced in response to a Congressional request to develop a strategy to reduce and prevent underage drinking. The committee reviewed a wide variety of government and private programs for the purpose of developing a comprehensive national strategy. We relied on the available scientific literature, commissioned papers, testimony and submissions from the public, and the expertise of committee members in public policy, public health, youth interventions, and substance abuse. Our starting point was the current national policy setting 21 as the minimum legal-drinking age.

Alcohol use by young people is an endemic problem that is not likely to improve in the absence of significant new interventions. Many more of the nation's youth drink than smoke cigarettes or use other drugs. And, young people tend to drink more heavily than adults, exacerbating the dangers to themselves and people around them. In the 2002 Monitoring the Future survey, a Federally sponsored study, nearly one-in-five 8th graders and almost half of 12th graders reported drinking in the last month. More than a quarter of high school seniors reported that they had five or more drinks in a row in the last 2 weeks. One-in-eight 8th graders reported the same thing. These underlying rates have remained basically unchanged for a decade. The social cost of underage drinking has been estimated at $53 billion each year, including $19 billion from traffic crashes alone. While traffic crashes are perhaps the most visible consequences of this problem, underage drinking is also linked with violence, suicide, academic failure, and other harmful behaviors. Heavy drinking also threatens youth's long-term development.

Although the public is generally aware of the problems associated with underage drinking, the nation's social response has not been commensurate with the magnitude and seriousness of the problem. This disparity is evident not only in the fact that the Federal Government spends 25 times more on prevention of illicit drug use by young people than on prevention of underage drinking, but also in the lack of sustained and comprehensive grassroots efforts to address the problem in most communities.

Some people think that the key to reducing underage drinking lies in finding the right messages to send to young people to instill negative beliefs and attitudes toward alcohol use. Others tend to focus on changing the marketing practices of the alcohol industry in order to reduce young people's exposure to messages designed to promote drinking. However, the problem is much more complicated than either of these positions would suggest because alcohol use is deeply embedded in the economic and cultural fabric of life in the United States. Annual revenues in the alcohol industry amount to $116 billion. The challenge, then, is how to reduce underage drinking in a context where adult drinking is widespread and commonly accepted and where billions of gallons of alcohol are in the stream of commerce. We believe that will require a broad, multifaceted effort.

The primary goal of the committee's recommended strategy is to create and sustain a strong societal commitment to reduce underage drinking. All of us, acting in concert—including parents and other adults, alcohol producers, wholesalers and retail outlets, entertainment media, and community groups—must take the necessary steps to reduce the availability of alcohol to underage drinkers, to reduce the attractiveness of alcohol to young people, and to reduce opportunities for youthful drinking. Underage drinking prevention is everybody's business.

The report emphasizes that adults must be the primary targets of this national campaign to reduce underage drinking. Most adults express concern about underage drinking and voice support for public policies to curb it. Yet behind the concern lies a paradox: Youth often get their alcohol from adults. And many parents downplay the extent of the problem or are unaware of their own kids' drinking habits. Thirty percent of parents whose kids reported drinking heavily within the last 30 days, think their kids do not drink at all. The sad truth is that many adults facilitate and condone underage drinking. We need to change the behavior of well-meaning adults in communities all over the nation—including people who are holding drinking parties for kids in their homes in violation of the law.

As the centerpiece of the committee's adult-oriented strategy, our report calls on the Federal Government to fund and actively support the development of a national media campaign designed to create a broad societal commitment to reduce underage drinking, to decrease adult conduct that tends to facilitate underage drinking, and to encourage parents and other adults to take specific steps in their own households, neighborhoods and businesses to discourage underage drinking.

The comprehensive strategy we suggest also includes a multi-pronged plan for boosting compliance with laws that prohibit selling or providing alcohol to young people under the legal drinking age of 21. Efforts to increase compliance need to focus on both retail outlets and social channels through which underage drinkers obtain their alcohol. For example, we urge State authorities to require all sellers and servers of alcohol to complete State-approved training as a condition of employment, and to increase the frequency of staged underage purchases by which they monitor retailer compliance with minimum drinking-age laws. The Federal Government should require States to achieve specified rates of retailer compliance with youth-access laws as a condition of receiving Federal funds. And States should beef up efforts to prevent and detect the use of fake IDs by minors who want to buy alcohol.

The committee also supports specific intervention and education programs aimed at young people as long as those programs have been evaluated and found to be effective. A good start in identifying evidence-based school programs has already been made by the Department of Education and the Substance Abuse Mental Health Services Administration in the Department of Health and Human Services. A recent report sponsored by the National Institute on Alcohol Abuse and Alcoholism has done the same for programs aimed at college students.

Community leaders need to mobilize the energy, resources and attention of local organizations and businesses to develop and implement programs for preventing and reducing underage drinking. These efforts should be tailored to specific circumstances of the problem in their communities. The Federal Government as well as public and private organizations should encourage and help pay for relevant community initiatives that have been shown to work.

The alcohol industry also has a vitally important role to play in the strategy we have proposed. The committee acknowledges the industry's declared commitment to the goal of reducing underage drinking and its willingness to be part of the solution. We believe that there is much common ground, and that opportunities for cooperation are now being overlooked. Specifically, we urge the alcohol industry to join with private and public entities to create and fund an independent, non-profit foundation that focuses solely on designing, evaluating, and implementing evidence-based programs for preventing and reducing underage drinking. Although the industry currently invests in programs that were set up with that stated goal, the results of these programs have rarely been scientifically evaluated, and the overall level of industry investment is modest in relation to the revenues generated by the underage market. We think it is reasonable to expect the industry to do more than it is now doing, and to join with others to form a genuine national partnership to reduce underage drinking.

We also urge greater self-restraint in alcohol advertising. We recognize, of course, that advertising is a particularly sensitive issue. However, a substantial portion of alcohol advertising reaches an underage audience or is presented in a style that tends to attract youth. For example, alcohol ads on TV often appear during programs where the percentage of underage viewers is greater than their percentage in the overall U.S. population. Building on an important 1999 report by the Federal Trade Commission, the committee's report urges industry trade associations to strengthen their advertising codes to prohibit placement of commercial messages in venues where a large portion of the audience is underage. For many years, the industry trade association codes permitted ad placements in media where adults were at least 50 percent of the audience. The FTC recently announced that the beer and distilled spirits trade associations have joined the wine industry to increase the threshold to 70 percent for the minimum proportion of adults in the viewing audience. This is a step in the right direction, but the committee believes that the industry should continue to move toward a higher threshold of adult viewers. In addition, trade associations and alcohol companies should create independent, external review boards to investigate complaints about ads and enforce codes. Furthermore, alcohol companies, advertising firms, and commercial media should refrain from marketing practices that have particular appeal to young people, regardless of whether they are intentionally targeted at youth audiences.

Companies and trade associations in the entertainment sector also have a responsibility to join in the collective effort to reduce underage drinking, and to exercise greater restraint in disseminating images and lyrics that promote or glorify alcohol use in venues with significant underage audiences. Officials in the music, TV, and film industries should use rating systems and codes similar to those used by some industries for drug abuse to reduce the likelihood that large numbers of young listeners and viewers will be exposed to unsuitable messages about alcohol consumption—even when adults are expected to make up the majority of the audience.

The Federal Government should periodically monitor advertising practices in the alcohol industry and review representative samples of movies, television programs, music recordings, and videos that are offered at times or venues likely to have significant underage audiences. This work should be conducted by the U.S. Department of Health and Human Services, and reported to Congress and the general public on a regular basis. The department also should issue a comprehensive report to Congress each year summarizing trends in underage drinking, and reporting on progress in implementing the proposed strategy and in reducing the problem. A Federal interagency coordinating committee, chaired by the Secretary of HHS, should be formed to provide national leadership and to better organize the multiple Federal activities in this area. HHS also should create a National Training and Research Center on Underage Drinking and collect more detailed data, including data on brands preferred by youth. State policy-makers should designate an agency to spearhead and coordinate their activities.

To help pay for the proposed public programs and to help reduce underage consumption, Congress and State legislatures should raise excise tax rates on alcohol — especially on beer, which is the alcoholic beverage that young people drink most often. Alcohol is much cheaper today, after adjusting for inflation, than it was 30 to 40 years ago. Higher tax rates should be tied to the Consumer Price Index to keep pace with inflation. Research indicates that changes in these tax rates can decrease the prevalence and harmful effects of drinking among youths, who tend to have limited discretionary income and are especially sensitive to changes in price.

In summary, we've proposed a comprehensive strategy that, taken as a whole, would foster a deep, unequivocal societal commitment to curtail underage drinking. As a national community, we need to focus our attention on this serious problem and accept a collective responsibility to address it. This is an admittedly difficult challenge, but the committee believes that our country can do much more than it is now doing. The nation needs to develop and implement effective ways to protect young people from the dangers of early drinking while respecting the interests of responsible adult consumers of alcohol. The committee's report attempts to strike the right balance.

Thank you for your interest and the opportunity to testify to the subcommittee. I'd be happy to answer any questions you may have about the committee's report.

Prepared Statement of Patricia J. Kempthorne, First Lady of Idaho

As the First Lady of Idaho, thank you for your invitation to speak to you today on behalf of the 34 current Governors' spouses and 11 Emeritus members of the *Leadership to Keep Children Alcohol Free* national initiative.

I would like to acknowledge the support shown by many of our members who are here today in commitment to this issue.

We are a non-partisan group devoted to increasing public awareness, engaging policy makers, and mobilizing action to stop childhood drinking. Our specific focus is the 9-15 year-old age group. The *Leadership to Keep Children Alcohol Free* was established to make childhood drinking prevention a national health priority. In addition to their role as Governors' Spouses, *Leadership* members are prosecutors, judges, educators, business leaders, substance abuse prevention specialists, and parents. Many of us have witnessed through our respective professions or personally the devastation early alcohol abuse can inflict on individuals, families, and society. We are here today to emphasize for the Committee the immediate and far reaching consequences of childhood drinking and also to offer our recommendations for action.

We are pleased that the Subcommittee on Substance Abuse and Mental Health Services understands the need to address underage drinking in all its complexity, including early onset of alcohol use by the most vulnerable members of our society— children.

On a personal note as a parent, as a community encourager, and as a proponent for the health and well-being of children I would like to express my thanks to the committee and acknowledge the need for your leadership in addressing this issue. During most of my childhood my father worked as a distributor of wine and distilled spirits. It was very clear to me at the time that alcohol was not meant for me as a child. Growing up I learned a respect for alcohol as an adult beverage but also saw some of the effects of the abuse of alcohol on members of my community. Seeing the hurt and confusion caused by the abuse of alcohol was instructive in helping me make choices in my life. I do not believe today the message in our society is as clear.

While it is unsettling to think that we have to consider elementary students when we think about drinking prevention, we do. The environment surrounding our children often contributes to their attitudes and expectancies about alcohol. In addition, drinking initiation most often begins at the age of 13. We know from research that behaviors adopted during adolescence set a lifelong trajectory.

Before you say "but I've never seen a drunk 12 year old," let me share some statistics. More than 29 percent of students report that they first drank alcohol (more than a few sips) before age 13. By the eighth grade (that's 13-14 year olds), more than 12 percent report having had five or more drinks in a row, that's binge drinking within two weeks prior of being surveyed. They are drinking with the goal of getting drunk.

Children are our top priority. We expend tremendous energy ensuring that they are vaccinated, use infant car seats, and have access to educational opportunities. Yet there is a serious disconnect when it comes to childhood drinking.

Some propose that the solution is to adopt the so-called European model in which drinking age laws and attitudes are more liberal. The argument is that these policies and attitudes in turn foster more responsible styles of drinking by young people. That is a myth.

In a study conducted in 1995, 15-16 year-olds in 22 European countries were asked about consuming five or more drinks in a row. Compared with the U.S., only a single country, Portugal, had a lower percentage of kids report this behavior. In addition, the World Health Organization report released in 2002 states that one in four deaths among European men aged 15-29 years is alcohol related. This is not the model we should emulate. Moreover, governments around the world, including in Europe, are beginning to take action to address underage drinking.

The phone call in the middle of the night is the fear of every parent. What may not be immediately obvious, but just as devastating, are the long-term irreversible consequences of heavy drinking during adolescence.

Research documents that forty percent of kids who begin drinking before the age of 15 will develop alcohol abuse or dependence at some point in their lives. The adolescent brain is still a work in progress and therefore vulnerable. More recent research demonstrated that children who engaged in heavy drinking by age 15, showed noticeable changes in the brain and that these children developed fewer learning strategies and remembered less than non-drinkers. In addition, those who begin drinking before age 14 are 12 times more likely to be injured after drinking, 7 times more likely to be in motor vehicle crash, and 11 times more likely to be in a physical fight. Alcohol use also leads to other risky behaviors with life changing consequences such as unplanned pregnancies or infectious sexually transmitted diseases. And finally, 28 percent of suicides and attempted suicides by children can be attributed to alcohol.

Starting to drink at an early age poses risk not only for those who drink, but there is a second-hand negative effect on the non-drinking adolescent.

While parents certainly bear responsibility for their own children, families do not live in a vacuum; our homes are not bunkers from reality. Parental guidance is constantly challenged by external influences. We are not here to place blame but to address a serious public health issue that is affecting a significant number of our nation's young people. The responsibility for solving this problem rests with all of us— individuals, families, schools, communities, policy-makers, opinion-leaders, retailers, and the industry. The National Academies of Science and the Institute of Medicine have identified opportunities for all of us to play a role in tackling the problem of underage drinking as we are all stakeholders in the future of our nation's youth. We need to be motivated by what is in the best interests of our youth.

On behalf of the Leadership to Keep Children Alcohol Free and speaking as a parent, I would respectfully offer four recommendations for action:

1) Please do not let this be the only hearing on this critical public health issue, but rather the impetus for a series of hearings leading to significant policy deliberations and proposals.
2) We request that the Subcommittee ask the Surgeon General to issue an independent evaluation and "Call to Action on Childhood Drinking" and that the resulting report be released in a timely way.
3) We request that national surveys begin to collect data on alcohol use and attitudes that include children as young as age 9.
4) When used by our youth alcohol is the number one illegal drug. Therefore, we urge the Subcommittee to support increased funding for research, prevention, and treatment. It is time to increase the nation's investment on this issue and to bring it in line with what is spent on illicit drugs and tobacco.

Each one of us can make a difference to ensure that our nation's children have a strong foundation for life. Delaying the start of alcohol use is a critical step in doing so. Please do not be swayed by those who argue this is not a serious problem. Our children are drinking at younger and younger ages and that should be a concern for all of us.

Thank you.

PREPARED STATEMENT OF JEFF BECKER

Good morning Mr. Chairman and distinguished Senators. My name is Jeff Becker and I'm the president of the Beer Institute, a national trade association of America's brewers. I am pleased to represent almost 900,000 men and women employed by our industry, including those who work in two of our nation's largest breweries in the Buckeye State. Our industry has a long and proud tradition of giving back to the communities where we live and do business, and we share the commitment of the members of this Subcommittee to combat illegal underage drinking.

Our commitment stems from two areas. First, it is no surprise to learn that many in our ranks are parents themselves—they share the concerns of all parents in this regard. But equally important, we do not like to see illegal underage consumption of the products that our members take such great care to make for adults of legal purchase age. We are joined in our commitment to be part of the solution to underage drinking by a large percentage of small and large businesses in the United States that would not be successful without a license to sell alcohol beverages. I can assure you that we have enlisted the commitment and the talents of personnel from our member companies, beer wholesalers, and retailers across the nation in the ongoing challenges posed by illegal underage drinking. We do not want the business of young people below the legal purchase age.

That phrase "ongoing challenges" is not a glib cliche, because each year, a new group of young people enter high school and college. Each year, our children are allowed more freedom in our highly mobile and open society. Some are allowed to take the bus or train to explore their cities. Some get a driver's license that allows them to travel to the next town for a school dance or a movie. Let us not forget that some of them, as young as 18, are off in Iraq and Afghanistan serving our country at war. The fact that our youth don't stop growing is only one of the fundamental challenges that confront parents, educators, law enforcement officials, and yes members of the beer industry. The stakes are high, and a second challenge is to get these disparate groups working together to find long and short-term ways to reduce illegal underage drinking.

Have our efforts, along with those of many others, made a difference? Let's look at the facts. While underage drinking has not disappeared, teen drinking and teen drunk-driving fatalities have declined significantly over the last two decades. According to the U.S. Department of Health and Human Services, 82 percent of today's adolescents do not drink.[1] Similarly, according to the University of Michigan survey called "Monitoring the Future," sponsored by the National Institute on Drug Abuse, the percentage of high school seniors who report having a drink in the last 30 days was 30 percent lower in 2002 than it was in 1982.[2] And beer drinking by college freshmen fell 37 percent in the same time frame according to the American Council on Education and researchers at the University of California at Los Angeles.[3]

In addition, the United States Department of Transportation reports that fatalities in crashes involving drunk drivers aged 16 to 20 have fallen 60 percent between 1982 and 2000. That progress has been achieved even though the number of 16 to 20 year olds licensed to drive has increased over 10 percent over the last decade to more than 12.6 million.[4]

While many factors explain this success, and there is still significant room for improvement, we believe that one of reasons for the progress of the last 20 years is that industry, government, and communities have cooperated to create programs that work. Brewers have committed hundreds of millions of dollars and substantial human, media, political and other resources to create effective anti-underage drinking programs.

A critical area in which I believe we have broad societal agreement is the importance of active parental involvement to prevent underage drinking. Brewers have long advocated and sponsored programs to facilitate parental discussions about drinking with their young children as well as their college-bound teens. By acknowledging the temptation associated with underage drinking and encouraging their children to

---

[1] *National Household Survey of Drug Abuse*, available at http://www.samhsa.gov/oas/p0000016.htm.

[2] Available at http://monitoringthefuture.org.

[3] *The American Freshman Survey* (2002), sponsored by UCLA and the American Council on Education, available at http://www.gseis.ucla.edu/beri/freshman.htm.

[4] National Highway Traffic Safety Administration, U.S. Dept, of Transportation (2002).

respect themselves and the law, parents can make an enormous difference. Brewer materials for parents are available in five languages with useful information to explain why drinking is inappropriate for youth. These efforts are effective because they draw on the strong influence parents have over their children's decisions about drinking.

For over a decade, according to a national poll conducted by the Roper Research organization, youth have identified their parents as the most powerful influence in their decision to drink or to refrain from drinking. I should point out that advertising has always been one of the choices offered in the survey. Every year, it has ranked dead last as an influential factor by the most important group in this discussion: youths themselves.

Because young people have so plainly told us that parents are the most effective way to reach them on the issue of underage drinking, we strongly believe in providing information and encouragement to help parents exercise this influence. And we do. Over the last several years, our members have distributed over 5 million pieces of material—guidebooks, videos, and others—to parents across the U.S. Brewers have also maintained on-going national advertising campaigns and comprehensive websites dedicated to this issue.

In addition to programs aimed at parents, our members sponsor or fund specific programs for those who sell our products in supermarkets, convenience stores, stadiums, concert venues, restaurants, and other retail outlets. As stated in the FTC Report to Congress released earlier this month, retailers play a vital role in stopping underage drinking by following their State laws and by checking and verifying IDs. Our members sponsor programs and provide materials in English, Spanish, Korean, and Vietnamese for servers of alcohol to teach them how to properly check IDs and to spot fake IDs. The Beer Institute and our members also disseminate "NAT ID" and other point-of-sale materials that remind customers that the establishment will ask for proper identification. In cooperation with retailers, police departments, county sheriffs, and other State and local agencies, brewers also have worked aggressively to help retailers and servers prevent the illegal underage purchase of alcohol.

Over the last decade, brewers have joined the National Highway Traffic Safety Administration, Major League Baseball, and other professional sports leagues in the TEAM Coalition to address underage drinking and abusive consumption at games and other major outdoor events.

And, at the college level, we have supported campus programs that focus student attention on education and awareness, emphasizing personal responsibility and respect for the law—which means not drinking if you are under 21, and drinking responsibly if you are above the legal drinking age and choose to drink. These programs include, among others, support for National Collegiate Alcohol Awareness Week programming, a nation-wide awareness effort that is taking place this month on hundreds of campuses across the country. Our industry has also supported research and programs collectively known as social norms, a positive approach that reminds college students that the large majority of their peers make healthy and responsible decisions about drinking.

Last year, the National Institute on Alcohol Abuse and Alcoholism (NIAAA) issued a comprehensive report on alcohol abuse on campus, a section of which categorized social norms and other approaches supported by the industry as effective or promising.[5]

And finally, in addition to the other programs I have discussed, brewers have created diverse national advertising campaigns including "Live Responsibly," "Let's Stop Underage Drinking Before It Starts," and "21 Means 21."

The recent Federal Trade Commission Report on alcohol beverage industry self regulation reviewed industry-sponsored programs favorably and pointed out that they are developed by professionals in the fields of education, medicine, or alcohol abuse and that they follow approaches recommended by alcohol research.[6]

---

[5] Task Force of the National Advisory Council on Alcohol Abuse and Alcoholism, *A Call to Action: Changing the Culture of Drinking at U.S. Colleges*, NIAAA, 2002, p. 24.

[6] Federal Trade Commission, *Alcohol Marketing and Advertising— A Report to Congress*, September, 2003, p. 21.

Since our industry's advertising activities have recently been the subject of Congressional interest, I would like to briefly touch on some other developments that underscore our commitment to market and sell our products to adults of legal purchase age. The FTC's 2003 Report unequivocally stated that beer industry members do not target underage consumers. Critics seek to use advertising as a lightning rod to divert attention from the real issues. Perhaps it is because they question the larger issue of beer's respected place in American society. But let's face it: drinking beer is not the only adult activity that youth should not engage in. In fact, this is just one of the many rules that society imposes on young people as they pass through maturity on their way to adulthood. And the most effective way to keep youth from engaging in adult behavior is not to pretend that adult products don't exist or that advertising causes people under 21 to drink. The way to address this issue is to help youth navigate through an adult world where there are many things—driving a car, voting in an election—not just drinking, that are not appropriate for them until they reach an age of maturity.

At the same time, our advertising is intended for adults, and our members voluntarily undertake extensive steps to avoid advertising and marketing that could be perceived as directed at youth. Self-regulation in this area is very important from a public policy perspective.

The 2003 FTC report further reinforces a statement from a 1999 agency report on alcohol beverage advertising: "Self-regulation is a realistic, responsive and responsible approach to many of the issues raised by underage drinking. It can deal quickly and flexibly with a wide range of advertising issues and brings the accumulated experience and judgment of an industry to bear without the rigidity of government regulations."[7] The FTC has conducted four comprehensive reviews of industry advertising

---

[7] *Self-Regulation in the Alcohol Industry: A Review of Industry Efforts To Avoid Promoting Alcohol To Underage Consumers*, A Report to Congress from the Federal Trade Commission (Sept. 1999), at p. 4. Furthermore, our review of the internal company documents did not find evidence that the products and their advertising are targeted to consumers under 21."[7] The Bureau of Alcohol, Tobacco and Firearms agreed these beverages "were placed appropriately with other alcohol beverages in retail outlets, and that available point of sale advertising was not targeting consumers under age 21."[7]

practices over the last 5 years.[8] The FTC recently indicated that, "Self-regulation practices in the alcohol industry have shown improvement since issuance of the 1999 Report…"[9] Its September 2003 report cited improvements in the area of ad placement, noting that industry members had shown 99 percent compliance with industry standards governing placement of broadcast advertising.[10] The FTC report discusses a number of important changes in our industry advertising code, which I will touch on in a moment. In the interest of full disclosure, the FTC also included some cautionary comments about advertising content and other issues, and we take the Commission's advice seriously.

In addition to the latest FTC report, the National Academies September report to Congress recognized the importance of self-regulation. The report does highlight the age-old scholarly debate over advertising and underage drinking, which clearly indicates that advertising is not a significant factor in underage drinking or the decision to drink at any age. Beyond that discussion, however, the National Academies panel states, "The industry has the prerogative indeed, the social obligation—to regulate its own practices in promotional activities that have a particular appeal to youngsters, irrespective of whether such practices can be proven to "cause" underage drinking." [Emphasis in original].[11]

We do have some fundamental differences with the National Academies recommendations and the process used to develop them. We believe the key to further progress in reducing underage drinking lies in family and community-based efforts. We are disappointed that the National Academies panel ignored the clear direction of Congress to evaluate existing Federal, State, and non-governmental programs. The panel focused heavily on costly and experimental government solutions with a

---

[8] The FTC has initiated the following: Orders to file special reports to several major industry members in 1998; the 1999 report cited above in footnote 7; 2001 investigation of advertising and marketing of flavored malt beverages; and *Alcohol Marketing and Advertising—A Report to Congress*, September, 2003.

[9] Federal Trade Commission, *Alcohol Marketing and Advertising—A Report to Congress*, September, 2003, p. 22.

[10] Id.

[11] National Research Council and Institute of Medicine of the National Academies, *Reducing Underage Drinking—A Collective Responsibility*, p. 137.

cursory review of existing programs, including many State efforts that combine education and enforcement to address unique challenges in different areas of our nation. The report does not provide the guidance Congress sought to determine policy and funding priorities to further reduce illegal underage access and consumption. This is unfortunate.

For over 50 years, Beer Institute's members have maintained socially responsible business practices including a policy of vigorous self-regulation of advertising and marketing. First adopted in 1943, the beer industry's advertising code has evolved over time to respond to societal and technological developments. We want our intentions to be clear to our consumers as well as to those who do not drink. Our primary goal as an industry is to reach out to those who can legally purchase our products with tasteful, contemporary advertising that increases awareness of our members' brands. Our ads are enjoyed by millions of Americans and rated highly in numerous surveys of adult consumers. Consistent with our longstanding policies, the Beer Institute Code was recently revised to incorporate some of the best practices of our member companies and to address several FTC recommendations.

I am pleased to inform you that our members have revised the standard for advertising placements in television, radio, and magazines to require placements only where the proportion of the audience above age 21 is reasonably expected to be 70 percent or higher. This standard reflects the demographics of the US population, in which approximately 70 percent of the public is age 21 or older. We have also expanded our code provisions covering marketing at or near college campuses and product placement in television programs and movies. The 2003 FTC report discusses these revisions in detail, and a copy of our full code is included with this testimony.

Although the recent National Academies recommendation to increase excise taxes is not part of our discussion here today, it is well known that the beer industry opposes such a measure; and I would like to take a brief moment to explain why. We oppose higher excise taxes because they are not an effective deterrent to abusive consumption or illegal underage drinking. A tax increase would force responsible adults on a budget—a large number of consumers who enjoy our products—to pass up the purchase of a six pack because it becomes less affordable. The science on this issue was examined by the NIAAA in its 10th Special Report to Congress. Their conclusion is that no consensus exists in this debate. Research conducted by Thomas Dee, and funded by the NIAAA, indicates that teens are not affected by higher taxes. In fact, Dee's research exposes methodological flaws in the research that the National Academies cited in support of raising excise taxes. If the research used to support higher beer taxes is flawed, we are surprised that the underage drinking committee ignored this important fact. Further, we note that Henry Weschler's research on the effects on college students is also cited in the NIAAA report, which concludes, "The results suggested that alcohol prices were a less salient determinant of the drinking behavior of college students than they were in other populations." Finally, a study coauthored by one of the National Academies' panelists indicates that the effects of tax increases may be "considerably smaller than suggested in previous literature."[12] The bottom line is that we do not support this recommendation because there is no scientific consensus to show that it will reduce teen drinking. It is also regressive and unfair to responsible adult consumers.

In closing, I'd like to leave you with this last fact. Brewers fully recognize that underage drinking is a problem that our society must embrace and tackle. We hope that we will be given the consideration to be a meaningful part of that fight, through our demonstrated commitment to this issue. As the father of two children, and I share this committee's concern—just like every other parent out there. Thank you for the opportunity to discuss these important issues.

---

[12] Cook, P.J. and Moore, M.J., "Environment and Persistence in Youthful Drinking Patterns," in *Risky Behavior Among Youths, An Economic Analysis*, edited by Jonathan Gruber, University of Chicago Press, National Bureau of Economic Research, 2001, pp. 375—437.

PREPARED STATEMENT OF WENDY J. HAMILTON, NATIONAL PRESIDENT, MOTHERS AGAINST DRUNK DRIVING

Introduction

Good morning, my name is Wendy Hamilton and I am the National President of Mothers Against Drunk Driving. MADD's mission is to stop drunk driving, support the victims of this violent crime and prevent underage drinking. I am honored to be here today to testify on the critical public health issue of illegal youth alcohol use.

I would like to take this opportunity to thank Chairman DeWine and Senator Dodd for holding this hearing today and for their continued commitment to protecting America's youth. Senators, your leadership has been and will be so important in bringing underage drinking prevention to the forefront of our nation's policy agenda.

I would also like to recognize and thank Senators Arlen Specter, Robert Byrd, Tom Harkin, John Warner, Harry Reid, and Representatives Lucille Roybal-Allard, Frank Wolf and Zach Wamp for requesting the National Academy of Sciences (NAS) report and for their efforts to reduce underage drinking. MADD looks forward to working with this committee and with Congress to develop prevention policies that provide adequate attention and funding—and employ effective strategies—to save young lives.

Today's hearing is truly historic—never before has the Federal Government considered action to develop a comprehensive strategy to prevent underage drinking, even though underage alcohol consumption is the nation's number one youth illegal drug problem. The NAS has assembled the nation's top public health researchers to examine a problem that has been overlooked for far too long. NAS has done an outstanding job cataloguing research and making science-based recommendations that if implemented will save lives.

The public health and safety community has been pursuing action at the Federal level for many years on this issue, but only now has the necessary national dialogue begun. With this committee's leadership, the national spotlight will finally shine on this sorely neglected issue.

The Problem

Without question, alcohol is the most widely used drug among America's youth. It is illegal for people under the age of 21 to drink alcohol, and yet currently there are 10.1 million underage drinkers in this nation (2002 National Household Survey On Drug Use and Health). Alcohol kills 6.5 times more kids than all other illicit drugs combined and is a major factor in the three leading causes of death of America's teens: motor vehicle crashes, homicides and suicides. Underage drinking does not just harm the drinker: half of the people who die in traffic crashes involving underage drinking drivers are people other than the drinking drivers. Underage drinking is not harmless fun. There is no such thing as "responsible" underage drinking.

Progress was made in the 1980's, most notably with the raising of the minimum drinking age to 21—a law that has saved over 20,000 young lives. But we still have a national mentality that accepts underage drinking as a mere "rite of passage," and underage drinking rates remain inexcusably high and have not improved for the past decade.

According to 2002 Monitoring the Future data, nearly half (48.6 percent) of all high school seniors report drinking in the last 30 days, a much larger proportion of youth than those who report either using marijuana (21.5 percent) or smoking (26.7 percent). The proportion of high school seniors who report drinking in the last 30 days was the same in 2002 as it was in 1993. Additionally, 29 percent of seniors report having five or more drinks on at least one occasion in the past two weeks, a percentage virtually unchanged since 1993.

To bring these statistics to life, I would like to raise a recent incident involving youth alcohol use that made national news. A Sunday morning touch football game between suburban Chicago high school girls turned into a brutal hazing incident resulting in the hospitalization of five students, one with a broken ankle and another who needed 10 stitches in her head. Video tape of the event revealed that younger girls were beaten, splattered with paint and had mud and feces thrown in their faces. About 100 students were involved, including onlookers who cheered while waving cups of beer before the camera.

In one segment of the home video, sixteen and seventeen year old girls are seen being held upside down over a keg of beer by several boys while they drink straight from the tap. In another segment, several girls can be seen pounding on one girl with their fists while they push her down into the mud.

School officials cited alcohol as a major factor in the violence, and in the weeks that followed, police charged two parents with providing three kegs of beer to minors.

As the nation watched these broadcasts in horror, many teens likely did not bat an eye. The Chicago incident could have been filmed in almost any town. Today, teens have easy access to alcohol. They are saturated with irresponsible alcohol ads. Underage drinking laws are not well enforced. And, parents and communities often look the other way when kids drink, in many cases even providing the beer. We've all heard the line: "Well, at least they're not using drugs." The fact is, alcohol IS the illegal drug of choice for kids.

Drunk Driving and Other Alcohol-Related Consequences Associated with Youth Alcohol Use

The consequences of youth alcohol use are staggering. Research demonstrates that the younger someone starts drinking, the more likely they are to suffer from alcohol-related problems later in life, including alcohol dependence and drunk driving. Children who drink before age 15 are four times more likely to become alcohol dependent than those who delay drinking until they are 21.

More than 17,000 people are killed each year in alcohol-related crashes and approximately one-half million are injured. In 2000, 69 percent of youth killed in alcohol-related traffic crashes involved underage drinking drivers. Although young drivers make up a mere 7 percent of the driving population, they constitute 13 percent of the alcohol-involved drivers in fatal crashes.

The 1999 National Survey of Drinking and Driving among Drivers Age 16-20 revealed that youth drove 11 million times after drinking in the past year. Their average blood alcohol level was 10 percent, three times the level of all drivers who drove after drinking. Forty percent of youth who drove after drinking had a least one passenger in the vehicle. Clearly young drivers are putting themselves at risk, but they are also putting others at risk. Society has an obligation to protect motorists from the risky behavior of underage drinkers. Society also has an obligation to protect kids from themselves.

Alcohol is also implicated in a large portion of deaths and injuries caused by dangers other than drinking and driving. According to the NAS, nearly 40 percent of youth under age 21 who died from drowning, burns and falls tested positive for alcohol. Youth alcohol use is also associated with violence and suicidal behavior. Individuals under 21 commit 45 percent of rapes, 44 percent of robberies, and 37 percent of other assaults, and it is estimated that 50 percent of violent crime is alcohol-related.

Sexual violence, as well as unplanned and unprotected sexual activity, is another consequence of youth alcohol use. A 2002 National Institute on Alcohol Abuse and Alcoholism (NIAAA) study titled “A Call to Action: Changing the Culture of Drinking at U.S. Colleges” found that each year more than 70,000 students aged 18-24 are victims of alcohol-related sexual assault or date rape. Additionally, the report found that 600,000 students were assaulted by another drinking college student annually.

Long-term consequences of youth alcohol use have become more and more clear as research on the adolescent brain continues to emerge. The human brain continues to develop into the early 20’s. Studies show that heavy alcohol use by youth has disproportionately negative effects on the physical development of the brain, and that alcohol use during adolescence has a direct affect on brain functioning.

In addition to the human costs associated with underage drinking, the economic cost to society is staggering. It is conservatively estimated that underage drinking costs this nation $53 billion dollars each year, including $19 billion from traffic crashes and $29 billion from violent crime. The NAS points out that this estimate is "somewhat incomplete" and "does not include medical costs other than those associated with traffic crashes" and other potential factors contributing to the social costs of underage drinking. The NAS concludes that "the $53 billion appears to be an underestimate of the social costs of underage drinking" (p. 70).

National Academy of Sciences Provides Roadmap for the Nation

The NAS report provides a significant and groundbreaking opportunity to help put the nation's number one youth drug problem on the national policy agenda and gives our nations' leaders the impetus for concrete action. All of the NAS recommendations should be seriously considered by Congress, the Administration, and State and local leaders. The NAS strategy includes components that will involve leaders at all levels of government, community activists, parents, educators, businesses, law enforcement, youth and society at large.

The NAS roadmap includes ten main components:

1. National Adult-Oriented Media Campaign
2. Partnership to Prevent Underage Drinking
3. Alcohol Advertising
4. Entertainment Media
5. Limiting Access
6. Youth-Oriented Interventions
7. Community Interventions
8. Government Assistance and Coordination

9. Alcohol-Excise Taxes
10. Research and Evaluation

While MADD supports the NAS report in its entirety, my testimony will focus on areas MADD believes will have the greatest impact on reducing youth alcohol use.

National Efforts to Combat Underage Drinking Woefully Inadequate

While illicit drugs and tobacco youth prevention have received considerable attention and funding from the Federal Government, underage drinking has consistently been ignored. NAS confirms this:

In fiscal 2000, the nation spent approximately $1.8 billion on preventing illicit drug use (Office of National Drug Control Policy, 2003), which was 25 times the amount, $71.1 million, targeted at preventing underage alcohol use." (p. 14)

Not only is there minimal funding available to States and local communities specifically targeted to reduce youth alcohol use, there is also no coordinated national effort to reduce and prevent underage drinking.

In May 2001 the General Accounting Office (GAO) released a report outlining Federal funds aimed at preventing underage drinking. The report provided concrete evidence that: (1) the Federal Government's approach to youth alcohol use prevention is disjointed and (2) funding for youth alcohol prevention is woefully inadequate.

GAO found that multiple Federal agencies play some role in underage drinking prevention, and that only a very small portion—7 percent—of total funds available for alcohol and other drug use both had a specific focus on alcohol and identified youth or youth and the broader community as the specific target population. Specifically, among the Departments of Health and Human Services, Justice and Transportation, a mere $71.1 million focused on youth or alcohol and youth and the broader community.

Citing the GAO and additional research, the NAS report concludes the following:

> … there is no coordinated, central mechanism for disseminating research findings or providing technical assistance to grantees or others interested in developing strategies that target underage drinking … the committee is not aware of any ongoing effort to coordinate all of the various Federal efforts either within or across departments. The multitude of agencies and initiatives involved suggests the need for an interagency body to provide national leadership and provide a single Federal voice on the issue of underage drinking, (p. 236-237)
>
> The NAS report also adds that "community efforts are most likely to succeed if they have strong and informed leadership" and that "resources are needed for training and leadership development for coalition and task force members as well as key decision makers." (p. 237-238)

NAS Recommendations 12-1 through 12-6 demonstrate a clear need for better "Government Assistance and Coordination" at the national level in order to reduce underage drinking. MADD strongly supports implementation of NAS Recommendations 12-1 through 12-6:

> 12-1: A Federal interagency coordinating committee on prevention of underage drinking should be established, chaired by the secretary of the U.S. Department of Health and Human Services.
>
> 12-2: A National Training and Research Center on Underage Drinking should be established in the U.S. Department of Health and Human Services. This body would provide technical assistance, training, and evaluation support and would monitor progress in implementing national goals.
>
> 12-3: The secretary of the U.S. Department of Health and Human Services should issue an annual report on underage drinking to Congress summarizing all Federal agency activities, progress in reducing underage drinking, and key surveillance data.
>
> 12-4: Each State should designate a lead agency to coordinate and spearhead its activities and programs to reduce and prevent underage drinking.

12-5: The annual report of the secretary of the U.S. Department of Health and Human Services on underage drinking should include key indicators of underage drinking.

12-6: The Monitoring the Future Survey and the National Survey on Drug Use and Health should be revised to elicit more precise information on the quantity if alcohol consumed and to ascertain brand preferences of underage drinkers.

National Adult-Oriented Media Campaign

Six years ago, Congress allocated $1 billion dollars to the White House Office of National Drug Control Policy (ONDCP) for an anti-drug media campaign designed to prevent youth drug use. Despite the fact that alcohol is the number one youth drug problem—both then and now—underage drinking prevention messages were excluded from the campaign.

MADD and other members of the public health and safety community pressed to have underage drinking prevention messages included in the ONDCP campaign. In May 1999, an amendment sponsored by Representatives Lucille Roybal-Allard (D-CA) and Frank Wolf (R-VA) was introduced that would change the authorizing legislation to allow ONDCP to begin including such messages. The proposed amendment came under attack and was eventually defeated due to intense pressure from the alcohol lobby.

Since 1998, Congress has considered creating a separate media campaign to prevent underage drinking, but those attempts also failed due to behind the scenes opposition from the alcohol industry. The alcohol industry instead pressured Congress to request a study as a means to delay action on a media campaign. The Congressional directive to NAS to develop a comprehensive strategy to prevent underage drinking dates back several years to repeated attempts by the public health and safety community to establish a media campaign that addresses youth alcohol use.

When the alcohol industry learned that the NAS might recommend prevention measures it opposes, alcohol interests tried to inappropriately influence the content of the report, fault the NAS expert panel, and criticize and discredit the findings while they were being formulated. Before the NAS report was even released, the beer industry took out full-page ads in Roll Call, the Hill, Congress Daily and other Capitol Hill publications in an attempt to discredit the report findings. The beer industry complained that they did not have enough influence on the NAS report.

MADD believes that the alcohol industry, and in particular the beer lobby, has not earned credibility on the issue of underage drinking prevention. As the nation attempts to get serious about employing effective, science-based strategies to curb the nation's number one youth drug problem, MADD urges the alcohol industry to stop its baseless opposition to proven public health measures and to stop relying on underage drinking as a source of revenue.

It is unacceptable that the alcohol industry has been the sole source of messaging to parents and teens on underage drinking. Congress decided that it wasn't a good idea to let tobacco companies be the sole voice in educating the public on smoking prevention. We believe the same should hold true for the alcohol companies on underage drinking.

MADD commends the NAS for calling for a national advertising campaign to prevent underage drinking and strongly supports NAS Recommendation 6-1:

> 6-1: The Federal Government should fund and actively support the development of a national media effort, as a major component of an adult-oriented campaign to reduce underage drinking.

The goals of the national media campaign, as explained by NAS, would be to instill a broad societal commitment to reduce underage drinking, to increase specific actions by adults that are meant to discourage underage drinking, and to decrease adult conduct that facilitates underage drinking.

The need for a comprehensive public education campaign aimed at underage drinking prevention is undeniable as most parents and teens are unaware of the dangers associated with youth alcohol use. Many parents do not recognize the prevalence of or the risks associated with drinking for their own children, and many parents even facilitate their underage children's drinking by giving kids access to alcohol, by not responding to children's drinking, and by not adequately monitoring their children's behavior.

NAS also concludes that an adult-oriented national media campaign is also important because it would support local efforts to reduce underage drinking. It is important not only because of what it will accomplish on its own, but also because its effects bolster local efforts.

Reducing Youth Exposure to Alcohol Advertising

Underage youth are bombarded with irresponsible alcohol marketing messages depicting alcohol consumption as cool, sexy and glamorous. The establishment of a national media campaign to prevent underage drinking is particularly important given the fact that in 2001 the alcohol industry spent 1.6 billion dollars on product advertising in the "measured media" (including magazines, newspapers, outdoor advertising, and radio and television). According to the Federal Trade Commission (FTC), at least twice that amount was spent on unmeasured promotion, including sponsorships and product placement in entertainment media and other venues.

A recent study by the Center on Alcohol Marketing and Youth (CAMY 2003) reported that in 2001 the alcohol industry spent $23.2 million dollars to air 2,379 "responsibility" messages, while in contrast the industry spent $812.2 million on 208,909 product advertisements. There were 179 product ads for every ad that referred to the legal drinking age. Quite significantly, a typical "responsibility" ad is branded with the alcohol company name, which leads many public health experts to conclude that "responsibility" ads are simply another means to promote brand recognition and loyalty.

MADD is not against alcohol advertising, but it is imperative that stricter standards be put in place to protect our children from constant exposure to alcohol messages. Although beer is the favorite alcoholic beverage among young people, the beer industry has advertised for years with little or no restrictions or standards from the networks. Strong alcohol advertising restrictions must be mandatory for all segments of the alcohol industry—including ads for beer, wine, liquor and malt-based beverages.

According to the Office of Juvenile Justice and Delinquency Prevention, underage drinkers consume about 10 percent of all the alcohol purchased in the United States, or 3.6 billion drinks annually. NAS reports that underage drinkers consume anywhere from 10 to 20 percent of all alcohol purchased in the U.S. Beer is the most common drink consumed in most cases of heavy drinking, binge drinking, drunk driving and underage drinking.

Now "malternatives" or "alcopops" have climbed onto the advertising bandwagon to capture more of the youth market (such as Smirnoff Ice, Bacardi Silver, and Skyy Blue). MADD is deeply concerned with the growing number of ads for liquor-branded, malt-based beverages that have a flavor and marketing plan that appeals to our kids. Just like beer, the distilled spirits industry is being given a "free pass" to establish brand recognition and loyalty among youth. NAS states that:

A particularly troubling illustration of the youth-specific attractions of an alcohol marketing campaign concerns so-called "alcopops," sweet, flavored alcoholic malt beverages. Recent survey data suggest that these products are more popular with teenagers than with adults, both in terms of awareness and use (p. 135).

Greater restrictions are also needed for print advertising. Despite the alcohol industry's claims, CAMY reports that young people under 21 are reached at a higher proportion to their numbers in the population by alcohol ads. Our youth see far more beer, distilled spirits and malternative advertising in magazines than adults. In 2001 alone, nearly one-third of all measured magazine alcohol ads were placed in 10 publications with a youth audience of 25 percent or more.

NAS points out that the dispute over whether alcohol advertising "causes" underage drinking is simply an "unnecessary distraction" from the most important task at hand: the alcohol industry must do a better job of refraining from marketing products or engaging in promotional activities that appeal to youth. NAS concludes that if the industry fails to respond in a meaningful way to this challenge, the case for government action becomes compelling.

MADD supports all of the NAS recommendations on alcohol advertising, but in particular MADD urges action on NAS Recommendations 7-4 and 12-6:

> 7-4: Congress should appropriate the necessary funding for the U.S. Department of Health and Human Services to monitor underage exposure to alcohol advertising on a continuing basis and to report periodically to Congress and the public. The report should include information on the underage percentage of the exposed audience and estimated number of underage viewers for print and broadcasting alcohol advertising in national markets and, for television and radio broadcasting, in a selection of large local or regional markets.
>
> 12-6: The Monitoring the Future (MTF) Survey and the National Household Survey on Drug Use and Health (NSDUH) should be revised to elicit more precise information on the quantity of alcohol consumed and to ascertain brand preferences of underage drinkers.

Both of these recommendations call for basic public health surveillance that is essential to identify and prevent the over-exposure of our youth to alcohol advertising. The availability of such data is needed to understand the actual youth impact of new products and the advertising campaigns that promote them.

Limiting Alcohol Access to Youth

Limiting youth access to alcohol is a proven way to decrease underage drinking. Most notably, increasing the minimum drinking age to 21 has been one of the most effective public health policies in history, resulting in a significant decrease in fatal traffic crashes, DWI arrests, and self-reported drinking by young people. However, the law alone does not preclude youth from gaining access to alcohol. General deterrence through sanctions, improved enforcement, and public awareness of enforcement is needed in order to effectively implement restrictions on youth alcohol use.

The NAS report points out that "[i]t is apparently not difficult for youth who want to drink to readily obtain alcohol. A majority of high school students, even eighth graders, report that alcohol is 'fairly easy' or 'very easy' to get, with the proportion increasing from eighth to tenth to twelfth grade." For eighth graders, 60 percent report that alcohol is fairly easy or very easy to obtain, while for twelfth graders the percentage is more than 90 percent. The NAS also reports that the "alcohol most favored by underage drinkers is beer."

A critical component of a comprehensive strategy to reduce underage drinking is to enact and strengthen laws designed to limit youth alcohol consumption. Although every State defines the legal minimum drinking age at 21, State laws vary in scope in terms of restrictions relating to underage purchase, possession, or consumption of alcohol and for the use of false identification. These weaknesses, as NAS points out, compromise the effectiveness of minimum drinking age laws.

The NAS recommendations to limit youth alcohol use focus on enacting and strengthening laws to: (1) reduce access through commercial sources; (2) reduce access through non-commercial sources; (3) reduce drinking and driving by underage drinkers; and (4) prescribe and enforce penalties on adult providers and underage drinkers.

In addition to closing loopholes in age 21 laws as mentioned above, NAS suggests, and MADD agrees, implementing key approaches to meeting these goals, including:

- Imposing more stringent penalties on retail licensees for violation of laws against sales to minors;
- Strengthening compliance check programs in retail outlets;
- Strengthening or enacting dram shop laws;
- Regulating internet sales and home delivery of alcohol;
- Holding adults responsible for illegal consumption of alcohol by minors;

- Implementing beer keg registration laws to deter the purchase of kegs of beer for consumption by minors;
- Strengthening enforcement of zero tolerance laws;
- Implementing the use of routine sobriety checkpoints to increase the deterrence of underage drinking and driving.

Enforcement of State and local laws has proven to be a highly effective tool in underage drinking prevention. Tougher enforcement of laws aimed at reducing underage drinking is greatly needed, and Congress can provide the impetus for action. In particular, MADD strongly supports NAS Recommendation 9-3:

> 9-3: The Federal Government should require States to achieve designated rates of retailer compliance with youth access prohibitions as a condition of receiving block grant funding, similar to the Synar Amendment's requirements for youth tobacco sales.

As part of a comprehensive strategy to reduce underage drinking, Congress should also provide additional resources to law enforcement in order to improve enforcement of underage drinking laws.

Expanding Youth-Oriented and Community Interventions

The NAS report underscores the need for expanding youth-oriented and community interventions, including: intensive research and development for a youth-focused national media campaign to prevent underage drinking; funding for and implementation of evidence-based education interventions, with priority given to those that incorporate effective elements and those that are part of comprehensive community programs; and improving assessment and treatment programs.

MADD strongly supports NAS Recommendation 11-2:

> 11-2: Public and private funders should support community mobilization to reduce underage drinking. Federal funding for reducing and preventing underage drinking should be available under a national program dedicated to community-level approaches to reducing underage drinking, similar to the Drug Free Communities Act, which supports communities in addressing substance abuse with targeted, evidence-based prevention strategies.

MADD's youth programs are rooted in the latest scientific research and strive to empower children, teens and parents with knowledge so that individuals will be able to keep themselves and others safe from harm. Programs encourage good decision-making and engage youth in specific interventions designed to reduce underage drinking.

One of MADD's most successful community based youth programs is called Youth In Action (YIA). MADD's YIA program partners young people with community adult leaders to work toward "environmental" prevention strategies. Projects focus on strengthening enforcement of underage drinking laws and policy change. YIA teams have been trained in more than 40 communities across the country. Their partnerships with local law enforcement agencies, schools and community leaders have helped pass key underage drinking legislation and saved young lives.

Youth In Action focuses on the community environment that condones underage drinking, from the store clerk who doesn't check IDs, to the police officer who might pour out the beer and send teens home, to an adult who doesn't mind buying beer for a kid who slips him an extra $10—YIA teams look for community solutions instead of focusing their attention on their peers. Youth In Action teams engage in very specific interventions because research says these projects work. YIA teams across the country conduct:

- Alcohol Purchase Surveys—A young looking 21 year old attempts to purchase alcohol without an ID. No actual purchase is made. It is merely a survey to see if the clerk would have sold alcohol to a presumed minor without ID.

- Compliance Checks—With the help of the police, young people act as underage buyers. They are instructed to go through with the sale, whether the clerks ask for ID or not. The police may cite or arrest the store clerk.
- Shoulder-Tap Surveys—With law enforcement present to ensure safety, a young person (or group of young people) approach strangers outside an alcohol retailer to see if these adults would willingly purchase alcohol for them because they are too young to legally buy. Those that answer yes receive instead of money, a card outlining the law and penalty for furnishing alcohol to a minor. Those that refuse to purchase alcohol are handed a card thanking them for serving their community by refusing to provide alcohol to a minor.
- Law Enforcement Recognition Programs—YIA teams publicly thank local law enforcement officials who are working to prevent underage drinking. This can be done many ways: a formal banquet, a media event, or even just by bringing food to officers at the station or out on location where police officers are working on the job. Either way, this is a unique opportunity for teens to thank police officers for doing their job.
- Roll Call Briefings—YIA teams set up meetings with their local police departments to make presentations at shift change meetings. Two or three YIA members go to the police station with an adult leader to encourage police officers to enforce the Zero Tolerance Law. Many YIA teams have printed cards or notepads to hand out outlining the law and declaring their support for it.

Two weeks ago while visiting New Orleans to attend the MADD National Conference, 20 young activists from YIA teams from across the country spent a Thursday night determining youth accessibility to alcohol in the “Big Easy” by measuring the number of adults willing to purchase alcohol for those under 21. The “shoulder tap” survey revealed that it is relatively easy for youth to get alcohol in New Orleans. Additionally, to help enforce the minimum drinking age law, YIA teams spoke at 10 New

Orleans Police Department roll call briefings to demonstrate to law enforcement officers that young people believe that the enforcement of the 21 minimum drinking age law will change behavior and save lives.

Protecting You/Protecting Me (PY/PM) is another program developed by MADD in response to educators, parents, and community leaders seeking an alcohol-use prevention program for elementary school students that could be incorporated in to the core curriculum. PY/PM was named a Model Program by the U.S. Department of Health and Human Services, Substance Abuse and Mental Health Services Administration (SAMHSA), Center for Substance Abuse and Prevention (CSAP).

PY/PM includes the latest brain research, provides all curriculum and training materials necessary for national replication and includes an evaluation component, which continually demonstrates significant results.

The PY/PM curriculum teaches first through fifth graders basic safety skills, alcohol's effects on the developing brain and shows kids how to protect themselves by making good decisions, such as what to do when riding in a car with an unsafe driver. The curriculum is designed to fill the gap in current prevention programs that have not yet incorporated the latest research on children's brains and the developmental risks associated with exposure to alcohol before the age of 21.

The goal of the curriculum is to prevent injury and death of children and youth due to underage consumption of alcoholic beverages, and vehicle-related risks, especially as passengers in vehicles in which the driver is not alcohol-free.

Evaluation of PY/PM has shown that students receiving the lessons are:

- more knowledgeable about their brains
- more media literate
- less likely to ride with a driver who is not alcohol-free
- less likely to drink when they are teenagers

PY/PM is endorsed by the American Academy of Pediatrics and the National Association of Elementary School Principals. By the end of 2003, nearly 200,000 elementary students will be exposed to MADD's PY/PM's lessons in over 1,200 schools across the country.

Increasing Alcohol Excise Taxes

Research shows that alcohol taxes and price affect youth alcohol consumption and associated consequences. Studies demonstrate that increased beer prices lead to reductions in the levels and frequency of drinking and heavy drinking among youth and lower traffic crash fatality rates among young drivers.

MADD strongly supports NAS Recommendation 12-7:

> 12-7: Congress and State legislatures should raise excise taxes to reduce underage consumption and to raise additional revenues for this purpose. Top priority should be given to raising beer taxes, and excise tax rates for all alcoholic beverages should be indexed to the consumer price index so that they keep pace with inflation without the necessity of further legislative action.

Revenue generated from increased alcohol excise taxes could be designated, as NAS suggests, to fund a broad prevention strategy to reduce underage drinking. NAS concludes that "the long downward slide in the actual cost of these taxes to consumers has considerably exacerbated the underage drinking problem" (p. 246).

Despite the public health ramifications, the alcohol industry continues to push for lower alcohol excise taxes. In 1991, for the first time in 40 years, the Federal excise tax on beer was raised from \$9 per barrel to \$18 per barrel (or 16 cents per six-pack to 32 cents per six pack).

MADD is strongly opposed to H.R. 1305 and S. 809, legislation seeking to "rollback" the 1991 beer tax increase. The National Bureau of Economic Research has estimated that the 1991 increase saves 600 young lives each year in reduced traffic crashes. Similarly, MADD is strongly opposed to H.R. 2950 and S. 1457, legislation seeking to roll-back the Federal excise tax on distilled spirits to its pre-1985 level.

Conclusion

It is time for our nation—from parents to communities to our political leaders at the national and State levels—to end the complacent attitude about underage drinking and to take action to end this public health epidemic. There is an urgent need to expand prevention, treatment and community programs and improve enforcement of existing laws to prevent underage drinking. More youth drink alcohol than smoke tobacco or use other illegal drugs, yet Federal investments in preventing underage drinking pale in comparison with resources targeted at preventing illicit drug use.

The media constantly reports on the countless numbers of alcohol-related deaths and injuries of today's youth, but our nation accepts and even enables these preventable tragedies. The future of our nation's youth continues to hang in the balance. Underage drinking is illegal, and yet millions of kids continue to engage in this high-risk behavior every month, every weekend, and even every day.

The NAS has reviewed the research and has recommended strategies that will significantly reduce and prevent underage drinking: a national media campaign to prevent underage drinking, tougher standards for alcohol advertising, improved teen drinking prevention laws, better enforcement and awareness of these laws, expanded youth and community interventions, and increased Federal and State excise taxes on alcohol—all areas that MADD's members view as critical to solving this problem.

MADD will continue to work with Members of Congress and with partners in the public health community to pursue introduction of a comprehensive, science-based legislative package designed to reduce and prevent underage drinking. I urge this committee to use the NAS recommendations as a roadmap to create a healthier future for America's youth.

The devastating effects of underage drinking are completely preventable. The NAS recommendations give us a new beginning and a fresh approach to attack this problem. We must, as a nation, ramp up our efforts, and today is a new beginning in that endeavor. Thank you.

Prepared Statement of David DeAngelis

Good morning. My name is David DeAngelis, and I am a senior at North Haven High School in North Haven, Connecticut. I would like to thank Senator Dodd, Senator DeWine, and the sub-committee for inviting me to be here this morning. I am honored to have the opportunity to speak on this issue.

Three summers ago, three classmates and I attended the Connecticut MADD Power Camp. One speaker left a lasting impression on us. Her teenage daughter had been killed by a drunk driver and she began speaking to young people about the perils of drinking and driving. The task grew increasingly difficult and on the way to our group, she prayed to her daughter for a sign to help her continue. A car passed. The license plate read "SAVE 1."

The four of us left the camp determined to address the problems of underage drinking in our community and started a newspaper column titled "SAVE 1." We decided to target adults, hoping to enlighten parents and encourage them to help their children make the right choices. After the other three students graduated, I continued to write it on my own.

Although I receive positive feedback about the column, I sometimes get frustrated. Last spring, I gave a presentation to parents at my town's middle school and only thirty people showed up. Trying to remain motivated became a challenge.

That changed this summer when I volunteered as a staffer at Power Camp and worked with students to develop a project for their town. I left the camp optimistic after watching them rally behind their idea to focus on passing a local ordinance against serving alcohol to minors at house parties.

Today I speak before you on the heels of the release of the NAS report on underage drinking. When I read the report, especially the committee's proposal for a national adult-oriented media campaign, the words Adult-oriented jumped out at me. Targeting adults is necessary to effectively address underage drinking. Parents often take on a "kids will be kids" attitude and think that drinking is part of growing up. Actually, young people try to emulate adults whose social lives revolve around alcohol. Many parents not only condone the use of alcohol but also provide liquor to their children and their children's friends.

Last May, a classmate of mine had an after-prom party where alcohol was included. To make sure the guests would be "safe," his parents confiscated their car keys. This summer, what started as a few kids banging out in a basement turned into a full-fledged party as more and more kids showed up with beer. The parents spent the entire evening upstairs never checking on the group.

Then, there are the times when parents are not home. Rids party, drink, and do stupid and dangerous things. One girl, hosting a party, jumped into her pool fully clothed after getting drunk. Three times. Another classmate celebrated his birthday by drinking at a friend's house and falling down the stairs.

Underage drinking is not a problem confined to the town of North Haven. It happens everywhere. This past July, I was here in Washington for Boys Nation. Standing in the airport, I met some of the other delegates and casually asked what they liked to do for fun. One promptly replied, "Drink" and began recounting stories that involved getting drunk with his friends.

A large number of high school students are affected by underage drinking, including those who have made the decision not to drink. These kids are often ostracized by students in the more popular drinking circles and fight daily pressures to join.

This initiative is extremely important. It will take a national movement to change the apathetic attitudes of parents. Blatant disregard for the drinking age simply cannot be tolerated. The youth of America are receiving the message that underage drinking is acceptable, not to mention the messages they receive from the media.

The alcohol industry spends over one billion dollars each year on advertising, portraying drinking as a ticket to good times. Most disturbing is the fact that alcohol companies advertise during TV programs viewed predominantly by teenagers. On the radio, more beer commercials are heard by children than by adults. These ads are clever, entertaining, and humorous. I can recite a radio commercial for Beck's Beer that I heard almost every day this summer.

When children are not getting bombarded with commercials, they are seeing images promoting drinking in the shows they watch. Who else is watching MTV at 4:00 in the afternoon? Or at 1:00 on a Saturday when shows like "Spring Break" and "Fraternity" are aired?

Connecticut has the highest rate of underage drinking. The average age that children begin drinking is 11 for boys and 13 for girls. The Connecticut Coalition to Stop Underage Drinking has been at work for the past seven years addressing these issues, focusing much of its energy on the role of adults. It has also begun work on each of the local recommendations in the NAS report.

But they only scratch the surface of the problem. We—the entire nation—need the federal government's guidance, direction, and resources. Underage drinking is a national crisis which is only getting worse. The NAS recommendations are too valuable to ignore.

PREPARED STATEMENT OF CATHERINE BATH, PROGRAM DIRECTOR, SECURITY ON CAMPUS, INC.

Dear Senator DeWine and Committee Members: We at Security On Campus, Inc., a national nonprofit organization concerned with the safety of college students, want to thank the Senate for supporting stronger Federal action on the serious problem of drinking among our youth. The recommendations of the NAS report need to be implemented to save the needless waste of young lives. I know. I lost my only son to an alcohol-related incident at Duke University in November 1999. There is no greater heartbreak. There is no loss more tragic or unnecessary!

Should we be surprised at the high percentages of college and high school students experimenting with alcohol and engaging in high-risk drinking? Our children have been exposed to the alcohol industry's public service announcements (AKA beer commercials) all of their young lives.

Other than the alcohol industry's advertisements to party with beer, bond with beer, be fun, popular and successful with beer, our children have had virtually no other education about alcohol. My son (now deceased) and his whole generation, now in college, grew up mesmerized by Spuds McKenzie and the Budweiser Frogs!

Why are alcohol advertisers not required to issue a long list of warnings (the truth—like the drug companies are required to do) on TV? Why are they allowed to advertise such a dangerous drug to our children at all?

The National Campaign to Prevent Underage Drinking Act of 2001 never got passed into law. Why? Because the alcohol industry lobby is more powerful than the voice of this country's parents. All of the efforts to effect some change in this culture are subverted at every juncture by the alcohol industry, a very powerful and cash rich presence and force at every level, including governmental. They are lobbying to lower beer tax to its 1951 level.

That is a slap in the face of every parent in this country. And it is a knife in the heart of parents such as myself who have lost their children to alcohol and there are SO MANY OF US!

Prepared Statement of Brandon Busteed, Founder and CEO, Outside the Classroom

I am so utterly frustrated and disappointed. I'm frustrated with the fact that this country has an underage drinking problem of epidemic proportions, yet the resources dedicated to solving it have been miniscule by any measure. I'm frustrated by the lack of leaders willing to address the problem. I'm especially frustrated that so many people don't care, and that some even want to keep things status quo. I'm disappointed that it has taken Congress so long to even consider doing something about it. I'm disappointed in myself in believing that very little will come of this hearing. I'm disappointed most of all that those leaders needed most to solve this problem—the college and high school students themselves—are completely missing from this dialogue.

You'll see and hear today from alcohol industry lobbyists seeking to protect their market and profits, researchers who are decades removed from college and high school, and activists who have lost family members and close friends to alcohol-related deaths. All these perspectives are critical and deserve to be heard. Indeed, they are typically the only ones heard. But unfortunately, you're not going to hear from some of the sources that most need to be heard. You're not going to hear from people like me, save if you take the time to read this—one of the many written testimonies submitted to this hearing.

I'm 26-years-old—about 4 years removed from my undergraduate experience at Duke University where I was a student activist advocating responsible drinking and nonalcoholic lifestyles. Different from most who get involved in this effort, I was not spurred into action by the death of a friend or an alcoholic relative. I was an NCAA Division I standout in track and cross-country. I was a public policy major. I am a white male athlete raised in an upper-middle class home. Based on those demographics, I'm in about the highest-risk category for high-risk drinking that there is. About the only thing missing is that I was not a member of a Greek organization in college. But my father is an active elder in his Greek organization, and there was every reason to believe I should have/could have/would have followed his footsteps.

What makes me unusual is that I fit all the standard stereotypes for being the opposite of who I am today. I should be a "binge" drinker. Instead, I'm the founder and CEO of an organization, Outside The Classroom, that has educated over 100,000 college students about alcohol through an online course called AlcoholEdu. I am a young person who has chosen to make a career out of tackling this social epidemic of high-risk drinking. And I'm extremely impatient.

The study by the National Academy of Sciences clearly articulated the problem and made some useful recommendations about a solution. But unfortunately its assessment of effective prevention programs simply regurgitated already outdated studies such as the now 3-year-old NIAAA study on college drinking. It did nothing to advance the knowledge of and evaluation of successful new programs that are up and running today. For example, AlcoholEdu did not yet exist when the NIAAA conducted their assessment of effective college prevention programs. In just 3 short years later, we've demonstrated success on hundreds of campuses.

The fact of the matter is that there are many programs already up and running that are working to reduce dangerous drinking on college campuses and in high schools today. These programs need better financial support along with more formal evaluation. AlcoholEdu, our online prevention program, is only one. Others include environmental management campaigns, stricter enforcement of alcohol policies, and more encouragement and funding of alcohol-free social alternatives. Our partner in delivering AlcoholEdu for High School, Mothers Against Drunk Driving, has a suite of prevention programs that are getting dramatic results in high schools and communities.

In fact, the new concept we have pioneered of "Population-Level Prevention," where an entire social group goes through a prevention program simultaneously, is one of the most important steps forward in prevention that we've seen in years. With AlcoholEdu, our research has shown that when all the first-year students in a college go through the online prevention experience together, overall consumption of alcohol declines from rates before the program, rates of abstention increase rather than decrease, and, most important, rates of dangerous, high-risk binge drinking — cause of the most harmful negative consequence of alcohol on campus—decline dramatically.

Such successful programs may be working today, but they need more economic support during the worst fiscal crisis colleges and high schools have faced in a generation.

Therefore the policy implications are clear. Congress should pay heed to the advice in the NAS report to raise taxes on alcohol. The money is needed to fund important prevention programs that are already available, and that will work when applied on a population basis. The real scandal is that this country is doing virtually nothing to fund and support prevention efforts. The statistics speak for themselves. We spend 25 times more money on anti-drug campaigns (other than alcohol) than we do on anti-drug campaigns related to alcohol. Yet, alcohol is by far the most widely used drug with the most death and destruction associated with it—far more than all other drugs combined. And it's clear the alcohol industry bears much of the responsibility simply by virtue of selling and marketing alcohol.

Therefore it's only right that the Federal Government should tax the industry to support public efforts to protect our young people from this danger. However, the taxes shouldn't go toward funding programs run or in any other way supported by the alcohol industry. Instead, Congress should use the money to authorize funding for proven programs delivered by nonprofit and for profit providers without any alcohol-industry affiliations, mimicking the same successful public policy we have learned from tobacco industry settlements.

Specifically, Congress should allocate funds to implement recommendations 10-1, 10-2, 10-3 and 10-4 in the NAS report focusing on Youth-Oriented Interventions. This funding would support planning for a youth-focused media campaign, implementation of evidence-based population-level education programs, and support for evaluations of evidence-based comprehensive prevention programs in colleges. Congress should also allocate funds to implement recommendations 11-1 and 11-2 in the section of the report focusing on Community Interventions, helping community leaders conduct comprehensive prevention programs utilizing evidence-based strategies and programs.

The NAS proposal that a grand public-private partnership be formed also is the right idea. With the right public funding to prime the pump, we will see an inflow of private capital from across the rest of the private-sector spectrum to address the problem. At Outside The Classroom, which is a private, for-profit company, we have forged an alliance with one of the world's best-known nonprofit organizations, Mothers Against Drunk Driving, and are calling on the private sector to do their share as well. We are issuing a challenge to the nation's CEOs to fund prevention programs for every high school student in the country by contributing to a new Youth Alcohol Prevention Partnership Fund. The cost of this program—

less than $5 per student per school for a school-wide Population-Level Prevention Program—gives real meaning to the old saying, "an ounce of prevention is worth a pound of cure." It is an innovative partnership between a for-profit and a nonprofit that is actively engaging the private sector to meet the demand for a solution to a problem that, by effectively disabling America's youth, is undermining our nation's future productivity and competitiveness.

The CEOs we've spoken with like the philosophy of our prevention partnership, because it attacks the problem at the source—by drawing the first line in the battle against underage drinking with the individual young people themselves. By educating young people about the problems of high-risk drinking, and by engaging them in leadership activities to attack the problem, we are inculcating the value of personal accountability and responsibility in our citizens and leaders of tomorrow which will be absolutely essential to any long-term effort to solve the problem. And, because beneficial results from a program like AlcoholEdu are so easily measured, it provides the kind of ROI measurement that the private sector needs. Finally, it is actually solving a problem that will directly affect the private sector's competitiveness and profitability in the future.

The Federal Government should assist with these prevention efforts not only by providing direct funding for them, but also by providing funding for the evaluation of programs necessary to rapidly discover which programs work best, and how, so that they might be propagated across the country all the more rapidly.

As a recent member of the underage population, I understand what will motivate young people to change their behavior. I had my first alcoholic drink on February 10, 1999, one month before my 22nd birthday, and three months before my graduation from college. The fact that I didn't drink never hurt my social life in college one bit. I was elected a class officer every year, and served as class president my junior year. My senior year—because of my efforts to provide an alternative lifestyle for campus—I was elected by my peers to serve as Duke's Young Trustee—a 3-year position on Duke's Board of Trustees. I wouldn't say that my actions were "popular" though. At one point during my undergraduate career, students were so upset by a non-alcoholic party I planned following a basketball victory that I had the door of my car kicked in along with death threats on my answering machine. Most people would have thrown in the towel. I only became more convinced that I was on the right track towards social change.

During my senior year, I founded a national nonprofit organization with two of my undergraduate colleagues. Its purpose was to work jointly with student leaders and administrators to find creative alternatives to social life on campus—that either did not involve alcohol or involved it in safe, responsible, legal, and "de-emphasized" ways. We had plenty of successes and plenty of failures. One of the biggest failures was in our capabilities as a nonprofit organization. We applied for and were denied 16 grants from 16 different foundations and government entities.

Although we were able to attract some private donations for our efforts, we had zero success at convincing grantors to fund our efforts. We were trying to do something innovative and ground-breaking, but unfortunately our nation's foundations and government agencies are not designed to support such initiative. We didn't have Ph.D.'s, we didn't have CVs and successful track records, and we didn't have operating history. What we did have was an idea that eventually found its way, but only through sheer willpower, true innovation, and an appeal to the private sector.

Since I couldn't find a way to do what I wanted as a nonprofit, I decided that I might have a compelling case to start a for-profit company. So, I took my innovative idea and went to the only place that rewards innovation: private industry and venture capital. I've since raised nearly $7 million for Outside The Classroom, Inc. and our program AlcoholEdu—a science-based, non-opinionated online course about alcohol. In only 3 years, AlcoholEdu is now the single most widely used course on the Internet. And because we built-in the evaluation and assessment of the course, we now have the world's largest evaluative database on college students and alcohol with nearly 15 million data points from tens of thousands of students from hundreds of colleges and universities.

After 3 years, I am confident that we are on to something extremely important. We have been pioneering the concept of "population-level prevention" whereby AlcoholEdu is mandated or required of all students in a population—namely all first-year students. When a college or university requires the course of all students, we can demonstrate dramatic reductions in high-risk drinking and related behaviors, and increases in abstention and the use of protective factors. Highlights include:

- Abstainers rose from 39.4 percent to 43.4 percent, a 10 percent increase.
- Heavy episodic drinkers dropped from 38.1 percent to 35.0 percent, an 8 percent decrease Problematic drinkers (who had 10-plus drinks at least once during the past two weeks) dropped from 12.1 percent to 9.9 percent, an 18 percent decrease.
- The average number of drinks consumed per week, for drinkers, dropped from 9.9 before the course to 8.6 a month after AlcoholEdu.

Population-level prevention is based on the theory that high-risk drinking is not an individual or addiction problem; rather it is a social epidemic that finds its home within social networks. And just as these social networks among young people can drive negative norms related to alcohol, they can also be used to drive positive, safe norms related to alcohol. In our research, we have found that when AlcoholEdu— an interactive, personal education related to alcohol—is given to entire population of students, it creates a viral and interactive reaction which results in more students talking to one another about the experience. Because all students are required to take AlcoholEdu and because AlcoholEdu evokes a very personal educational experience from each student, the school creates a common bond or shared experience among this population. That common bond is exactly what drives the dialogue among students, and when students are creating their own dialogue about what they've learned, they are essentially engineering a new cultural norm around alcohol. A norm that is less tolerant of high-risk drinking and negative consequences, and more supportive of abstention.

I don't need to espouse the validity and power of what AlcoholEdu is doing. Its results are speaking loud and clear, and at the end of the day results will drive what our approach to solving this problem will be. I'm confident I'll be a part of the solution and so will Outside The Classroom—despite the fact that I'm not a Ph.D., and my organization is for-profit. And I also know that finding a solution will require many leaders and many organizations collaborating on a truly comprehensive approach to addressing the problem.

Let me be clear: I'm not a prohibitionist. I never have been and never will be. But let me also be clear about another point: I think alcohol, specifically the abuse of it, is the number one cause undermining the future success of America and our competitiveness in the world. It is keeping college students from realizing their true potential, and it has essentially diminished the value of higher education as a process to train the leaders of tomorrow. A vast number of college students are literally "pissing away" their education. And, increasingly, a vast number of our high school and middle school students are on the way to squandering their promising futures too.

I'm willing to help. I'm here to solve the problem. And I'm looking for support. All of us in the prevention field are looking for support. And we're waiting to see how you're going to respond. Please don't do what's expected and disappoint us. The answers to solving this epidemic are clear and present. The leadership from government is not. But it can be. And I urge you to take action now.

PREPARED STATEMENT OF PETER H. CRESSY, ED.D., PRESIDENT/CEO, THE DISTILLED SPIRITS COUNCIL OF THE UNITED STATES

Mr. Chairman and Members of the Subcommittee, on behalf of the Distilled Spirits Council of the United States (DISCUS), a national trade association representing U.S. producers, marketers, and exporters of distilled spirits products, I commend you for initiating the hearing on national strategies to reduce underage drinking. As a former university president, parent and now CEO of a major beverage alcohol trade association, I appreciate the opportunity to discuss this serious and complex problem.

Code of Responsible Practices for Beverage Alcohol Advertising and Marketing

For decades, DISCUS and its members have been deeply committed to social responsibility and have worked aggressively to fight underage drinking. Since the 1930's, DISCUS members have adhered to a voluntary code of advertising and marketing practices. The overriding principle of the Code is to market our products to adults in a responsible and appropriate manner.

A major component of the Code is the Code Review Board (Board). The Board serves as an enforcer by quickly responding to complaints from both the public and competitors alike. DISCUS is proud to note that member companies have fully and readily complied with the decisions rendered by the Board. Moreover, non-DISCUS members have been largely responsive as well.

During the hearing, some discussion focused on examples of inappropriate alcohol advertising content. Senator Dodd referenced a print advertisement by Bacardi tagged "Vegetarian By Day. Bacardi By Night" that provides an excellent example of the effectiveness of the DISCUS Code review process. In 2001, following publication of the ad, a competitor within the industry filed a complaint with the Code Review Board. The Board subsequently determined the content inconsistent with provisions of the Code. Shortly thereafter, Bacardi withdrew the advertisement from circulation.

In 2003, DISCUS adopted major revisions to the Code to underscore a commitment to the most responsible advertising and marketing practices in the industry, including:

- All drinks Code covering over 2,800 brands of spirits, beer and wine
- 70 percent adult demographic for all ad placements and promotional events
- Transparency through public reports of complaint decisions
- Participation by external advisors
- Continuation of ban on advertising in college newspapers
- Age verification mechanisms for websites
- Explicit restraints regarding sexual content
- Minimum of 25 years old for all models/actors in advertising

Virtually all of the available research makes it clear that parents and peers have the greatest influence on a minor's decision to drink. Similar studies also prove that advertising affects brand choice rather than the decision to drink illegally or to abuse beverage alcohol. Nonetheless, DISCUS and its members have taken the steps outlined above in response to changing technologies and societal concerns. A leading public health professional—Dr. Robert Reynolds, Director of Policy Analysis and Training at the Pacific Institute for Research and Evaluation reinforces this point:

"There can be no public confidence in alcohol industry self-regulation until the results of the complaint process are open to public review. DISCUS, by adopting new standards for transparency and public reports about complaints, promises sunshine to previously secret decisions. As a public health professional, I must applaud the new commitment by DISCUS to provide the American people with the information necessary to judge their actions, not just their words."

DISCUS and its member companies are proud of the Code review process and the expeditious and just manner that complaints are handled. The Federal Trade Commission, offering a similar assessment in a report to

Congress last month, found the Code review process "rigorous and effective."

The Century Council

Since 1990, The Century Council, an independent organization funded by America's leading distillers, has spent $130 million on programs developed with multiple academic, government and community partners. Many of these programs and strategies are similar to those recently advocated in the 2003 National Academy of Sciences report.

American Campus and Alcohol Conferences

In October 2000, DISCUS initiated an effort among universities to reduce drinking on college campuses throughout the country. Together with Eastern Connecticut State University, The George Washington University, University of Massachusetts Dartmouth, University of Massachusetts Amherst, and University of Louisville, DISCUS convened a 3-day working conference where campus and community teams developed realistic plans to combat campus drinking. Representatives from 34 universities, including Connecticut College and Bowling Green State University, attended the conference with teams comprised of students, faculty, community leaders, local law enforcement, and beverage alcohol retailers. At the conclusion of the conference, each team was encouraged to apply for grants to implement their plans. As a result, roughly $300,000 was distributed in program grants to seventeen universities who submitted requests.

This model program has resulted in a nationwide series of regional conferences. We have now completed four and have worked with nearly 200 colleges and universities. Additional conferences are scheduled at Eastern Connecticut State University in November and DePauw University in Indiana next February.

Again, Mr. Chairman, allow me to commend you, your staff and the Subcommittee for addressing underage drinking. DISCUS and its members are determined and dedicated to ensuring that our products are consumed responsibly and in moderation by those of legal drinking age who choose to drink. I look forward to further collaborative partnerships that make a real impact on this complex and serious issue.

Prepared Statement of George A. Hacker, Director, Center for Science in the Public Interest, CSPI and Kimberly Miller, Manager of Federal Relations Alcohol Policies Project Center for Science in the Public Interest

Introduction

Thank you for the opportunity to submit testimony regarding one of the most damaging and neglected public health and safety threats facing our society. Underage drinking is by far the nation's costliest and most neglected youth drug problem, and CSPI commends the Committee for focusing much needed attention on this important public health issue. Underage the hearing is especially timely given this month's release of two major reports to Congress on underage drinking and related issues, from the National Academy of Sciences and the Federal Trade Commission, respectively.

For more than 20 years, CSPI's Alcohol Policies Project has worked to prevent and reduce alcohol problems at the national, State and local levels, collaborating with thousands of organizations and individuals to promote a comprehensive, prevention-oriented policy strategy to improve public health and safety and help save young lives. During that time we have developed the strong conviction that Federal efforts to prevent and reduce underage drinking have been sorely underfunded, woefully fragmented, fundamentally invisible and largely ineffective. Numerous obstacles have thwarted the creation of a comprehensive, highly focused, clearly identified, and hard-hitting Federal effort to address underage drinking. We hope that the work of this Committee will begin to help overcome some of those long-standing barriers.

First, we would like to review the legislative and policy context which gave rise to the National Academy of Sciences' ground breaking report, recommending a comprehensive national strategy to reduce underage drinking. Second, we will address the longstanding absence of, and glaring need for, a stronger, more visible, consistent, and effective Federal leadership role in reducing underage drinking and its widespread public health and safety harms. Third, we will outline why a media and communications campaign to prevent underage drinking needs to be the centerpiece of a comprehensive, aggressive national prevention-oriented public health and safety strategy. Finally, we will highlight two other priority areas for Federal action to reduce underage drinking in the areas of taxation and advertising.

Legislative and Policy Context of Underage Drinking Prevention Efforts

CSPI was part of a broad coalition of national and local public health and safety organizations that for 2 years supported Congressional efforts to include underage drinking prevention messages in the Office of National Drug Control Policy's billion-dollar Youth Anti Drug Media Campaign (see attached list of organizations). Although ultimately unsuccessful, efforts by Representatives Wolf and Roybal-Allard in the House and by Senator Frank Lautenberg in the Senate generated substantial support and hotly contested debate on the issue.

Despite votes that excluded alcohol from ONDCP's media campaign, Congressional debate on the issue strongly affirmed the clear and compelling need for a parallel, but comparable national media campaign to prevent underage drinking. Numerous members of Congress recognized the incongruity of spending hundreds of millions of dollars to prevent illicit drug use, while ignoring underage alcohol use, widely recognized as the far more devastating, severe, and widespread drug problem for young Americans. Congressional debate reflected strong support[13] —and recognition of the need—for an underage drinking prevention campaign to raise awareness of the problems associated with underage drinking and deliver prevention messages to young people, parents, community leaders, and public health and safety officials.

In this context, on April 4, 2001, Representatives Lucille Roybal-Allard (D-CA) and Frank Wolf (R-VA) introduced legislation to establish a "National Media Campaign to Prevent Underage Drinking" (H.R. 1509). Shortly thereafter, Senators Harry Reid (D-NV) and John Warner (R-VA), and others, introduced companion legislation in the Senate (S. 866). The proposed legislation would create a discrete underage-drinking media campaign focused on alcohol and housed in the Department of Health and Human Services. These bills are backed by a broad array of public health and safety groups, including CSPI, the American Medical Association (AMA), Mothers Against Drunk Driving (MADD), Consumer Federation of America, Latino Council on Alcohol & Tobacco, the Trauma Foundation, and the American Academy of Pediatrics, as well as by the Advertising Council and the National Partnership for a Drug-Free America. Countless local and statewide groups also support the measure. The bipartisan bills have garnered 82 co-sponsors in the House and 18 in the Senate.

While the legislation was not enacted in the 107th Congress, report language in the fiscal year 2002 Labor, Health and Human Services and Education appropriations bill represented an important first step in moving the media-campaign issue forward. With support from the National Beer Wholesalers Association and the Distilled Spirits Council of the United States, appropriations language provided 8500,000 for the National Academy of Sciences and Institute of Medicine to develop a strategy to reduce and prevent underage drinking. Congress charged the Academy to

[13] Congressional Record, Volume 145, July 1, 1999 (Senate)] [Page S7987-S8010], Floor debate on Lautenberg Amendment No. 1214 to S. 1282 fiscal year 2000 Treasury Postal Appropriations bill).

produce a comprehensive policy and prevention strategy to combat underage drinking and its consequences, with emphasis on the role a media campaign could play in such a strategy.

The NAS Report's Media Campaign Recommendations

Based on a review of available research, the NAS report strongly recommends that the Federal Government fund and actively support the development of a national media effort targeted at adults, as a major component of a campaign to reduce underage drinking. It states that the goals of the national media campaign would be to instill a broad societal commitment to reduce underage drinking, to increase specific actions by adults that are meant to discourage or inhibit underage drinking, and to decrease adult conduct that tends to facilitate underage drinking.

The report also calls for intensive research and development for a youth-focused national media campaign relating to underage drinking. It stipulates that if this work yields promising results, the inclusion of a youth-focused campaign in the strategy should be considered.

These recommendations provide strong backing for a renewed push to pass Federal legislation creating a national media campaign to prevent underage drinking. This goal has been a top alcohol-policy priority for public health, consumer, religious, and substance abuse prevention groups for several years, and a media campaign should be a top priority for legislative action flowing from the NAS report.

The Glaring Absence of a Visible, Cohesive Federal Voice on Underage Drinking

For too long, the Federal Government has been far too silent on underage drinking and the promise of many policy interventions and communications strategies to reduce problems that have devastating economic and public health and safety consequences. We believe that the longstanding absence of a visible, effective, coordinated Federal voice and role in addressing underage drinking and its harms contributes to a social norm of acceptance, tolerance, and even accommodation of underage drinking.

Worse yet, this abdication of Federal responsibility on underage drinking has left alcohol producers primarily in charge of educating young people and the public, both about alcohol use and about how to combat underage drinking. Despite wildly self-serving industry propaganda, those efforts to address underage drinking have been unevaluated and generally ineffective. Although more visible than Federal media programs to prevent underage drinking, industry's investment in those messages— both financial and creative—pales in comparison with what it spends promoting drinking. For example, Anheuser-Busch, the world's largest brewer, claims to have spent some $350 million since 1982 on public awareness and social responsibility messages. That's about what the company spends in just 1 year on advertising.

One way to measure the government's lack of commitment to this issue is to look at the resources devoted to preventing alcohol problems among young people. A May, 2001 report released by the U.S. General Accounting Office (GAO), Underage *Drinking: Information on Federal Funds Targeted at Prevention,* concludes that only $71 million of the Federal Government's fiscal year 2000 budget was allocated specifically to the prevention of underage drinking. This pitiful allocation is dwarfed by the $18 billion our government spends on the drug war, the $52 billion in estimated costs of underage drinking, and the $2 billion alcohol producers spend per year on alcohol advertising and promotion. To make matters worse, these woefully inadequate resources are scattered among disparate Federal agencies, and many programs have been developed with little coordination among the agencies and no unifying vision or strategy.

Unlike with tobacco, for which the Department of Health and Human Services has been designated as the lead agency for the government's efforts in the area of smoking and health and chairs a statutorily established Inter-Agency Committee on Smoking and Health, there's no lead agency for the development or implementation of a strategy on underage drinking or combating societal alcohol problems.

The Surgeon General has issued several widely publicized reports on the public health hazards of tobacco, and regularly issues reports on the marketing of tobacco products to young people. Despite numerous appeals over the years from an array of public health and safety groups, the Surgeon General has never held a single workshop or issued any report on underage drinking. In fact, the 1988 Surgeon General's Workshop on Drunk Driving stands out as the Department's sole high-visibility forum on alcohol, period.

Similarly, the Federal Government's efforts to combat the devastation of illicit drugs are backed by a well-funded, cohesive, publicly articulated, national drug-control strategy. That strategy is coordinated by ONDCP, an executive-department agency that reports directly to the President. Since the mid-1990s, Congress has appropriated billions to that agency, including hundreds of millions of dollars for a national youth anti-drug media campaign.

Nothing remotely resembling such a concerted effort has ever existed to address underage drinking, or alcohol abuse. Yet, according to DHHS, alcohol is the most costly of all drug problems, imposing economic costs of more than $185 billion on the nation each year and causing more than 100,000 deaths. According to the Centers for Disease Control, alcohol is a key factor in the three leading causes of death among young people in America: accidents, homicides, and suicides. Unlike tobacco, which kills its users in middle age and later, alcohol is a drug that actually kills thousands of young people each year, many more than die from the use of all other drugs combined.

The Need for a Media Campaign as the Centerpiece of Federal Efforts to Prevent Underage Drinking

According to the Department of Health and Human Services, prevention efforts are beginning to pay off in declining rates of teen smoking. However, in part due to the absence of comparable efforts to combat underage drinking, alcohol use and binge drinking among teens continue at alarmingly high rates. The latest National Household Survey data suggest that alcohol use among American youth has even increased. Ten million 12- to 20-year-olds reported drinking alcohol in the year prior to the survey. Of those, nearly 6.8 million (19 percent) reported binge drinking and 2.1 million (6 percent) were heavy drinkers. Among the 12- to 17-year-olds, 10.6 percent binge drink and 2.5 percent say they're heavy drinkers. In fact, previous month alcohol use among 12- to 17-year-olds increased more than 5 percent since 2000; 17.3 percent reported alcohol use in the past month.

As a society, we have invested heavily in massive public awareness campaigns designed to deter young people from taking up smoking and experimenting with illicit drugs. Those campaigns have provided an effective backdrop for a myriad of revolutionary public and private reforms that range from the imposition of advertising restrictions on cigarettes to the prohibition—even in bars—of indoor tobacco use. There is little doubt that they have helped to change the social and political conversation about smoking and drugs, and have empowered citizens and communities to take effective action on behalf of young people and society.

Recently, it has become increasingly apparent that comprehensive communications programs have actually played an important role in steering young people away from tobacco use. Evidence from Florida, California, and Massachusetts demonstrates that reaching young people with the right messages can make a difference. Although perhaps more complicated to implement, a similarly effective media campaign to prevent and reduce underage drinking is both imperative and achievable.

Of course, not even the best media campaign would magically eradicate underage drinking, any more than ONDCP's campaign has eliminated youth drug use. Nor is it realistic to imagine that sufficient resources would be available for a media campaign that, independently, could compete with more than $2 billion dollars a year in aggressive alcohol advertising and promotion, much of which appeals directly to underage youth. However, a highly visible media campaign that reaches mass—and target—audiences with consistent, powerful, credible, and persuasive messages on underage drinking can help in many ways. As the centerpiece of an integrated prevention strategy, it would:

- Provide a clear, consistent Federal voice and message on underage drinking that would highlight government interest in, leadership for, and commitment to reducing the widespread harms of underage drinking.
- Focus public attention on underage drinking as a significant public health and safety issue and elevate it on the public's and policy makers' radar screens. A well-financed, focused, appropriately targeted, creative, and provocative media campaign can generate discussion and debate, challenge complacency, and prompt State and community action for needed policy and practice reforms. Media involvement will help motivate and bolster community members working to change those community norms that contribute to youth alcohol use.
- Communicate highly visible, culturally imbedded media messages that (when effectively crafted and delivered) can help shift attitudes, shape perceptions, and change the national conversation about underage drinking, both among youth and adults. Administered effectively, a national media campaign would put to good use the enormous creativity and talent of willing participants in the media and advertising industries. Those professionals pride themselves on their prowess in influencing youths' attitudes and behaviors.

For too long, the absence of cohesive, well-researched, coordinated, and highly promoted prevention messages has allowed alcohol producers free reign to poison the airwaves, both with seductive product appeals and with ineffective, vague, and self-serving "socially responsible" public relations pitches. Those generally untested and unevaluated messages serve more to inoculate alcohol marketers from potential legal liability and Congressional and regulatory scrutiny than they do as real prevention.

Despite our reservations about industry's public awareness campaigns, we would not expect a national, government-sponsored media campaign on underage drinking to supplant those messages. Industry efforts would and should continue, given the alcoholic-beverage industry's undeniable responsibility to discourage the misuse of its products. However, just as we would never delegate the responsibility for youth smoking prevention efforts primarily to cigarette companies, we should not continue to allow vested interests in the alcoholic-beverage industry to have the principal voice when it comes to communicating with young people and adults about preventing underage drinking.

If the alcoholic-beverage industry is sincere in its commitment to prevent underage drinking, it should embrace public efforts to educate adults and young people about alcohol. A media campaign on underage drinking will not be about prohibition. It would not be about stigmatizing drinkers or alcohol producers. It would not, we would hope, be about communicating simplistic and self-defeating messages that heighten youth rebellion and interest in alcohol. It should be about ending our national denial of underage drinking as a major public health and safety issue and instilling a broad societal commitment to reducing underage drinking. A national media campaign would help increase public awareness and understanding of the destructive role of alcohol in young people's lives, and it would strengthen community resolve and capacity to take effective action to reduce and prevent underage drinking and its myriad harms.

Other Key Priorities for Federal Action on Underage Drinking: Taxes and Advertising

Among the NAS report's many worthy recommendations, those concerning taxation and advertising deserve brief mention.

Alcohol Taxes

One of the report's more controversial outcomes was a recommendation that Congress and State legislatures raise excise taxes to reduce underage consumption and to raise additional revenues for prevention programs. The report cites three arguments for higher taxes to combat underage drinking. "First, underage drinking imposes particularly high average social costs. Second, raising excise tax rates is a strategy that has strong and well-documented prevention effects on underage drinking. Third, a designated portion of the funds generated by the taxes can be earmarked for preventing and reducing underage drinking."

At the Federal level, this recommendation sends a clear message to lawmakers that—at the very least—lowering Federal excise taxes on alcoholic-beverages (in particular, beer—the primary alcoholic drink of choice for young people) is a bad idea. Supporters of legislation to reduce the Federal excise tax on beer and other alcoholic beverages now have a clear choice between protecting young people's health and safety or padding the bottom line of a politically-connected industry.

At the State level, the NAS report's tax recommendations firmly support and provide fresh impetus for State's initiatives to raise excise taxes on alcoholic-beverages to reduce underage drinking and raise revenues for prevention and treatment.

Alcohol Advertising

The NAS report urged the alcohol industry to strengthen its current voluntary advertising codes, refrain from marketing practices that have substantial appeal to youth, and be more careful to place ads to reduce youthful exposure. Even though the NAS report acknowledged the lack of direct evidence for a causal link between advertising and alcohol consumption, it supported better industry self-regulation and recommended that Congress appropriate necessary funding for the U.S. Department of Health and Human Services (DHHS) to monitor underage exposure to alcohol advertising on a continuing basis and to report periodically to Congress and the public. It also urged that the DHHS's principle annual survey on youth substance use be amended to include the collection of data on underage drinkers' product and brand choices.

Some industry representatives have alleged that the Federal Trade Commission's (FTC's) recent report to Congress, "makes the NAS report moot" on alcohol advertising. Nothing could be further from the truth. Although the FTC's report is quick to congratulate the alcoholic-beverage industry's promised voluntary adoption of a "70 percent adult audience" placement standard (up from 50 percent), the practical effects of this change will be minimal. The revised standard essentially mirrors what the industry is already doing. In fact, several years ago, when NBC considered running liquor ads using an even higher 85 percent adult-audience placement standard, advertising trade professionals pointed out that an 85 percent benchmark would be virtually meaningless, because nearly every NBC show would qualify (given that 72 percent of the U.S. population is 21 or older). In short, the shift to a 70 percent threshold is cosmetic, and will afford no real reduction in the extent of youth exposure to alcohol advertising.

The FTC's report also conspicuously punts on the critical issue of "spillover"—that is the impossibility of designing ads that appeal to 21-year-olds without also appealing to younger persons as well. The FTC's failure on this point (other than its almost offhand acknowledgements that ads reach significant numbers of underage persons and appeal to them) reflects an underlying legal conclusion that industry's right (given the paucity of evidence that advertising and consumption and harm are causally linked) to target legal-age consumers trumps society's responsibility to protect children and adolescents.

We think industry can do better, by eliminating youthful themes, concepts, and characters, by imposing stricter placement standards, and by more prominently promoting only the moderate use of its products. It's worth noting that some stores that sell alcohol exercise extra caution, for example, by carding everyone up to the age of thirty. Advertisers could do likewise by designing ads that skew "age-upwards" in appeal, rather than "age-downwards." Advertising content issues present challenging legal and business questions, but need to be addressed more seriously by producers than they have been.

The FTC's report also fails to respond to Congress' specific request to examine the impact of expanded broadcast advertising of the new generation of liquor-branded “alcopops” (such as Smirnoff Ice, Bacardi Silver, and Skyy Blue) on underage persons. The report instead fatalistically states that “there is no information to show the extent to which teens drink these beverages,” and proceeds to base its conclusions solely on a review of industry-supplied marketing materials. That is simply not good enough.

“Alcopop” producers openly acknowledge that their products are specifically aimed at “entry level” drinkers, and that the use of liquor brand names on these products is aimed at drawing young drinkers to the parent brands of hard liquor. The FTC’s failure to seriously examine the appeal of such products to underage consumers underscores the need to implement the NAS recommendation that the DHHS’s principle annual survey on youth substance use be amended to include the collection of data on underage drinkers’ product and brand choices. The availability of such data is essential to understanding the actual youth impact of new products and the advertising campaigns that promote them.

In sum, on the advertising front, we urge Congress to:

- Act on the NAS recommendations to encourage better voluntary placement standards;
- Require regular Federal monitoring of and reporting on the impact of alcohol advertising on underage consumers;
- Require the DHHS to amend its annual national survey on youth substance use (known as the “Monitoring the Future” Survey) to include the collection of data on underage drinkers’ product and brand choices.
- Establish a national media campaign on the risks and harms of underage drinking to balance the messages parents and young people receive from alcohol advertising.

We thank the Committee for its consideration of our views, and would be pleased to assist its efforts in any way we can.

PREPARED STATEMENT OF GENERAL ARTHUR T. DEAN, MAJOR GENERAL, U.S. ARMY, RETIRED CHAIRMAN AND CEO COMMUNITY ANTI-DRUG COALITIONS OF AMERICA

Underage drinking is a national epidemic affecting our nation's children. Community Anti-Drug Coalitions of America (CADCA) strongly supports a major Federal role in the funding and implementation of policies, strategies and programs aimed at preventing underage drinking. It is essential for every community in the nation to have the necessary tools and resources to protect their children from the harmful effects of underage drinking. Community coalition efforts that involve multiple sectors of a community working together to implement comprehensive strategies have proven effective in changing norms and reducing underage drinking.

Underage drinking is a serious, pervasive public health issue that must be seriously addressed at the Federal, State and local levels. Federal policies and programs need to include an increased focus on the importance of collaborative, comprehensive community responses to underage drinking. Multiple strategies, that include regulation, enforcement, training, community education and media campaigns need to be implemented in every State and community in the nation.

Many of CADCA's coalition members have had major successes implementing community-wide strategies that have markedly reduced underage drinking. For example in Ohio, the Coalition for a Drug-Free Greater Cincinnati has established comprehensive policies, strategies and programs to help lower alcohol consumption by youth. Due to those efforts alcohol use among 7th to 12th graders decreased by 23 percent between 1993 and 2000. In the same region where a coalition did not exist, alcohol use remained constant. Community coalitions can and do provide the community-wide synergy to decrease the consumption of alcohol among youth.

In Troy, Michigan, the Troy Community Coalition documented the impact adult alcohol consumption had on youth behavior. The Coalition worked with local businesses to encourage them and their employees to be positive role models for their children. They also established a campaign, "Do Your Part to Prevent Alcohol Tragedy" in which the Coalition convinced insurance companies to reduce insurance premiums for bars and bar owners that consistently checked ID's, refused to provide alcohol to adults who have had too much to drink, and whose employees received server training through coalition sponsored workshops. Due to these strategies, binge drinking among Troy's high school students was reduced by 10 percent between 1999 and 2000. In the 12 years since the Troy Community Coalition has been in operation the percentage of 8th grade students reporting they had consumed an alcoholic beverage in their lifetime was reduced by 22.5 percent.

In Vallejo, California, the Vallejo Fighting Back Coalition is working with the local police department to train teens to attempt to purchase alcohol at local outlets. These "teen decoys" also conduct assessments of outlets and encourage operators to create youth "safe" zones within the stores. The Vallejo Alcohol Policy Coalition has implemented environmental strategies to reduce the harm caused by alcohol in the community. These strategies include: a teen party ordinance, a conditional use permit ordinance, server/seller training and review of all new applications to sell alcohol in Vallejo. Finally, each family with a middle or high school student is provided with a copy of the teen party ordinance and drug and alcohol information, along with a request to sign a parent pledge that their children will not be permitted to attend or give parties where alcohol is served. Due to these in-depth community strategies, Vallejo reduced past month alcohol use by 11th graders by 9 percent from 37 percent in 1999 to 28 percent in 2001; Vallejo's 2001 rate for past month alcohol use by 11th graders is 13 percent lower than the comparable statewide rate.

CADCA knows firsthand that the most effective way to achieve reductions in underage drinking is through the consistent application of comprehensive communitywide strategies that focus on policy and environmental changes. CADCA therefore recommends that the Federal Government focus more attention and financial resources on effective strategies to combat underage drinking such as those outlined in the recently released report by the National Academy of Sciences entitled Reducing Underage Drinking: A Collective Responsibility.

Prepared Statement of Juanita D. Duggan, CEO and Executive Vice President, Wine and Spirits Wholesalers of America, Inc.

Mr. Chairman: Thank you for the opportunity to submit testimony to your subcommittee for this important hearing. I represent the Wine and Spirits Wholesalers of America, Inc. (WSWA), a national trade organization and the voice of the wholesale branch of the wine and spirits industry. Founded in 1943, WSWA represents more than 400 privately held, family owned and operated companies in 44 States, the District of Columbia and Puerto Rico that hold State licenses to act as wine and/ or spirits wholesalers.

The purpose of the National Academies of Sciences report and today's hearing is to look at how we can increase safeguards to prevent underage access to alcohol so that, for example, a 14-year-old girl or boy can't easily get beer, wine or liquor. As industry, government, parents and others work to strengthen these measures, there are those who want to weaken and ultimately dismantle the very heart of these longstanding safeguards.

These counterproductive forces include direct shipments of alcohol to homes from retailers and producers, as well as a series of court cases specifically intended to undermine local control of alcohol. If they succeed, the system of checks and balances we now have in place to guard against underage access—like a basic face-to-face transaction—will go away. Left in the wake of this vital system will be a freewheeling alcohol trade that will thrive in anonymous, faceless alcohol purchases which cannot be tracked or otherwise monitored.

When it comes to alcohol, our society recognizes its unique nature and need for a unique system to control its distribution. After all, the selling of beer, wine and liquor is not the same as selling cars, books or CDs.

Now, I would like to turn to the NAS report itself. David Rehr, President of the National Beer Wholesalers Association, Inc. may have said it best in an opinion column printed in the September 26, 2003 Washington Times:

"Illegal underage drinking deserves the nation's serious attention. It doesn't deserve a non-scientific study focusing on unproven methods that fail to identify real solutions. Congress took the first step in asking for a credible, scientific, unbiased study to attack underage drinking. They stepped up to the plate. Unfortunately, the NAS struck out."

There is a nugget of gold, however, that can be mined from the NAS report. In section two of the report entitled "The Strategy," the NAS focuses on the issue of underage access, in particular, Internet Sales and Home Delivery. The report states that underage purchase of alcohol over the Internet or through home delivery is a method of illegal access to alcohol used by 10 percent of underage drinkers. That figure, however, is based on data reported in the 2000 Journal of Studies on Alcohol, and the report correctly concludes that increasing utilization of the Internet may have increased that percentage greatly over the last 3 years. Finally, the NAS report goes so far as to suggest that the significance of these illegal underage sales is so great that:

> "…an argument can be made for banning Internet and home delivery sales altogether in light of the likelihood that these methods will be used underage purchasers…" (Page 176)

The NAS, in an otherwise flawed report, has struck gold in highlighting a point of access of alcohol for underage drinkers that is statistically significant and growing. Moreover, this point of access is one that public policy makers have the power to control. Recently, the wholesale tier has taken upon itself the role of safeguarding the three-tier system against those who seek to undermine it through direct shipment sales of alcohol, such as the ones cited by the NAS. To truly understand the dangers presented by an unregulated alcohol distribution system, it is helpful to illustrate how underage access to alcohol is different in these circumstances.

First and foremost, sales made via the phone or through the Internet, since they are not face-to-face, cannot positively establish the age of the purchaser. There is no guarantee that the person ordering the alcohol is of age. Most young people between the ages of 18 and 21 years of age (and many who are even younger) possess credit cards allowing them to order online-still others have the use of their parents' cards; there is no way for the online supplier to accurately verify the age of the person ordering.

Moreover, there is no way to ensure that a minor does not ultimately receive a shipment of alcohol. The suppliers wash their hands of the alcohol once it leaves their premises, and there is no guarantee that the delivery service will require an I.D. upon delivery—or that they will not simply drop the box off at the door unattended.

That is exactly what happened when scores of media outlets conducted stings over the past several years to determine the safety of direct sales. Those stings showed how easy it was for minors to order alcohol online-and how sloppy the carriers were who delivered the alcohol, often without checking I.D. or often just leaving the alcohol on the front doorstep. Perhaps more telling, a sting by the Michigan Attorney General's office ensnared 79 different companies who illegally shipped 1,020 bottles of wine, 318 bottles of beer and 20 bottles of spirits, many of those sales going to underage buyers.

At a 2002 forum on the issue of online commerce hosted by the Federal Trade Commission, Michigan Assistant Attorney General Irene Mead testified that not only were minors caught purchasing beer and wine online during stings to bust retailers breaking the law, but they also had made the startling discovery that minors were able to purchase high-proof grain alcohol as well. She told the frightening story of a teen in a rehabilitation facility that actually succeeded in having a case of bourbon delivered to the facility—straight to him via the Internet. When he finished that case he contacted the Internet site and said all the bottles were broken on delivery. A free case was promptly shipped to him, again without detection.

Separately, the owner of the 877 Spirits catalog told an audience at a legal conference on alcohol beverage law that minors were constantly trying to buy alcohol online through his company. He said they were often able to detect minors through their buying methods. Meaning, 877 Spirits bills itself as on online gift catalog. Therefore, when orders are placed for delivery within the same zip code as the purchaser, it indicates a potential concern, since his products would be available locally.

The catalog often asks the potential purchaser to send a fax copy of their I.D. and credit card and though the person says it is on the way—the proof never arrives.

Proponents of direct shipping alcohol beverages discount the implications of these enforcement actions and reports, claiming they are somehow tainted and the product of wholesaler orchestration. While we would like to claim credit for these illuminating stings, wholesalers do not control news reporters and certainly do not control the Michigan Attorney General's office. But that really isn't the point; the fact is that companies do exist that do business with remote consumers, and either do not have adequate controls in place, or simply do not care if they sell to minors.

The three-tier, wholesaler supported system for controlled distribution of alcohol provides for the quick identification and apprehension of a retailer who sells to minors, a safeguard that is impossible to implement with respect to direct-shipped sales.

Keep in mind, the genesis of the wine and spirits wholesaler, a key component in the modern system of controlled beverage alcohol distribution, can be traced back to the decision by State lawmakers at the end of Prohibition to establish the three-tiered system for the distribution of beverage alcohol—a decision that was theirs to make as a result of the ratification of the 20 Amendment in 1933.

The 21st Amendment is unambiguous in its enumeration of power to the States to regulate the importation and controlled distribution of alcohol within its borders. And no Supreme Court decision interpreting that amendment over the past 70 years has ever diminished that authority. The simple fact is, as noted by respected jurist Frank Easterbrook in a compelling 7th Circuit opinion upholding Indiana's right to determine and control the channels of distribution, alcohol is not cheese and its sale and distribution should be treated specially.

Principal among the reasons that the three-tiered system was established was consumer protection; it was determined that there should be an intermediary separating the supply and retail tiers to ensure that large suppliers with market power did not dominate individual retailers by establishing "tied-houses." These pre-prohibition tied-house retailers made their profits not by-the-glass, or by-the-bottle, but rather through winning incentives for moving large quantities of alcohol. In other words, the imposition of a mandatory wholesale tier served to end many unhealthy and unsafe practices that prevailed prior to Prohibition.

The wholesale tier functions as a partner with State regulatory systems that are designed to promote the core 21st Amendment concerns—ensuring orderly market conditions, promoting temperance, including keeping alcohol out of the hands of minors and collecting tax revenue. By requiring that every drop of alcohol passes through the three-tiered system, States are assured that every bottle of alcohol is properly labeled, taxed and sold only to adults.

In order to understand how the three-tiered system operates as a partner with the State and Federal regulatory communities and serves the interests of consumer protection, I would ask you to follow a bottle as it flows through the three-tiered system.

A supplier must obtain approval for the label from the Alcohol and Tobacco Tax and Trade Bureau (TTB) to ensure that it contains truthful and non-misleading information and that it contains mandatory health warnings. That bottle must then be sold to a State and federally licensed wholesaler who is responsible for maintaining and filing detailed records of each bottle brought into the State, pays the excise taxes due on the alcohol, and delivers the alcohol to a State licensed retail establishment. The retailer is responsible for paying over to the State the sales taxes generated by each sale, and is directly responsible for ensuring that alcohol does not fall into the hands of minors or other prohibited individuals. Since both the wholesaler and the retailer must be licensed by the State, they are fully accountable for any dereliction of their duties. They are subject to on-site inspections, auditing and compliance checks, and any violation can result in a loss of license, fines and other potentially more severe penalties.

Wholesalers believe that the three-tier system is our nation's premier safeguard against underage access to alcohol. As an industry, we are not only committed to this system, but also to its philosophy. We work diligently to uphold the letter and spirit of the stringent laws of each State in which we do business.

Congress has recently recognized the need for legislative action to support the safeguards and accountability mechanisms of the three-tier system. Mr. Chairman, you, along with Senators Hatch and Kohl authored the landmark Federal legislation that made it more feasible to prosecute an illegal direct shipper. "The 21st Amendment Enforcement Act," passed by the 106th Congress and signed into law in 2000, provides State Attorneys General with a powerful means by which to protect their citizens and prosecute illegal direct shippers.

However, the contributions of the wholesalers to the communities in which they live and work go far beyond protecting the three-tier system of alcohol distribution. Our commitment as good corporate citizens is also unwavering.

Last year, WSWA conducted the first-ever survey of our members' broader contributions to their communities. We found that our members donate more than $55 million a year to charitable causes throughout this country. They include:

United Way, Boys and Girls Clubs of America, YMCA/YWCA, The Sober Ride Project, D.A.R.E. (Drug Abuse Resistance Education), Ronald McDonald House, MADD, Make a Wish Foundation, Project Graduation, Center for Women and Families, Crusade for Children, Sky Ranch, Big Brother Project, Camp Braveheart and many others.

Our members not only contribute to organizations that confront the problems some people face with alcohol abuse and other risky behaviors, but to other organizations that contribute to the greater good of us all—artistic endeavors, environment enrichments and developmental teachings that exemplify responsible behavior. These efforts promote social connectedness and help dissuade inappropriate behavior such as alcohol abuse and underage consumption. For example, the youth groups I listed help disadvantaged kids make the right choices about drugs, alcohol and risky behavior in general. You cannot overlook our commitment to these organizations.

Instead, the proponents of direct shipping are posing a growing threat to preventing underage alcohol access. Led by a handful of powerful retailers and elite wineries, these direct shipping advocates want to dismantle the three tier-system of safeguards and instead ship directly to consumers—with little or no controls in place. These groups are suing in several States and the Supreme Court will likely take up the case. The bottom line issue that must be addressed is simply this: Should leaders in local communities control how alcohol is marketed and sold within their State, or will wineries and large international alcohol conglomerates make that decision? We think local communities should have more control, not less—and we think most Americans would agree.

In conclusion, Mr. Chairman, we as wholesalers of wine and spirits recognize— as did Judge Easterbrook—that our product is not cheese and must be treated specially. We recognize alcohol's unique consideration in our society and support—even defend—the regulation and control of its distribution. We also believe that we are good partners to the communities in which we live and work. As such, we are appreciative of the opportunity to provide testimony at this hearing and would hope that the Chairman will continue to consider Wine and Spirits Wholesalers of America a resource as you work to prevent underage consumption and access to alcohol.

Thank you again for this opportunity to provide testimony today for this important hearing.

Prepared Statement of the Governors Highway Safety Association (GHSA)

The Governors Highway Safety Association (GHSA) is a nonprofit association whose members administer Federal highway safety grant programs, including those that are aimed at reducing underage drinking and driving. Although underage drinking and driving is only one facet of the complex underage drinking issue, it is a serious and costly problem for the country and a priority for the organization. GHSA has received Federal grants from both the National Highway Traffic Safety Administration (NHTSA) and the Office of Juvenile Justice and Delinquency Prevention (OJJDP) to develop materials and training on underage drinking.

Significant progress has been made in underage drinking and driving over the last 20 years, largely due to the 1984 enactment of the National Minimum Drinking Age law. Nonetheless, young drivers are still being killed in motor vehicle crashes at an unacceptable rate. According to NHTSA, 17 percent of all underage drivers in fatal crashes were intoxicated and 24 percent of young drivers killed in fatal crashes in 2002 were intoxicated. Further, 69 percent of young drinking drivers involved in fatal crashes were unrestrained, and 77 percent of those drinking and killed in crashes were unrestrained. Clearly there is much work to be done to prevent this unnecessary loss of young life.

GHSA firmly believes that the problem of underage drinking and driving must be addressed as part of a comprehensive approach to underage drinking. The National Academy of Sciences recently released report, "Preventing and Reducing Underage Drinking," advocates such an approach, and GHSA strongly supports it. We believe that the NAS report is a landmark study that lays out the blueprint for future action on underage drinking. Implementation of the report will take a concerted, coordinated effort by all levels of government as well as considerably more resources from the Federal and State governments and the alcohol industry.

GHSA also supports a number of specific recommendations in the NAS report.

We laud the recommendation that Federal agencies form an interagency committee to coordinate their efforts on underage drinking. Different Federal agencies approach the problem of underage drinking differently, and there is little coordination between them. These agencies have working relationships with different State agencies, but there is no attempt to develop a comprehensive approach at the State level. For example, State highway safety agencies are eligible to use their NHTSA impaired driving grants for underage drinking programs. OJJDP funds

State programs aimed at enforcing underage drinking laws. Some State highway safety offices are grant recipients, but so are State criminal justice and health agencies. The Center for Substance Abuse Prevention (CSAP) of the U.S. Department of Health and Human Services (HHS) directs funds to State substance abuse agencies for underage drinking prevention. The National Institute of Alcohol Abuse and Alcoholism conducts research on underage drinking but disseminates the results largely to the prevention and health communities. The Center for Injury Prevention and Research of the Centers for Disease Control conducts research on impaired driving and disseminates the results to the public health and highway safety communities but not necessarily to the law enforcement community. If the Federal Government took a leadership role on this issue and developed a coordinated approach, then it is more likely that the States would respond in a similar manner.

Further, the NAS report recommends that a national training and research center should be established in HHS, presumably to serve the constituent Federal and State agencies with a responsibility for reducing underage drinking. If there were a single center, then the kind of duplicate Federal research and training programs that currently exist could be eliminated. Two years ago, GHSA recommended to NHTSA, CSAP, OJJDP and the HHS program on Drug Free Schools that they fund a joint underage community-based training program and a research effort to evaluate the effectiveness of the training. Without direction and resources from Congress, however, the suggestion was not followed. A national center is needed since training and research are integral parts of any underage drinking solution.

Another recommendation that GHSA strongly supports is the one calling for community interventions. The NAS report recommends that community leaders assess the underage drinking program in their communities and consider effective approaches to reducing underage drinking. GHSA was fortunate to receive a grant from NHTSA to develop a pilot project on underage drinking prevention. GHSA identified six communities and worked with their existing coalitions to assess their underage drinking problems and develop strategic plans for addressing the problems. Out of the pilot project, eight underage drinking guidebooks (on topics similar to those recommended by NAS) and one resource book was produced, and a training program was developed. (The guidebooks may be accessed on NHTSA's website, www.nhtsa.dot.gov/injury/alcohol. Click on youth and then on "Community How to Guides on Underage Drinking Prevention.") The guidebooks have been so popular with community organizations that NHTSA is on its third printing of them. Unfortunately, however, NHTSA did not have the resources to continue the community intervention effort and the pilot project has languished.

We believe that a community-level approach to underage drinking is critical and have proven successful in the prevention and criminal justice fields. (The Center for Substance Abuse Prevention, for example, has developed a Model Communities program which has been thoroughly evaluated and found successful.) Once a community has recognized the need to address the issue and put the resources and institutional infrastructure in place to address it, then there is a higher likelihood that underage drinking will be reduced and will remain reduced after Federal funding has disappeared. GHSA strongly urges this Committee to consider funding community intervention efforts such as the one developed by GHSA.

Restricting access to alcohol is an area with which GHSA members are very familiar since they provide the leadership on underage drinking legislation and enforcement and on education programs about the legislation and enforcement. Therefore, the NAS recommendations on access are ones which the Association strongly supports. State highway safety offices use Federal highway safety grants to fund sobriety checkpoints and saturation patrols (for those States constitutionally prohibited from conducting checkpoints), enforcement of zero tolerance laws, compliance checks, server training, programs to discourage adults from providing minors with alcohol, and educational programs to discourage underage purchase of alcohol.

GHSA members have also been very supportive of graduated licensing laws: 38 States now have these very effective laws. The Association has encouraged its members to review existing graduated licensing laws and strengthen them by restricting the number of underage passengers and by enacting nighttime driving curfews. Our proposal for reauthorization of the Transportation Equity Act for the 21st Century (TEA-21) would provide incentives to States that enhance their graduated licensing laws, among other actions.

GHSA also supports keg registration and dram shop laws, and many State highway safety agencies have provided information that has helped legislatures enact these laws. In addition, GHSA members have been supportive of State efforts to modify existing laws to allow passive alcohol testing since research has shown that these low-cost devices are very effective in providing a preliminary indication of a drunk driver.

There is one access issue in the NAS report that has not gotten much attention: the issue of Internet alcohol sales and home delivery. According to the report, surveys show that 10 percent of young people report obtaining alcohol through the Internet or home delivery and that this percentage is likely to grow. This direct shipment effectively puts the delivery person in the role of having to screen for underage access, thereby eliminating the State alcohol beverage control systems and reducing accountability. The panel indicated that a case can be made to ban this type of sale and GHSA believes that this should be explored further. We are concerned that, as the Federal Government and others work to curtail underage access through current channels, another door not be opened through the Internet and home deliveries. The issue deserves increased attention by the committee.

GHSA also supports the NAS recommendations on youth-oriented interventions. The Association concurs that only evidence-based youth-focused education programs should be funded. As noted previously, however, not enough is being done at the Federal level to ensure that the research results are being disseminated to all agencies—including State highway safety agencies—with a responsibility for underage drinking prevention.

GHSA is pleased that NAS has recommended a comprehensive approach to college-based interventions—an idea that fits nicely with its community-level intervention recommendation and with the GHSA underage drinking prevention pilots. The Association concurs that college interventions should also be carefully evaluated and a list of evidence-based programs published. At the same time, it is important not to discard potentially effective programs based on limited research findings. College age "social norming" is a case in point. Under this approach, colleges seek to create a new campus social norm around the positive behavior of students who drink moderately or not at all. A recent report by the Harvard School of Public Health cast doubt on the effectiveness of this approach and urges colleges and universities to cease funding such programs. GHSA feels, however, that social norming has many potential benefits and that further demonstration programs and evaluative research must be conducted.

One of the most controversial recommendations in the NAS report is the one to increase Federal alcohol excise taxes. While GHSA does not have explicit policy supporting such an increase, the Association strongly opposes any effort to reduce alcohol excise taxes, as has been proposed in S. 809 and H.R. 1305. Under these legislative initiatives, Federal beer taxes would be rolled back to their 1951 level, effectively reducing the taxes by 50 percent. Economic studies have shown that the price of alcoholic beverages, particularly beer, is very elastic: the lower the price, the higher the demand for the product. Conversely, the higher the price, the lower the demand. These studies estimate that the 1991 increase in beer taxes saved more than 600 young lives in alcohol-related crashes each year. Hence, if beer is the alcoholic drink of choice of young persons, and if the price is reduced, it is predictable that young persons will drink more beer. From GHSA's perspective, this will lead to more underage drinking and driving and more needless loss of young lives. GHSA therefore strongly believes that lowering the price of alcoholic beverages is very poor public policy and should be avoided at all costs.

Another controversial recommendation focuses on alcohol advertising and urges that alcohol companies refrain from marketing practices that have a substantial underage appeal. The report also recommends that alcohol trade associations strengthen their voluntary advertising codes so that commercial messages are not placed in venues that have a substantial underage appeal. GHSA strongly concurs with both recommendations.

The Association was very disappointed with the recent Federal Trade Commission's (FTC) report which concluded that the alcohol industry is complying with a previous FTC order that limited advertising to media with at least a 50 percent adult audience. While we applaud the actions of the Beer Institute and the Distilled Spirits Council of the United States to immediately raise the voluntary standard to 70 percent, GHSA believes that even that standard is too low. GHSA was particularly disappointed that the FTC did not use the Congressional-mandated review of industry advertising practices as an opportunity to convene the alcohol industry, safety groups, and prevention organizations to hammer out revised advertising standards that could be acceptable to all parties. We believe that the solution to the alcohol advertising problem must be a joint effort between the industry as well as agencies and organizations that are responsible for halting underage drinking.

This concludes the statement of the Governors Highway Safety Association. Thank you for the opportunity to submit our views on such an important issue and one that is of high priority to the Association and Congress.

PREPARED STATEMENT OF RALPH HINGSON, SC.D., PROFESSOR, ASSOCIATE DEAN FOR RESEARCH, BOSTON UNIVERSITY SCHOOL OF PUBLIC HEALTH

My name is Dr. Ralph Hingson. Last year I was asked by the Committee on Developing a Strategy to Reduce and Prevent Underage Drinking of the National Academy of Sciences to write a background paper "Social and Health Consequences of Underage Drinking" for their report released September 10, 2003 Reducing Underage Drinking: A Collective Responsibility. They also asked me to present at their committee hearings the Report of the National Institute on Alcohol Abuse and Alcoholism (NIAAA) "A Call to Action: Changing the Culture of Drinking at U.S. Colleges." This report to which I contributed (Hingson et al. 2002; Hingson and Howland 2002) was prepared by a task force of college presidents, researchers, and students convened by NIAAA to:

1. review the magnitude and dimensions of college student drinking problems in the United States; and
2. explore what prevention and treatment strategies have been tested and found in scientific research to reduce those problems.

I would like to review findings on 1) the magnitude and consequences of underage drinking, and 2) strategies established through scientific research to reduce those problems.

Magnitude and Consequences of Underage Drinking

To assess the magnitude and consequences of underage drinking in the United States, we examined data from:

- The Fatality Analysis Reporting System (FARS) for the year 2002 of the National Highway Traffic Safety Administration (NHTSA).
- Injury mortality statistics from the U.S. Centers for Disease Control and Prevention (2003).
- U.S. Census population statistics.
- Smith, et al. Fatal non-traffic injuries involving alcohol: A meta-analysis. Annals of Emergency Medicine, 1999, a review of 331 published medical examiner studies from 1975 to 1995 in the United States.
- The 2002 National Household Survey on Drug Use and Health conducted in person with over 68,000 randomly selected persons age 12 and older by the Substance Abuse and Mental Health Services Administration (2003).

- The 2001 Youth Risk Behavior Survey, a self-administered in school study of a random sample of 13,600 U.S. high school students with an 83 percent response rate conducted by the U.S. Centers for Disease Control and Prevention (Grunbaum et al. 2002).
- The 1999 National Survey of Drinking and Driving conducted for NHTSA in 1999, with 5,733 respondents of age 16 and older (Royal 2000).
- The 1992 National Longitudinal alcohol Epidemiologic Survey conducted with over 40,000 adults 18 and older in 1992 by the U.S. Census Bureau for the National Institute of Alcohol Abuse and Alcoholism.

Key Findings

1. The average age that American youth begin drinking has declined from 17.6 in 1965 to 15.9 in 1999. Among persons 12-20 years old in 1990, 2.2 million or 11 percent started drinking before the age 18. By 2000 that number nearly doubled to 4.1 million, 17 percent of the 12-20 age group (2002 National Household Survey on Drug Use and Health, U.S. Census Bureau).
2. Among U.S. high school students, 29 percent (over 4.3 million) started drinking alcoholic beverages before age 13 (2001 Youth Risk Behavior Survey).
3. Among high school students nationwide, those who begin drinking at younger ages are much more likely than those who wait until they are older to drink heavily and drink heavily more frequently. Those who start to drink at age 10 or younger are 11 times more likely than those who wait until they are 17 or older to have consumed 5 or more drinks on at least 6 occasions in the past month, 22 percent vs. 2 percent (2001 Youth Risk Behavior Survey).

4. Those high school students who drink 5+ drinks at least 6 times per month, nearly one million students, compared to those who don't drink are much more likely in a given month to engage in behavior that places them and others at risk for injury, death, or illness. Those frequent heavy drinkers are:
   - more likely to drive after drinking, 41 percent vs. 0 percent.
   - 5 times more likely to ride with a drinking driver, 80 percent vs. 14 percent.
   - 5 times more likely to never wear a seatbelt, 15 percent vs. 3 percent. (Thus they are more likely to be in traffic crashes and if in a crash, seriously injured or killed).
   - 4 times more likely to carry a weapon, 44 percent vs. 10 percent.
   - 7 times more likely to carry a gun, 22 percent vs. 3 percent.
   - 6 times more likely to be injured in a fight, 13 percent vs. 2 percent.
   - 9 times more likely to be injured in a suicide attempt, 9 percent vs. 1 percent.
   - 27 times more likely to have used marijuana, 27 percent vs. 1 percent, much more likely to use cocaine 26 percent vs. 0 percent.
   - 13 times more likely to have injected drugs, 13 percent vs. <1 percent.
   - 8 times more likely to have had sex with 6 or more partners, 31 percent vs. 4 percent.
   - less likely to use condoms during their last sexual intercourse, 54 percent vs. 63 percent. In the U.S. 138,000 persons ages 13-29 have been diagnosed with HIV/ AIDS (U.S. Department of Health and Human Service 2000).
   - nearly 4 times more likely to have been or gotten someone else pregnant, 19 percent vs. 5 percent. Annually there are over 900,000 unplanned teenage pregnancies (Henshaw 1998).

5. High school students who drink 5+ drinks on at least six occasions per month, were 3 times more likely to report that their grades at school in the past year were mostly D's and F's, 15 percent vs. 5 percent. While their risky violent behaviors, illicit drug use and sexual behavior may also contribute to their poor academic performance, new research indicates that the teenage brain is developing throughout adolescence and is disproportionately vulnerable during adolescence to adverse effects of alcohol on memory, planning, and spatial relations. Magnetic resonance imaging studies have shown decrements in frontal lobe activity associated with heavy adolescent alcohol consumption (Brown, Tapert, Granholm, and Delis 2000; Tapert, Brown, Meloy et al. 2001).
6. These newly identified effects of alcohol on the brain may help explain why alcohol impairs the driving ability of people under 21 more than it does for adults. A review of over 100 experimental scientific articles on alcohol and driving skills published from 1981-1997 (Moskowitz and Fiorentino 2000) revealed that alcohol impairs some driving skills beginning with any significant departure from zero blood alcohol content (BAC). The majority of experimental studies examined reported significant impairment at BACs of 0.05 percent and all drivers can be expected to experience impairment in some critical driving skills by a BAC 0.08 percent or less. Research comparing drivers in single vehicle fatal crashes to those stopped in national roadside surveys on similar roadways at the same time of day and day of the week who were not in crashes reveal each 0.02 percent increase in blood alcohol level nearly doubles the single vehicle fatal crash risk (Zador et al. 1991). The most recent national crash and survey analysis reveals that at BACs of 0.08 percent-0.099 percent compared to zero BAC in all age and gender groups, there is at least an 11-fold increase in single vehicle fatal crash risk, but for males 16-20 there is a 52-fold increased risk relative to same age sober drivers. Compounding their heightened single vehicle fatal crash risk at

each blood alcohol level relative to older drivers, when they drive after drinking, drivers under 21 have higher blood alcohol levels, on average BAC of 0.10 percent, 3 times the average level consumed by adults who drive after drinking. Young drinking drivers are also more likely to have passengers in the vehicle than adult drunk drivers (Royal 2000). In 2002 nationwide over 2,200 people died in crashes involving drinking drivers under the age of 21. Half of the people who died in those crashes were persons other than the underage drinking driver. Over half were under the age of 21 while nearly 500 were over age 21 (Fatality Analysis Reporting System 2002).

7. Based on medical examiner studies of alcohol involvement in non-traffic injury deaths among persons under 21, there may be another 2000 non-traffic alcohol-related injury deaths annually caused by falls, drownings, burns, overdoses, as well as, nearly 2000 alcohol-related intentional injury deaths, homicides and suicides (CDC 2003; Smith 1999; Levy, Miller, Lox 1999).

Implications

There is a strong need to increase education and enforcement of laws that exist in every State making it illegal to sell alcohol to persons under 21 and for persons under 21 to drive after any drinking. There is also a clear need to improve our measurement of underage drinking and related problems.

- We need to collect information in our national surveys on harms underage drinkers cause to others just as we have collected information on harms drinking college students cause other college students (600,000 assaults caused by drinking college students annually and 70,000-80,000 sexual assaults/date rapes perpetrated by drinking college students) (Hingson et al. 2002).

- We need to conduct national surveys about alcohol consumption and related health risks with respondents at younger ages starting at early as 9 or 10 to more accurately understand when drinking begins, what contributes to early alcohol use and to prospectively examine associated immediate and long-term consequences.
- Every unintentional death should be tested for alcohol just as most fatally injured drivers in fatal crashes are tested for alcohol. The alcohol testing of fatally injured drivers has provided a valuable yardstick against which to measure the impact of laws to reduce drinking and driving. States passing laws can be compared to States that do not pass these laws to see if there are post-law reductions in alcohol-related deaths. Knowledge gained from studies like this have productively guided our efforts to address this problem. We need a similar yardstick to better assess the impact of interventions to reduce alcohol-related falls, drownings, burns, overdoses, homicides and suicides.

Strategies to Prevent Underage Drinking

Fortunately there are strategies scientifically tested and demonstrated through rigorous studies to reduce underage drinking and related problems. These include:

- Individually-oriented strategies
- Environmental strategies
- Comprehensive community intervention

Individually-Oriented Strategies

Strategies to change knowledge, attitudes, beliefs and behaviors of person whose drinking places themselves and others at risk have been shown to reduce drinking and related problems. Particularly effective have been brief counseling behavior modification strategies in Trauma Centers and Emergency Departments. Gentilello et al. (1999) screened all patients treated at the Harborview Trauma Center in Seattle, Washington. Forty-six percent had been injured under the influence of alcohol. Similar proportions have been found at other Trauma Centers (Rivara 2000).

Half of those injured under the influence were randomly allocated to receive a 30-minute brief intervention during which time they were advised: 1) how their drinking compared to people of the same age and gender nationwide; 2) what their increased risk of subsequent injury or illness was if they continued to drink at levels recorded at intake into the study; 3) where they could obtain counseling and other assistance in reducing their drinking. One year later, those in the intervention group were averaging 3 drinks less per day and over a 3 year follow-up period those in the intervention group relative to the control group experienced 23 percent fewer drunk driving arrests, a 47 percent reduction in emergency department admissions for injury and a 48 percent reduction in hospital in-patient injury admissions. Most of the reductions occurred among patients who did not meet diagnostic criteria for alcohol dependence.

A similar experimental study was completed in a Pediatric Emergency Department by Monti et al. (1999) at Providence Hospital. In both, the brief counseling intervention and standard care group drinking declined 6 months after intake into the study, but the brief intervention group reported one-quarter the number of drinking driving incidents, one-seventh the number of traffic violations, and one-quarter the number of alcohol-related injuries. A key to the remarkable success of both studies was that the patients were queried and counseled about their drinking at a teachable moment when they had just been so severely injured under the influence of alcohol that they needed to be treated in an emergency department or given life support in a trauma center.

Larimer (2002) has recently reviewed a similar series of experimental studies that screened college students for drinking problems and reported significant reductions in drinking and alcohol-related problems among those offered brief interventions. Fleming (1999) similarly reviewed over 30 experimental studies of brief interventions in primary care and hospital settings that also indicated brief interventions were followed by reductions in drinking and alcohol-related problems.

Thus, while there are clearly numerous, rigorous experimental evaluations that indicate brief interventions and counseling can help persons with risky drinking behaviors, a limitation is that most adolescents do not believe they have drinking problems, do not attend screening programs, are not queried about their drinking by their physicians and health care providers and are not receiving the sort of brief intervention counseling demonstrated to reduce alcohol problems. There is an urgent need to expand screening and brief intervention counseling of adolescents with drinking problems.

However, before this can be accomplished a major policy impediment must be addressed. In over 35 States, there are laws that permit insurance companies to withhold medical reimbursement for the treatment of patients injured under the influence of alcohol (Rivara 2000). These laws create a disincentive for physicians and health care providers to screen for the underlying factor "alcohol" that may be contributing to many of the injuries that bring patients to emergency departments and trauma centers.

Environmental Intervention

In addition to individually-oriented intervention, efforts to reduce alcohol availability in the environment can reduce underage drinking. The most important such intervention has been raising the legal drinking age to 21. Over the past two decades alcohol-related traffic deaths have declined 56 percent in 16-20 year olds. During the same time period, traffic deaths in that age group where alcohol is not a factor have increased 42 percent as the numbers of drivers under 21 has increased as has the distance they travel (Figure 1). In 1984 Congress passed and President Reagan signed legislation that would withhold Federal highway construction funds from States that did not raise the legal drinking age to 21. At that time 25 States had a legal drinking age of 21. By 1988 all States adopted that law.

A review by the U.S. Centers for Disease Control and Prevention of 49 studies published in the scientific literature found that in States where drinking ages were lowered in the 1970s on average experienced a 10 percent increase in alcohol-related crashes in the targeted age group of drivers. Conversely, in States where drinking ages were raised there was a

16 percent decrease in alcohol-related crashes in the target age groups of drivers. The National Highway Traffic Safety Administration (NHTSA) estimates that annually 700-1000 traffic deaths are prevented by the adoption of the minimum legal drinking age of 21, bringing the total number of lives saved by that law to more than 21,000 by 2002.

I believe the NHTSA estimate is conservative for two reasons. First, it does not take into account other causes of death associated with alcohol misuse among young persons—unintentional injuries, falls, drownings, burns, overdoses, homicides, suicides, HIV/AIDS infection, etc. Second, it does not take into account a new body of scientific studies that indicate the younger people are when they start to drink the greater their likelihood not only as adolescents but as adults of experiencing a myriad of life-threatening alcohol-related problems.

Analyses of the National Longitudinal Alcohol Epidemiologic Study reveals that persons who begin drinking at age 14 or younger are 4-5 times more likely in their life to experience alcohol dependence (Grant 1998); 7 times more likely to as adults to drink to intoxication on a weekly basis (Hingson et al. 2000); 12 times more likely to be unintentionally injured under the influence of alcohol (Hingson et al. 2000); 7 times more likely to be in motor vehicle crashes because of drinking (Hingson et al. 2002); and, 11 times more likely to be in physical fights while or after drinking (Hingson et al. 2001) [Figures 2-6]. The statistically significant relationships between starting to drink at a younger age and unintentional injury, motor vehicle crash, and involvement in physical fights after drinking persist even after analytically controlling for personal history of alcohol dependence, frequency of heavy drinking, illicit drug use, smoking, family history of alcoholism, race and ethnicity and other respondent characteristics associated with early onset of alcohol use (Hingson et al. 2000, 2001, 2002).

These findings raise the possibility that delaying drinking onset or preventing alcohol use during adolescence may have benefits in reducing alcohol-related unintentional and intentional injuries and deaths not only during adolescent but also adult years. This possibility is of great importance because unintentional injuries are the leading cause of death in the United States from ages 1-34 and intentional injuries are the second leading cause of death from ages 10-34 (CDC 2003). In 2000, there were 97,900 unintentional injury deaths in the United States (CDC 2003) of which 41,944 were traffic crash deaths. In 2000, 17,380 traffic deaths (40 percent) were alcohol-related (involving a driver or pedestrian who had been drinking). The meta-analysis of medical examiner studies conducted by Gordon Smith (1999) revealed that 39 percent of non-traffic unintentional injury deaths tested positive for alcohol at the time of death. Thirty-one percent of traffic crash deaths and 31 percent of other unintentional injury deaths involved persons with blood alcohol levels above 0.10 percent meaning they would have been legally intoxicated. These data on blood alcohol concentrations of non-traffic unintentional injury deaths indicate there are over 20,000 alcohol-related non-traffic unintentional injury deaths annually in the U.S.

The meta-analysis of medical examiner studies of Smith (1999) indicated that 47 percent of homicide victims and 29 percent of suicide victims had positive blood alcohol levels. In 2000 there were 16,765 homicide deaths and 39,350 suicide deaths indicating that at least 7,800 homicide deaths and 8,500 suicide deaths were alcohol related. Thus, all total each year over 50,000 people die in the United States from alcohol-related unintentional or intentional injuries. Alcohol is a major if not the leading contributor to the top 2 leading causes of death among young people in the United States, unintentional and intentional injuries.

Price of Alcohol

The National Academy of Sciences in its Report to Congress in 2003 reviewed the literature on price of alcohol and alcohol-related problems and recommended that Congress and State legislators should raise excise taxes to reduce underage alcohol consumption and to raise additional revenues for this purpose.

The research literature on the effects of price on alcohol consumption indicates that as price increases, consumption decreases (Toomey and Wagenaar 2002). Among moderate drinkers, it has been estimated that a 1 percent price increase results in a 1.19 percent decrease in consumption

(Manning 1995). Younger, heavier drinkers tend to be more affected than older, heavier drinkers (Kenkel 1993; Godfrey 1997; Chaloupka and Wechsler 1996; Sutton and Godfrey 1995). Younger drinkers have less discretionary income and that may contribute to their heightened sensitivity to alcohol prices.

Higher alcohol prices have also been found to reduce alcohol-related problems such as motor vehicle fatalities (Kenkel 1993), robberies, rapes, and liver cirrhosis deaths (Cook and Moore 1993; Cook and Tauchen 1982; Ruhm 1996).

If, as recommended by the National Academy Report (2003) revenues generated by alcohol tax increases to raise beverage prices are in turn earmarked for programs and enforcement of policies known to reduce underage drinking that could be further reduce underage drinking problems.

Legislation to Reduce Alcohol-Related Traffic Deaths

A variety of laws have also been found to reduce alcohol-related traffic deaths (Voas et al. 2000; Hingson, Heeren, Winter 1994, 1996, 2000; Hingson and Winter 2003 in press; Shults 2001; Wells-Parker 1995; Wagenaar 2001; Zador et al. 1989). These include criminal per se laws, enacted in all States, that stipulate that having a blood alcohol level above the legal limit is evidence by itself that a person was driving while legally intoxicated, a criminal offense; administrative license revocation, the law in 40 States that permit police to immediately confiscate the license of any driver operating a motor vehicle with a blood alcohol level above the legal limit in that State; mandatory assessment and alcohol treatment if warranted for persons convicted of driving while intoxicated, the law in 32 States; 0.08 percent legal blood alcohol limits for drivers age 21 and older, the law in 44 States; zero tolerance laws making it illegal for driver under age 21 to drive with any measurement amount of alcohol, the law in all States; and primary enforcement safety belt laws, the law in 20 States that allow police to stop and give a citation to drivers of vehicles containing unbelted or unrestrained motorists. Sobriety checkpoints are a particularly effective enforcement strategy to assist in the life-saving implementation of these laws (Castle et al. 1995; Lacey et al. 1999; Shults et al. 2001). We need each of these laws in every State and they should be coupled with active education and enforcement efforts.

Comprehensive Community Interventions

Implementation of environmental strategies has to occur at the community level. The just released National Academy of Sciences report (2003) emphasized the importance of community based efforts to reduce underage drinking and related problems. The report indicates comprehensive initiatives are the most effective and recommends community organizing, coalition building and use of mass media. They also recommend communities and States undertake regular and comprehensive compliance check programs including notification of retailers concerning the program and follow-up communication to them about the outcome (sale/no sale) for their outlet.

Research supports these recommendations. Several carefully conducted school based and community based initiatives have been found in rigorous research evaluations, most sponsored by the National Institute on Alcohol Abuse and Alcoholism, to have had particular success in reducing drinking and/or related alcohol problems among young people (Hingson and Howland 2002). These programs typically coordinate efforts of city officials from multiple departments of city government, school, health, police, alcohol beverage control, etc. which include concerned private citizens and their organizations, as well as, parents, students and merchants who sell alcohol. Often, multiple intervention strategies are incorporated into the programs including school based programs involving students, peer leaders and parents, media advocacy, community organizing and mobilization, environmental policy change to reduce alcohol availability to youth and heightened enforcement of laws regulating sales and distribution of alcohol and laws to reduce alcohol-related traffic injuries and deaths.

The Mid Western Prevention Project attempted to prevent abuse of alcohol, tobacco, and illicit drugs, such as cocaine, among adolescents age 10-14 in Kansas City, Missouri and later in Indianapolis, Indiana. A quasi-experimental design in Kansas City and a randomized experimental design in Indianapolis were used to evaluate the program (Pentz 1989). In Kansas City, a 10-session youth training program on skills for resisting substance use included homework sessions involving active interviews and role plays with parents and family members about family rules regarding the use of these substances, and successful techniques to avoid their use, and counteract media and community influences to use these substances. Approximately 80 percent of students completed the exercises with parents or adult family members. Mass media coverage was also initiated as part of the intervention. Topic areas included psycho social consequences of the use of alcohol, tobacco, and other drugs, correction of perceptions about the prevalence of peer drug use, recognition of adult media and community influences on substance use, peer and environmental pressure resistance, assertiveness in practicing pressure resistance, problem solving for difficult situations that involve potential substance use, and statements of public commitments to avoid alcohol, tobacco and other drug use. Modeling and role playing of resistance skills, feedback with peer reinforcement, peer leader facilitation and discussion of homework results were part of the program.

Forty-two schools participated in the study. When students in the 24 intervention schools were compared at 1 year follow up to students in 18 delayed intervention schools, prevalence of use of alcohol, cigarettes and marijuana was lower in the intervention schools 11 percent vs. 16 percent for alcohol use, 17 percent vs. 24 percent for cigarette use and 7 percent vs. 16 percent for marijuana use.

Project investigators (Chou et al. 1998) also tracked 1904 students exposed to the program in Indianapolis. They were compared with a sample of 1608 in the control group. Schools were randomly assigned to groups, and students were followed at 6 months, 1.5 years, 2.5 years and 3.5 years after baseline. After analytically controlling for ethnicity, gender, socioeconomic status, father's occupation, school type and grade, the researchers found that among subjects using alcohol, tobacco or other drugs at baseline, secondary prevention effects reducing alcohol use were found at the 6 month and 1.5 year follow up, and for tobacco at 6 month follow up. The authors concluded the social influence based primary prevention program produced benefits not only among students who are non-users at baseline but also among those using substances at baseline.

Project Northland in Minnesota (Perry et al. 1996) was designed to reduce alcohol use among young adolescents. Sixth, seventh and eighth graders were exposed to 3 years of a behavior curriculum, that educated them to communicate with their parents about alcohol, deal with peer influence and normative expectations about alcohol, and understand methods that bring about community level of change in alcohol-related programs and policies. Students learned skills to resist alcohol use and skills for bringing about social, political and institutional change. A "Town Meeting" was conducted by students making recommendations for community action for alcohol use prevention.

Community task forces included a cross section of community government officials, law enforcement personnel, school representatives, health professionals, youth workers, parents, concerned citizens, and adolescents. Community task forces stimulated passage of several local alcohol-related ordinances to prevent sales to minors and intoxicated patrons. Businesses provided discounts to students who pledged to be alcohol and drug free. A theater production was also undertaken.

A higher percentage of students in the intervention group were alcohol users at baseline prompting stratified follow up analyses of users and non-users at baseline. At follow up, the percentages that used alcohol in the past week and past month were significantly lower in the intervention group. No significant follow up differences between groups were found on measures of cigarette smoking or marijuana use.

DARE and DARE Plus. DARE Plus took the traditional DARE program involving police education with 7th and 8th grade students about alcohol and drugs and enhanced it with a peer-led parental involvement classroom program, youth-led extracurricular activities, community adult action teams and postcard mailings to parents. Evaluation of this program randomly allocated 24 middle and junior high schools to receive DARE Plus, DARE or a control intervention. Over 6,200 students were enrolled and 84 percent were followed for 2 years.

In schools receiving DARE Plus relative to control schools, boys showed less increase in alcohol use, other drug use and tobacco use. Girls showed less increase in drunkenness when DARE Plus and DARE schools were compared. No significant differences between students' behavior in DARE schools and controls schools were observed over time (Perry C., Komro K., Veblen-Mortenson S., et al. 2003).

In Communities Mobilizing for Change (Wagenaar 2000), 15 communities were randomly allocated to intervention or comparison groups. The intervention used a community organizing approach to reduce the accessibility of alcoholic beverages to youth under the legal drinking age.

The intervention communities sought to reduce the number of alcohol outlets selling to young people, availability of alcohol to youth from non-commercial sources such as parents, siblings, older peers, and community tolerance of adults providing alcohol to underage youth. Action was encouraged through city councils, school and enforcement agencies, as well as private institutions such as alcohol merchants, business associations, and the media.

Relative to the comparison communities the intervention communities achieved a 17 percent increase in outlets checking the age identification of youthful appearing alcohol purchases, a 24 percent decline in sales by bars and restaurants to potential underage purchasers, a 25 percent decrease in the proportion of 18-20 year olds seeking to buy alcohol, a 17 percent decline in the proportion of older teens who provided alcohol to younger teens and a 7 percent decrease in the percentage of respondents under age 21 who drank in the last 30 days.

The Community Trials Program (Holder et al. 2000) was a 5-year initiative designed to reduce alcohol involved injuries and death in 3 experimental communities. The program had 5 mutually reinforcing components.

The first component tried to mobilize the community support for public policy interventions by increasing general awareness, knowledge, and concern about alcohol-related trauma. Initiatives jointly planned by project organizers and local residents were implemented by the residents.

Second, a Responsible Beverage Server component sought to reduce sales to intoxicated patrons and increase enforcement of local alcohol laws by working with restaurants, bar and hotel associations, beverage wholesalers, the Alcohol Beverage Control Commission and local law enforcement.

Third, a DWI component sought to increase the number of DWI arrests by a combination of special officer training, deployment of passive alcohol sensors, and the use of DUI checkpoints. News coverage publicized these activities.

Fourth, the media brought attention to underage drinking. Sales clerks, owners, managers were trained to prevent sales of alcohol to minors and enforcement of underage drinking laws increased. Compliance check surveys detected sales of alcohol to underage purchasers and police gave citations to violators. Fifth, local zoning powers regarding alcohol outlet density were used to reduce availability of alcohol.

The percentage of alcohol outlets that sold to underage drinkers declined in each intervention community (Grube 1997). Alcohol related crash involvement as measured by single vehicle night crashes declined 10 percent-11 percent more in program than comparison communities. Alcohol related trauma visits to Emergency Departments declined 43 percent (Holder et al., 2000).

The Massachusetts Saving Lives Program (Hingson et al. 1996) was a 5-year (1988-1993) comprehensive community intervention designed to reduce alcohol impaired driving and related traffic deaths. Six program communities were selected to receive financial support for their initiatives based on a competitive proposal process (Haverhill, Lowell, Marlborough, Medford, Plymouth, and North Hampton). These were compared with five matched communities whose applications also satisfied selection criteria but were not funded. The rest of the State of Massachusetts also served as a comparison. Outcome data was collected for the period 5 years before and 5 years after the intervention.

In each program community, a full time coordinator from the Mayor or City Manager's office organized a task force of concerned private citizens and organizations and officials representing various city departments (e.g.,

School, health, police, and recreation). Each community received approximately $ 1 per inhabitant per year in program funds. Half the funds were spent to hire the coordinator and the balance for increased police enforcement and other program activities and educational materials. Voluntary activity was also encouraged. Active task force membership ranged from 20 to more than 100 persons in each community. An average of 50 organizations participated in each city.

Most of the initiatives were developed by the communities. The program sought to reduce drunk driving as well as behaviors disproportionately exhibited by drunk drivers, related risks, such as speeding, running red lights, failure to yield to pedestrians in crosswalks, and failure to wear safety belts. To reduce drunk driving and speeding, communities introduced media campaigns, checkpoints, business information programs, speeding and drunk driving awareness days, speed watch telephone hotlines, police training, high school per led education, Students Against Drunk Driving Chapters, College Prevention programs, alcohol free prom nights, beer keg registration, and increased liquor outlet surveillance by police to reduce underage alcohol purchase. To increase pedestrian safety and safety belt use, program communities conducted media campaigns and police check points, posted crosswalk signs warning motorist of fines for failure to yield to pedestrians, added crosswalk guards, and offered preschool education programs and training for hospital and prenatal staff. Coordinators engaged in numerous media advocacy activities to explain trends in local traffic safety problems and strategies the communities were implementing to reduce traffic injury and death. The proportion of drivers under age 20 who reported driving after drinking in random digit dial telephone surveys, declined from 19 percent during the final year of the program to 9 percent in subsequent years. There was little change in comparison areas. The proportion of vehicles observed speeding through use of radar was cut in half, whereas there was also little change in comparison cities. There was a seven percent increase in safety belt use, a significantly greater increase than shown in comparison area.

Fatal crashes declined from 178 during the 5 preprogram years to 120 during the 5-program years. This was a 25 percent greater reduction than in the rest of Massachusetts. Fatal crashes involving alcohol declined 42 percent and the number of fatally injured drivers with positive blood alcohol levels declined 47 percent relative to the rest of Massachusetts (90 percent of fatally injured drivers in Massachusetts are tested annually for alcohol). Visible injuries per 100 crashes declined 5 percent more in Saving Lives Cities than the rest of the State during the program period. The fatal crash declines were greater in program cities particularly among younger drivers age 15-25. All six-program cities had greater declines in fatal and alcohol-related fatal crashes than comparison cities or the rest of the State.

Conclusion

Alcohol is a leading contributor to the leading causes of death for persons under 21 and up to age 34 unintentional and intentional injury. Each year over 50,000 people nationwide die from alcohol-related injuries. The average age that young people begin to drink in the U.S. is declining with 29 percent of high school students, 4.3 million starting to drink before age 13. Alcohol has a disproportionately deleterious effect on the developing brain during adolescence producing decrements in memory, planning, and spatial relations. The younger the age people begin to drink the greater their likelihood of developing alcohol dependence and frequent heavy drinking patterns, and experiencing unintentional injuries under the influence of alcohol, motor vehicle crashes because of drinking, and physical fights while or after drinking. These relationships are found not only during adolescence, but carry over into adult life.

Underage drinking is associated with a variety of health risks not only to adolescent drinkers but other adolescents and adults as well. Half the people who died in motor vehicle crashes involving drinking drivers under 21 are persons other than that underage drinking driver. Our government at all levels, Federal, State and local, has an obligation to protect its citizens from harms posed to them by underage drinking drivers. There is a clear need to expand screening, counseling, environmental and comprehensive community efforts to reduce underage drinking and onset of drinking at very young ages.

Fortunately, there is a sizeable research literature that has identified individually oriented counseling strategies that can reduce problematic drinking as well as environmental approaches such as greater enforcement of the age 21 drinking age law, zero tolerance laws making it illegal for persons younger than 21 drive after any drinking, increased price of alcohol with tax revenues earmarked for prevention and treatment programs with proven effectiveness, and heightened enforcement of other alcohol service and anti-drinking driving laws. The enforcement of these laws is best accomplished at the community level and several rigorously evaluated comprehensive community intervention studies have demonstrated these efforts can markedly reduce drinking and associated alcohol-related injuries and deaths among young persons.

There is an urgent need to adopt interventions along these lines proposed in the National Academy of Sciences 2003 report, Reducing Underage Drinking: A Collective Responsibility.

REFERENCES

Brown S., Tapert S., Granholm E., and Delis D. Neurocognitive function of adolescents: Effects of protracted alcohol use. *Alcoholism Clinical and Experimental Research,* 24 (2): 164-171, 2000.

Castle S.P., Thompson J.D., Spataro J.A., et al. Early evaluation of a statewide sobriety checkpoint program. Paper presented at the *39th Annual Conference of the Association for the Advancement of Automotive Medicine*, Chicago, 1L, pp. 65-78, October 16-18, 1995.

Centers for Disease Control and Prevention. *National Center for Injury Prevention and Control Web-based injury statistics query and reporting system (WISQARS).* http://www.cdc.gov/ncipc/wisqars/, 2003.

Chaloupka F.J. and Wechsler H. Binge drinking in college: The impact of price, availability, and alcohol control policies. *Contemporary Econ. Policy,* 14 (4): 112-124, 1996.

Chou CP. et al., Effects of a community based prevention program on decreasing drug use in high risk adolescents. *American J. of Public Health* 88 (6) 944-948, 1998.

Cook P.J. and Moore M. Economic perspectives on reducing alcohol-related violence. In: Martin S.E., ed. *Alcohol Interpersonal Violence: Fostering Multidisciplinary Perspective*. NIAAA Research Monograph No. 24. NIH Pub No. 93-3496. Rockville, MD, pp. 193-212, 1993.

Cook P.J. and Tauchen G. The effect of liquor taxes on heavy drinking. *Bell J. Econ*, 13 (2): 379-390, 1982.

Fleming M.F. and Manwell L.B. Brief intervention in primary care settings: a primary treatment method for at-risk, problem, and dependent drinkers. *Alcohol Research Health,* 23: 128-137, 1999.

Gentilello L., Rivara F., Donovan D., Jurkovich G., Daranciang E., Dunn C., Villaveces A., Copass M. and Ries R., Alcohol interventions in a trauma center as a means of reducing the risk of injury recurrence. *Annals of Surgery,* 230 (4): 473-483, 1999.

Godfrey C. Can tax be used to minimize harm? A health economist's perspective. In: Plant M., Single E., Stockwell T. (eds.) *Alcohol: Minimising the harm: What works?* London, England: Free Association Books, pp. 29-42, 1997.

Grant B. The impact of family history of alcoholism on the relationship between age at onset of alcohol use and DSM III alcohol dependence. *Alcohol Health and Research World,* 22: 144-147, 1998.

Grube J.W. Preventing sales of alcohol to minors: results from a community trial. *Addiction,* 92 (S2): S251-S260, 1997.

Grunbaum J.A., Kann L., Kinchen S.A., Williams B., Ross J.G., Lowey R. and Kolbe L. Youth risk behavior surveillance—United States, 2001. *J. School Health,* 72 (8): 313-328, 2002.

Henshaw S.K. Unintended pregnancy in the United States 1982-1993. *Family Planning Perspectives,* 30: 24-29, 1998.

Hingson R. and Winter M. Epidemiology and consequences of drinking and driving. *Alcohol Research and Health,* in press, 2003.

Hingson R., Heeren T., Levenson S., Jamanka A. and Voas R. Age of drinking onset, driving after drinking and involvement in alcohol related motor vehicle crashes, *Accident Analysis and Prevention*, 34: 85-92, 2002a.

Hingson R. and Howland J. Comprehensive community interventions to promote health: Implications for college-age drinking problems. *J. Studies on Alcohol, Supplement* 14: 226-240, 2002.

Hingson R., Heeren T., Zakocs R.C., Kopstein A. and Wechsler H. Magnitude of alcohol-related mortality and morbidity among U.S. college students ages 18-24. *J. Studies on Alcohol*, 63 (2): 136-144, 2002.

Hingson R., Heeren T. and Zakocs R., Age of drinking onset and involvement in physical fights after drinking. *Pediatrics,* 108: 872-877, 2001.

Hingson R., Heeren T., Jamanka A. and Howland J. Age at drinking onset and unintentional injury involvement after drinking *JAMA,* 284 (12): 1527-1533, 2000.

Hingson R., Heeren T., and Winter M. Effects of recent 0.08 percent legal blood alcohol limits on fatal crash involvement. *Injury Prevention*, 6: 109-114, 2000.

Hingson R., Heeren T., and Winter M. Lowering State legal blood alcohol limits to 0.08 percent: The effect on fatal motor vehicle crashes. *American J. Public Health,* 86 (9): 1297-1299, 1996.

Hingson R., McGovern T., Howland J., Hereen T., Winter M. and Zakocs R. Reducing alcohol-impaired driving in Massachusetts: The Saving Lives Program. *American J. of Public Health,* 86: 791-797, 1996.

Hingson R., Heeren T. and Winter M. Lower legal blood alcohol limits for young drivers. *Public Health Reports* 109(61:738-744, 1994.

Holder H., Gruenwald P., Ponicki W., Treno A., Grube S., Satz R., Voas R., Reynolds R., Davis J., Sanchez L., Gaumont G., and Rolper P. Effects of community based intervention on high risk driving and alcohol-related injuries. *JAMA,* 284 (18): 2341-2347, 2000.

Kenkel D.S. Drinking, driving, and deterrence: The effectiveness and social costs of alternative policies. *J. Law Econ.,* October: 877-913, 1993.

Lacey J.H., Jones R.K. and Smith R.G. *Evaluation of Checkpoint Tennessee: Tennessee's statewide sobriety checkpoint program.* DOT HS 808-841. U.S. Department of Transportation, National Highway Traffic Safety Administration, Washington, DC, 1999.

Larimer M.E. and Cronce J.M. Identification, prevention and treatment: A Review of individual-focused strategies to reduce problematic alcohol consumption by college students. *J. Studies on Alcohol, Supplement* 14: 148-163, 2002.

Levy D., Miller T. and Lox K. *Costs of underage drinking.* U.S. Department of Justice, Office of Justice Programs, Office of Juvenile Justice and Delinquency Prevention, Washington, DC, 1999.

Manning W.G., Blumberg L. and Moulton L.H. The demand for alcohol: The differential response to price. *J. Health Econ.,* 14 (2): 123-148, 1995.

Monti P., Colby S., Barnett P., Spirito A., Rosenhow D., Myers M., Wooland R. and Lewander W. Brief intervention for harm reduction with alcohol positive older adolescents in a hospital emergency department. *J. of Consulting and Clinical Psychology*, 67 (6): 989-994, 1999.

Moskowitz H. and Fiorentino D. *A review of the literature on the effects of low doses of alcohol on driving related skills*, DOT HS 809-028. U.S. Department of Transportation, National Highway Traffic Safety Administration, Springfield, VA, 2000.

National Academy of Sciences. *Reducing underage drinking: A collective responsibility.* Committee on Developing a Strategy to Reduce and Prevent Underage Drinking. Institute of Medicine, National Research Council, National Academies Press, Washington, DC, 2003.

National Center for Injury Prevention and Control. *Division of Unintentional Injury Prevention Annual Report 2000.* Centers for Disease Control and Prevention, National Center for Injury Prevention and Control, Atlanta, GA, 2003.

National Highway Traffic Safety Administration. *Traffic Safety Facts 2002: Overview.* DOT HS 809-612. U.S. Department of Transportation, Washington, DC, 2003.

National Institute on Alcohol Abuse and Alcoholism. *A Call to Action: Changing the culture of drinking at U.S. colleges*. NIH Publication No. 02-5010, p. 19, April 2002.

National Institute on Alcohol Abuse and Alcoholism. *Drinking in the United States: main findings from the 1992 National Longitudinal Alcohol Epidemiologic Survey (NLAES)* NIH Publication No. 99-3519, 1998.

Pentz M., Dwyer J., MacKinnon D., Flay B., Hensen W. and Wang E., Johnson A., A multi community trial for primary prevention of adolescent drug abuse. *JAMA,* 261(22): 3259-3265, 1989.

Perry C.L., Komro K.A., Veblen-Mortenson S., Bosner L., Farbrakhsler K., Munsen K., Stigler M. and Lytte L. A randomized controlled trial of middle and junior high school DARE and DARE Plus programs. *Archives of Pediatrics and Adolescent Medicine,* 157 (2): 178-184, 2003.

Perry C.L., Williams C.L., Veblen-Mortenson S., Toomey T.L., Komro K.A., et al.. Project Northland: Outcomes of a community-wide alcohol use prevention program during early adolescence. *American J. of Public Health,* 86: 956-65, 1996.

Rivara F., Tollefson S., Tesh E. and Gentilello L. Screening trauma patients for alcohol problems: Are insurance companies barriers? *J. of Trauma Injury Infection and Critical Care,* 48 (1): 115-118, 2000.

Royal D. 1999 *National Surveys of Drinking and Driving Attitudes and Behaviors.* Volume One: Findings; Volume Two: Methods. U.S. Department of Transportation, National Highway Traffic Safety Administration, Washington, DC, 2000.

Ruhm C.J. Alcohol policies and highway vehicle fatalities. *J. Health Econ,* 15 (4): 435-454, 1996.

Shults R., Ekder R., Sleet D., et al. Reviews of evidence regarding interventions to reduce alcohol-impaired driving. *American J. Preventive Medicine,* 21 (S4): 66-68, 2001.

Smith G., Branngs C. and Miller T. Fatal non-traffic injuries involving alcohol: a meta-analysis. *Annals of Emergency Medicine,* 33: 699-702, 1999.

Substance Abuse and Mental Health Services Administration. *Results from the 2002 national survey on drug use and health: National findings.* Office of Applied Statistics, NHSDA Series H-22, DHHS Pub. No. SMA 03-3836, Rockville, MD, 2003.

Sutton M. and Godfrey C. A grouped data regression approach to estimating economic and social influences on individual drinking behaviour. *Health Econ.,* 4: 237-247, 1995.69.

Tapert S.F., Brown G., Meloy M., Dager A., Cheung E. and Brown S. MRI measurement of 471rain function in alcohol use disordered adolescents. *Alcoholism: Clinical and Experimental Research*, 25, 80A, 2001.

U.S. Department of Health and Human Services. *Health United States with Adolescent Chart Book*. DHHS Pub No. 0012317, Hyattsville, MD, 2000.

Voas R.B., Tippets A.S. and Fell J. The relationship of alcohol safety laws to drinking drivers in fatal crashes. *Accident Analysis Prevention*, 32: 483-492, 2000.

Wagenaar A., O'Malley P. and LaFond C. Lowered legal blood alcohol limits for young drivers: Effects on drinking drivers and driving after drinking behaviors in 30 States. *American J. Public Health*, 91 (5): 801-804, 2001.

Wagenaar A., Murray D., Gehan J., Wolfson M., Forster J., Toomey T., Perry C. and Jones-Weber R. Communities mobilizing for change: Outcomes from a randomized community trial. *J. Studies on Alcohol,* 161 (1): 85-94, 2000.

Wells-Parker E., Bangert-Drowns R., McMillen R. and Williams M. Final results from a meta-analysis of remedial intervention with drink/drive offenders. *Addiction,* 90: 907-926, 1995.

Zador P.L., Krawchuck S. and Voas R. Alcohol-related relative risk of driving fatalities and driver impairment in fatal crashes in relation to driver age and gender: An update using 1996 data. *J. Studies on Alcohol,* 61: 387-395, 2000.

Zador P.L. Alcohol-related relative risk of fatal driver injuries in relation to driver age and sex. J. *Studies on Alcohol*, 52 (4): 302-310, 1991.

Zador P., Land A., Fields, et al. Fatal crash involvement and laws against alcohol impaired driving. *J. Public Health Policy*, 10: 467-485, 1989.

A Note on the Effects of Lower Legal Drinking Ages in Europe

The National Academy of Sciences report (2003) noted the belief held by some people that in Europe, where drinking ages are lower than in the U.S., young people learn to drink in a more responsible manner and that lowering the legal drinking age would reduce underage drinking.

The National Academy report provided clear evidence that this notion has no basis in fact. In 1999 random surveys 15-year-olds in 29 European nations were asked the same questions about drinking as used in the Monitoring the Future national surveys of U.S. 10th grade students. In 28 of 29 European nations, a greater percentage of the adolescents surveyed drank in the past 30 days than in the U.S. In 21 of the European nations, a greater proportion of youth surveyed drank to intoxication in the past year. Since 1995, the proportions of U.S. youth under 21 who report drinking to intoxication has remained constant whereas in half the European countries, studies have shown the proportion has increased. Lower legal drinking ages do not reduce the proportion of underage drinkers; rather they reduce the age of initiation of alcohol use.

We as a Nation should examine why most European nations have lower legal blood alcohol limits that the U.S., a higher age of driving licensure, and the effects on youth drinking and driving of their often more widespread public transportation. The European nations might benefit from an examination of our history of raising the legal drinking age to 21 and the benefits of those changes in reducing alcohol-related traffic and other injury fatalities.

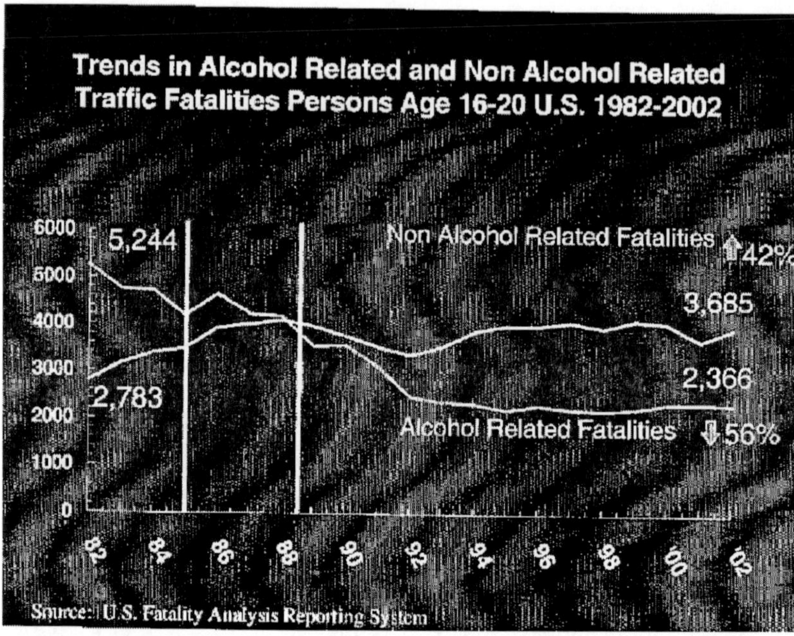

Figure 1.

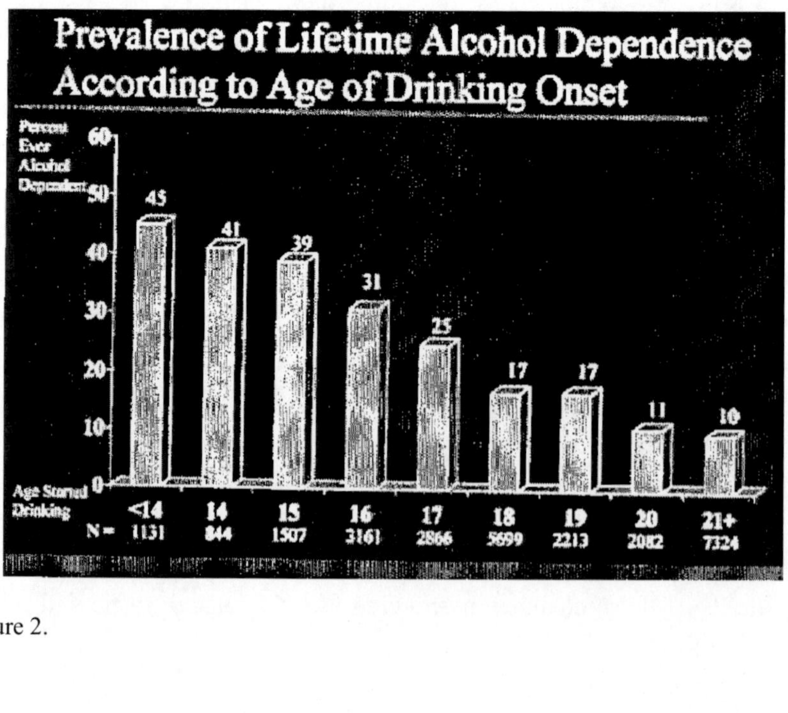

Figure 2.

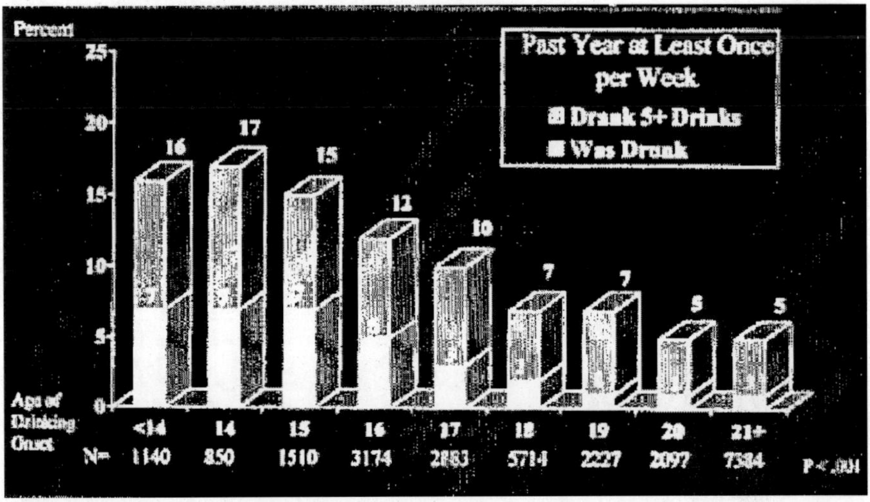

Figure 3.

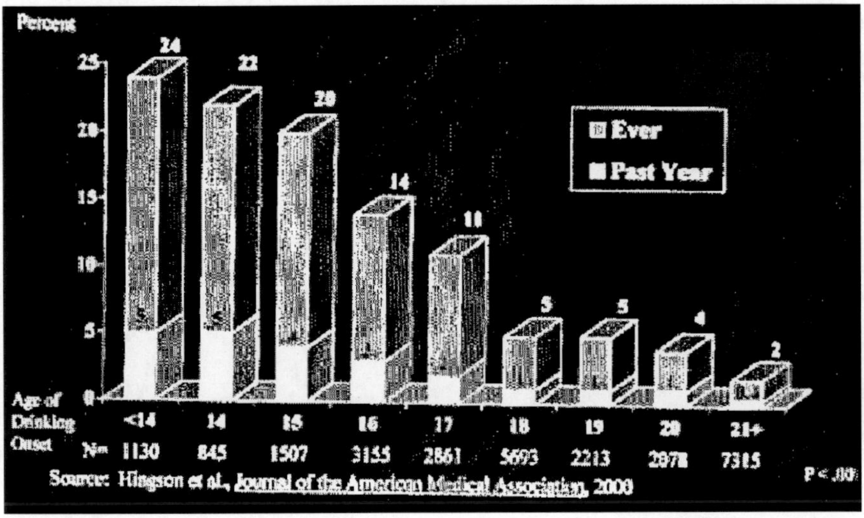

Figure 4.

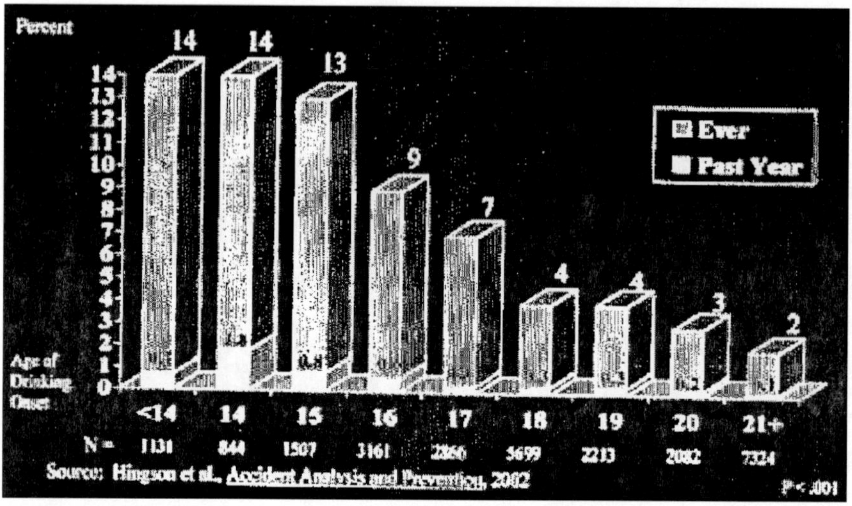

Figure 5.

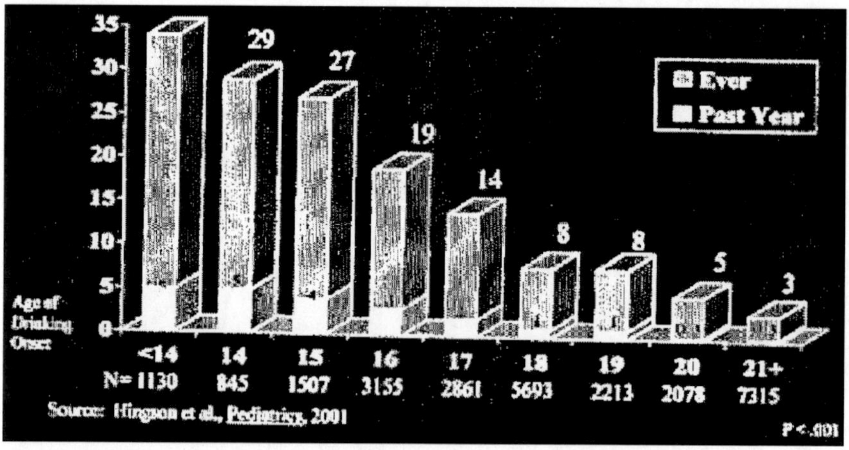

Figure 6.

Independent State Store Union, ISSU,
Harrisburg, PA 17108,
September 29, 2003.

Hon. Mike DeWine,
U.S. Senate,
Washington, DC 20510.

Dear Mr. Chairman: I have worked in the alcohol beverage industry for 32 1/2 years as a State store manager of the Pennsylvania Liquor Control Board.

We see daily the hands of old people and young people from every economic and social class shake as they scrounge their dollars and cents to buy their half pints of whiskey or pints of vodka.

We see billboards in poor neighborhoods extolling $30.00 bottles of cognac where children fight to go to bed early to get a mattress.

We see heavily advertised quarts of beer sold in hoagie shops cheaper than a quart of water.

We have watched 25 years of alcohol advertising on Super Bowl Sunday validate to every 8-21 year old male that drinking beer is the American male rite of passage.

I have read that 63 percent of all adults favor a law that would ban all advertisements of alcoholic beverages on billboards in the country. Let's do it.

As an American citizen, a liquor store manager, a president of a union representing State liquor store managers in Pennsylvania and a member of the Global Alcohol Policy Alliance, I encourage your committee to ban all alcohol advertising in the USA.

Alcohol is a factor in the four leading causes of death for people under 21—car fatalities, homicide, suicide and other accidental deaths.

A child is six times more likely to die from alcohol than all the other drugs combined.

The only argument against the ban of alcohol advertising is that too many dollars pass through too many hands and that allows the six-fold youth alcohol death ratio to live on and on.

Sincerely,
Ed Cloonan,
President, Independent State Store Union (ISSU).

PREPARED STATEMENT OF HON. SUSAN M. MOLINARI, CHAIRMAN, THE CENTURY COUNCIL

Mr. Chairman and Members of the Subcommittee: The Century Council is an independent, national not-for-profit organization dedicated to fighting drunk driving and underage drinking. Headquartered in Washington, DC, and funded by America's leading distillers, the Council's mission is to promote responsible decision-making regarding drinking, or not drinking, of beverage alcohol and to discourage all forms of irresponsible consumption through education, communications, law enforcement and other programs. Since 1991, The Council's funding companies (Allied Domecq Spirits & Wine North America, Bacardi USA., Inc., Brown-Forman, DIAGEO, Future Brands LLC, Pernod Ricard USA) have invested $130 million to support the Council's efforts to develop and implement alcohol education and prevention programs.

The Century Council is chaired by the Honorable Susan Molinari. An independent Advisory Board comprised of distinguished leaders in business, government, education, medicine and other relevant disciplines assists the Council in its' development of programs and policies. Additionally, the Council maintains advisory panels in the areas of education and traffic safety that provide related guidance in those areas.

The recently released National Academy of Sciences (NAS) report on underage drinking clearly accomplishes an extremely important goal and one that is central to The Century Council's mission. The report shines a spotlight on this critically important issue and hopefully as a result, decreases the awareness gap that exists in our country regarding underage drinking and the important relationship that parents have in solving this problem.

Since 1991, the Council has been on the front lines of developing programs, strategies and tactics that both highlight the issues and develop promising practices that result in long-term positive impact and many of the points covered in the NAS report are in concert with the philosophies, and actions, of The Century Council. As an independent organization, dedicated to fighting drunk driving and underage drinking, staffed with professionals in these areas, the Council is now, and has been in the past, providing many of the programs and services that the report recommends.

The Century Council, operating on the philosophy that collective action can have a greater impact than individual efforts, involves all sectors of the community including beverage alcohol wholesalers and retailers, law enforcement, public officials, educators, insurers, health care professionals and private citizen organizations in the fight against drunk driving and underage drinking.

In pursuit of these goals, The Century Council identifies areas of concern in the fight against drunk driving and underage drinking, coordinates the development of initiatives to address such areas, and implements education and public awareness campaigns and promotes legislation through strategic partnerships.

Hand-in-hand with all sectors of the community, The Century Council develops innovative, award-winning programs focused on the following core activities:

- Promoting alcohol educational programs for middle school-through college aged students and for their parents, teachers, and adult supervisors;
- Creating law enforcement and retailer programs with materials and promotions designed to deter minors from purchasing beverage alcohol;
- Researching and identifying solutions for drunk driving and underage drinking and advocating for effective laws and policies at the state and Federal levels;
- Developing programs that target drunk drivers, with a special emphasis on the hardcore drunk driver, and creating promising strategies and legislation to eliminate the problem;
- Delivering blood alcohol education to inform the public about State laws for blood alcohol concentration (BAC) and how and individual's BAC level is affected based on gender, weight, and number and type of beverage;

Clearly the issue of underage drinking is an important one. Many organizations highlight high-profile incidents involving underage drinking and call for action. Unfortunately, many of those same organizations do little to actually develop and implement programs to effectively combat and correct the problem. The Century Council focuses much of its efforts on programs, strategies and tactics to combat underage drinking. As always, our efforts are guided by noted professionals working in the field of alcohol education and prevention who ensure that our activities hold promise in effecting a long-term positive shift in the behavior of our youth.

These programs in both the education and traffic safety arenas include:

Ready or Not® Talking With Kids About Alcohol is a community program created in partnership with Boys & Girls Clubs of America, Ready or Not ® helps parents and other adults prevent underage drinking problems among middle-school age children (ages 10 to 14). The program includes a 30-minute video illustrating five concrete steps adults can take to prevent illegal underage drinking and a facilitator kit for use in workshops or at home. Spanish-language Sin Rodeos®: Hablando con los ninos sobre el alcohol and Native American adaptations are also available free-of-charge.

Brandon Tells His Story is a high school program that features Brandon Silveria, a permanently disabled young man who crashed his car after having a few drinks at age 17. Brandon and his father, Tony, tour America's high schools to educate students—over one million to date—about the dangers and consequences of underage drinking. In addition to the lecture program, The Century Council reaches thousands more students with a half-hour video and accompanying classroom activity guide that brings Brandon's story to high schools across the country. Three video messages focusing on back-to-school, spring break, and prom/graduation are available to keep Brandon's story alive throughout the school year. The video has won the education field's prestigious Chris award and a FREDDIE first-place in the American Medical Association's International Health & Medical Film Competition.

Alcohol 101 for High School Seniors is an interactive CD-ROM program with a companion Educator's Guide designed to aid educators in preparing students to make informed choices about alcohol. By demonstrating the negative outcomes of bad decisions and providing safe and healthy alternatives, Alcohol 101 for High School Seniors encourages students to maintain safety and control in situations involving alcohol. Alcohol 101 for High School Seniors was developed through a partnership between the American School Counselor Association (ASCA). Additional information can be found at www.Alcl01forHSseniors.org.

"Parents, You're Not Done Yet" is a brochure designed to encourage parents of incoming college freshmen to discuss college drinking with their kids before they leave home and during the first weeks of the school year. With input from educators, alcohol policy administrators and other higher education professionals, The Council created and has distributed more than 3 million free brochures to over 1,300 colleges. A downloadable version of the brochure, in both English and Spanish, is available online at www.centurycouncil.org.

Alcohol 101 Plus™ is an innovative, interactive CD-ROM program aimed at helping students make safe and responsible decisions about alcohol on college campuses. Set on a "virtual campus," Alcohol 101 Plus combines the core elements of the award-winning Alcohol 101 program, including the "Virtual Bar," with new content targeted to at-risk populations—first year students, Greeks, student-athletes, and judicial policy offenders. The realistic scenarios highlight the specific issues, challenges, and decisions these groups face when it comes to alcohol in a college setting and provides students and educators with the opportunity for reflection and discussion. The program also includes an interactive alcohol education game developed in partnership with SONY, which provides the user with an opportunity to learn about how alcohol affects an individual's health, performance, and decision-making. A website, www.alcohollOlplus.org, complements the Alcohol 101 Plus CD by providing a wealth of additional information for students, facilitators, and the media.

Promising Practices identifies constructive ways to fight alcohol abuse on university and college campuses. Developed through a grant from The Century Council, David Anderson, Ph.D. and Gail Gleason Milgram, Ed.D. developed a sourcebook of promising practices. This sourcebook, the only kind in the country, included two updates and companion materials such as task force and action planners. This resource includes nearly 300 proven alcohol abuse prevention programs at both public and private schools throughout the country and policies and programs included in the Sourcebook are in use on campuses nationally.

"Speak Up" is a joint project between The Century Council and the National Collegiate Athletic association (NCAA) that focuses on delivering alcohol education and prevention to student athletes. Through NCAA's Champs Life Skills coordinators, facilitated discussions dealing with alcohol issues are conducted with Division I, II and III student athletes.

Cops in Shops® — a cooperative effort, involving local retailers and law enforcement, designed to deter minors from attempting to illegally purchase alcohol and adults who purchase alcohol for minors. Undercover officers are assigned to participating retail locations; often one works inside the store while a second is positioned outside to apprehend adults who procure alcohol for youth.

Point of Sale Materials — more than ten million posters, decals, buttons and employee information brochures have been distributed free of charge to over 100,000 retailers in all 50 states. Based on recent survey data stating that 65 percent of youth who drink obtain alcohol from their family and friends, The Century Council, working with the American Beverage Licensees (ABL), created a new campaign that highlights the point of access to alcohol by underage youth and encourages parents to play a more active role in keeping alcohol out of the hands of our nation's youth. The key component to the campaign is a 30 second Public Service Announcement, buttons and informational cards, distributed at the point of purchase, that provide tips for parents on how to talk with their kids about alcohol. To raise awareness of the industry's efforts, The Council continues to host local events brining together retailers, wholesalers, and community leaders to deter underage purchasing.

The Blood Alcohol Educator CD-ROM is an interactive CD-ROM for adults that provides the blood alcohol concentration (BAC) limit for driving in a user's particular state and educates the user on how their personal BAC level changes based on their gender, weight and number and type of drink. Once in the program's "Virtual Bar," the user can select from a variety of drinks to determine their BAC level and a clock calculates how long it will take for the user's BAC level to return to zero. The BAE CDROM is the centerpiece of a national campaign that includes a BAE Van tow that has distributed over 100,000 BAE CD-ROMs to the public free-of-charge. The BAE Van is outfitted with the colorful BAE logo and builds out into a cyber-cafe with three computer terminals to allow visitors to use the program. The BAE CD-ROM is available in both English and Spanish and, in addition to the CD-ROM and Van tour, can be used on the web at www.b4udrink.org.

The Century Council believes that in educating parents, youth and educators in alcohol prevention and education, outreach to the Hispanic community is of utmost importance. As a result, the Council has a variety of Hispanic programs including;

The Century Council's award-winning Hispanic program—"Si Toma, No Maneje" was the first comprehensive program in the nation to provide the large, growing Hispanic population with Spanish-language anti-alcohol-abuse information. The Century Council's commitment is to provide the Hispanic community with culturally sensitive messages about the dangers of drunk driving and underage drinking. As a result of this approach, The Council has designed a complete array of educational programs that are easy to use and adaptable to the individual needs of the community.

Hice La Promesa! (I Made the Promise) —This program, a pledge to not drive drunk, to serve as designated drivers and to encourage families and friends to do the same, was created in partnership with the Catholic Archdiocese of Los Angeles. Over 2,000 parishes have conducted Hice La Promesa! events reaching more than 1 million Catholics.

Sin Rodeos: hablando con los nifios sobre el alcohol —A Spanish language version of The Council's Ready or Not: Talking With Kids About Alcohol program was produced in partnership with the Los Angeles Unified School District (LAUSD). Sin Rodeos presents the key messages of Ready or Not through culturally sensitive situations. The program is also supported by the ASPIRA Association, the Cuban American National Council, League of United Latin American Citizens (LULAC), National Association of Latino Elected and Appointed Officials Education Fund (NALEO), National Council of La Raza (NCLR), and the National Puerto Rican Coalition.

Public Service Announcements (PSA's) — In 1994, The Century Council's public service announcement "El Nino" received an award from Hispanic Business Magazine as Best Public Service Announcement.

Vive, por nuestro futuro! Si tomas, no manejes! is the title of our most recent campaign developed in partnership with Recording Artists, Actors and Athletes Against Drunk Driving (RADD) and the National Association of Broadcasters (NAB). More than a dozen radio and television PSAs were produced featuring Hispanic celebrities such as: Edward James Olmos, Chayanne, India, Shakira and Tito Puente. The NAB distributed the TV and radio PSAs nationwide in mid-September 2000, in conjunction with Hispanic Heritage Month.

Other Programs Available in Spanish—The Century Council also offers the Blood Alcohol Educator (BAE) program, the "Parents, You're Not Done Yet" brochure and some Point of Sale materials in Spanish.

The Century Council also has an ongoing PSA program featuring well-known public figures and celebrities discussing the dangers of drunk driving and the need for alcohol education; many are produced in both English and Spanish.

It is important to note that The Century Council also focuses on combating drunk driving and has similar programs, strategies and tactics to attack this important problem. As the focus of this statement surrounds the issue of underage drinking, an overview of those programs will not be included in this packet.

The Century Council constantly conducts research and focus groups to assist us in developing new programs and to gauge the effectiveness of our efforts. Attachments are included at the end of this statement that are relevant to any discussion on underage drinking.

Simply highlighting the problem and promoting action plans that are not data-driven are not in the best interest of solving this important issue. Since 1991, The Century Council, and America's leading distillers who fund us, have had a longstanding commitment in the fight to stop underage drinking. Our belief is that science-based, programs developed by professionals and widely distributed to parents, educators and youth is the best action towards the goal of stopping underage drinking. We will continue our efforts and as always, stand ready to work with any strategic partners and members of the Committee to accomplish this task.

Thank you.

ATTACHMENTS

Underage Alcohol Access Youth and Parent National Research Conducted May, 2003

Survey Highlights

A survey of 10-18 years olds shows an overwhelming majority of today's youth are not linking.

In a recent on-line survey of 10-18 year olds, 8 out of 10 youth between 10 and 18 years of age report they did not drink in the past month and 7 out of 10 youth report they did not drink in the past year.

Eighty-one percent of 10-18 year olds said there were zero occasions in the last 30 days when they drank alcoholic beverages, however, 19% still reported they drank, on average, once during the past month. Not surprisingly, reported alcohol use increases proportionally with age -1% of 10-12 year olds drank in the past month compared to 23% of 13-15 year olds and 35% of 16-18 year olds.

Additional results of the survey reveal 70% of 10-18 year olds report they have not had an alcoholic beverage to drink in the last 12 months. Drinking and drinking occasions increase significantly and proportionally with age - 4% of 10-12 year olds, 38% of 13-15 year olds, and 50% of 16-18 year olds report they drank alcoholic beverages in the past year. On average, 10-18 year olds drank alcohol in the past year four times, with an average of less than one occasion among 10-12 year olds, five occasions among 13-15 year olds and six occasions among 16-18 year olds in the last 12 months.

> Reported 30 day and past year drinking is higher among females than males 23% compared to 15% during the past month and 38% compared to 22% during the past 12 months, respectively.

Family and Friends are the leading source of alcohol for today's youth.

When 10-18 year olds were asked the question, "How do you and your friends get the alcohol you drink" a majority (65%) of today's youth who have consumed alcohol in the past year report family and friends as the leading source from which they get alcohol. Contributing family and friend sources include older siblings or friends, patents allow me to have it, and taking it from my home or a friend's home without permission.

In a separate study, parents with children ages 18 and younger were also asked how do you think kids today get the alcohol they drink. A majority (55%) of parents said family and friends is the leading source of alcohol for today's youth. Overall, kids and parents alike identify the same sources of alcohol for today's youth.

Only 7% of tweens and teens who drink report they are getting the alcohol they drink from a store or bar/club that does not check identification-Additional sources of alcohol for teens include asking a stranger who is 21 (5%) and my own fake id (3%).

From the parent perspective, the secondary sources of alcohol include own fake id (19%), a store or bar/club that does not check id (18%), and asking a stranger who is 21 or older to buy it (10%).

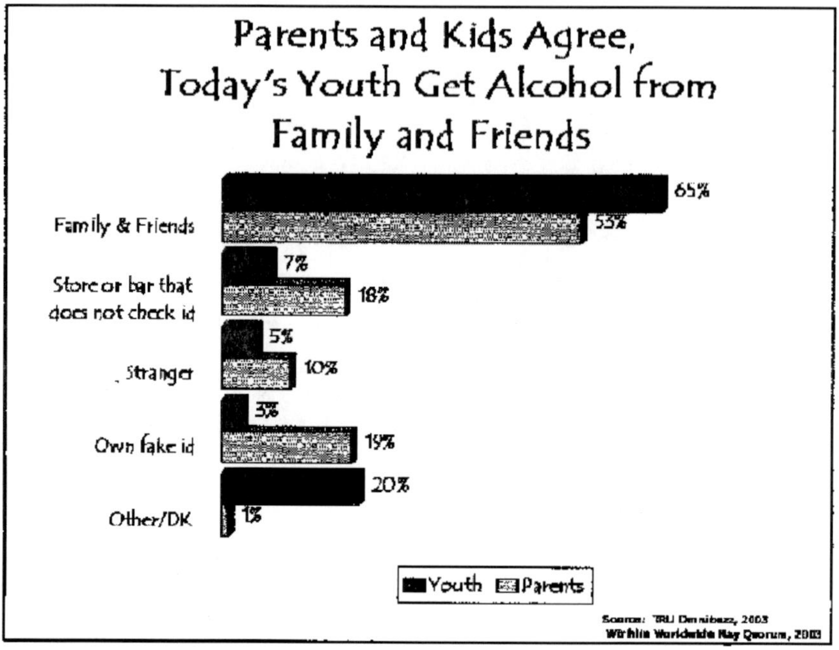

Parents are the leading influence in tween's and teen's decision not to drink.

Despite being identified by youth as one of their primary sources of alcohol, hand down, parents are the most influential person or thing in a child's decision not to drink at all or not to drink on occasion. Among 10-18 year olds, 65% cite parents as the leading influence for them not to drink- While top among all age groups, parental influence does appear to wane with age - 21% of 10-12 year olds, 58% of 14-15 year olds and 43% of 16-18 year olds cite parents as the leading influence in their decision to not drink alcohol. Friends and peers follow as a distant second to parents with 32% citing them as an influence on their decision not to drink. Friends and peers maintain an even level of influence - about one-third - among all age groups.

Perhaps as an expression of their independence, older teens 06-18 year old males and females) cite nobody's one of the top three leading influences in their decision not to drink at all or not to drink on occasion (33% and 22%, respectively).

While significantly more influential among non-drinking youth, drinkers and non-drinkers, alike, name parents as the leading influence in their decision not to drink (46% and 73%, respectively).

While effective, punishment is less of an influence on the decision to not drink of 16-18 year olds (20%), than it is among 10-12 (32%) and 13-15 year olds (30%).

Teachers and Police lose influence with age.

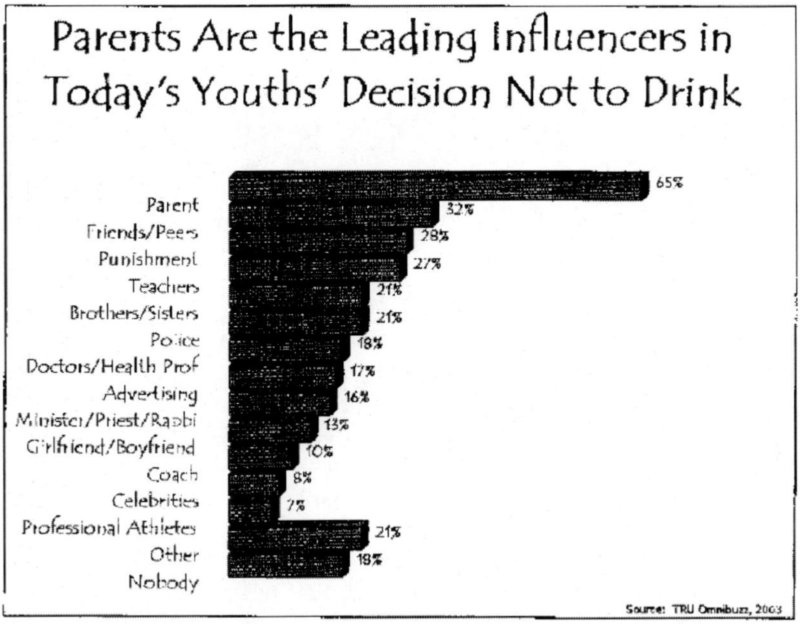

	Teachers	Police
10-12 year olds	40%	31%
13-15 year olds	24%	14%
16-18 year olds	14%	16%

Comparison with recent Roper Youth Report data reveals these survey results of the key influences on a young person's decision of whether to drink alcohol or not is relatively consistent. Parents top the list of influences on young people regarding their decision to drink alcohol or not followed by friends on both studies.

Methodology

Teenage Research Unlimited (TRU) conducted a self-administered online omnibus survey, Omnibuzz$_{TM}$, among 1,100 8 to 18 year olds May 14-21, 2003, For the purpose of The Century Council's research, a skip pattern was utilized to interview 974 youth between the ages of 10 and 18. The data were weighted for key demographic variables (gender, age, ethnicity, parent education, region and community-type of place of school.) to reflect the national population. The margin of error for a sample this size is ± 3.1 percent at the 95 percent confidence level. That is, if this survey were to be replicated 100 times, in 95 instances the results would be within four percentage points of the data reported here.

Within Worldwide conducted two national omnibus surveys, of 1,000 adults, 18 years of age or older in the contiguous United States (each wave). Telephone interviews were conducted May 9-12, 2003 and May 30-June 2, 2003 using a Computer Assisted Telephone Interview (CATI) system. The CAT1 system uses a random digit dialing CRDD) sampling method that insures a true random selection among all telephone numbers and provides a truly independent sample for each wave. The data are weighted on an individual multi-dimensional basis (age, gender, ethnicity, income and region) to give appropriate representation of the US. National population. For the purposes of The Century Council's research, The Council participated in two waves of the omnibus survey to collect data from 659 parents and/or guardians of children 18 year old and younger. The margin of error for the parent sample is ± 3.8 percent at the 95 percent confidence level and ±2.2 for the full sample of adults. That is, if this survey were to be replicated that the true values will 611 within four percentage points of the results shown here for parents and two percentage points for the full adult sample.

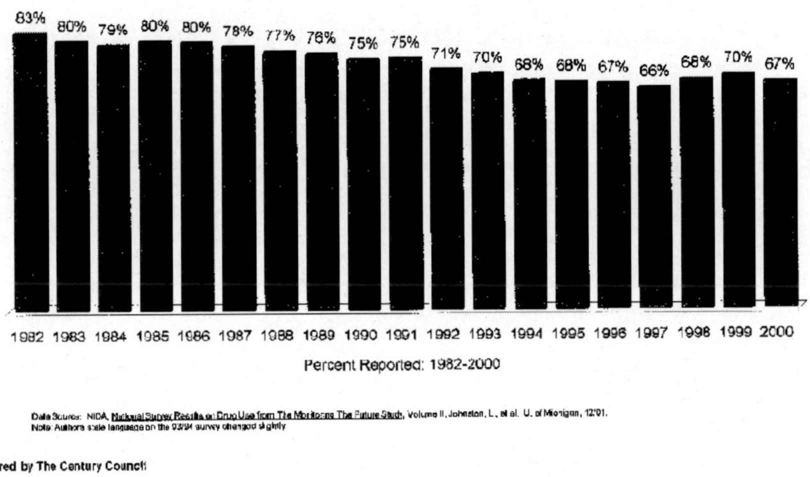

College Students Who Reported Drinking in the Past Month Declined 19% Proportionally from 1982 to 2000.

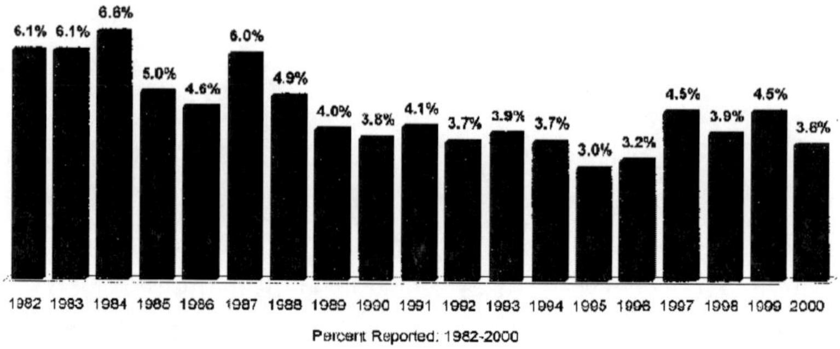

Data Source: NIDA, National Survey Results on Drug Use from The Monitoring The Future Study Vol.I, Johnston, L., et al, U. of Michigan, 12/01
Note: Authors state language on the 93/94 survey changed slightly

Prepared by The Century Council

College Students Who Reported Daily Drinking in the Previous 30 Days Declined 41% Proportionally from 1982 to 2000.

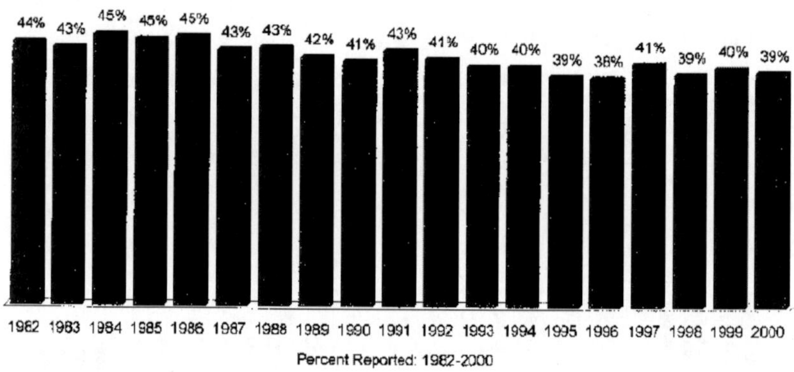

Data Source: NIDA, National Survey Results on Drug Use from The Monitoring The Future Study Vol.II, Johnston, L. et al, U. of Michigan, 12/01. *Five or more drinks in a row in the previous two weeks
Note. Authors state language on the 93/94 survey changed slightly.

Prepared by The Century Council

College Students Who Reported Binge Drinking* in the Previous Two Weeks Declined 11% Proportionally from 1982 to 2000.

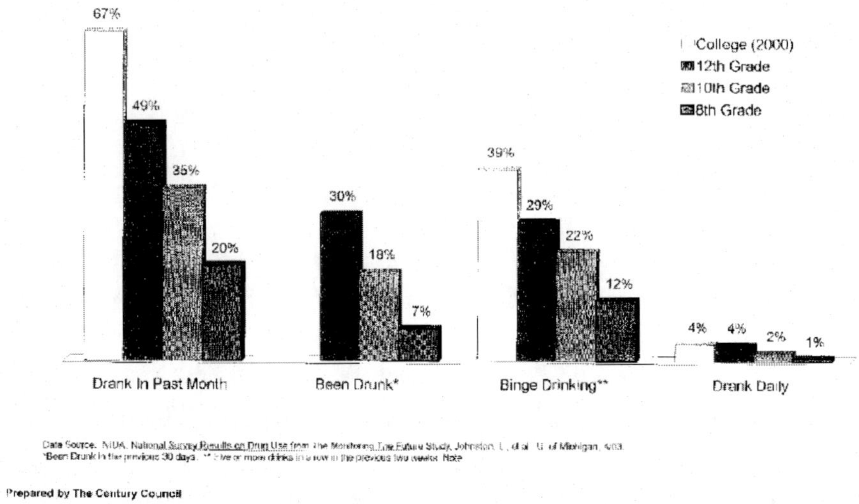

Reported Drinking Patterns Among 8th, 10th, 12th Grade and College Students: 2002.

PREPARED STATEMENT OF STACIA MURPHY, PRESIDENT, NATIONAL COUNCIL ON ALCOHOLISM AND DRUG DEPENDENCE, NCADD

Thank you for providing this opportunity to present written comments to the Senate Subcommittee on Substance Abuse and Mental Health Services, and we hope this statement will be made part of the hearing record.

As indicated in the recent report from the Institute of Medicine titled "Reducing Underage Drinking—A Collective Responsibility," underage drinking is a critical public health issue. Through this testimony, we hope to give support to the conclusions of the report. Furthermore, we urge implementation of the report's key findings and agree that there should be:

- Greater allocation of government resources to address underage drinking;
- Stronger constraints on alcohol advertising aimed at youth audiences;
- Stricter enforcement for regulations banning the sale of liquor to underage drinkers;
- An increase in the excise taxes on alcohol to promote a campaign to reduce underage drinking, much as has been done to reduce smoking.

To achieve these important goals, NCADD would support a strong Federal voice on underage drinking. As individuals and as a nation, we can't afford to look the other way any longer. America's youth are our future and we need to insure that they are no longer drowned in a whirlpool of negative consequences.

Founded in 1944, the National Council on Alcoholism and Drug Dependence is the oldest advocacy organization in the country addressing America's most widely used drug, alcohol. With over 95 Affiliates in 28 States, we work at the national level on policy issues related to barriers in education, prevention and treatment for alcoholics, other drug dependent persons and their families.

Prepared Statement of the National Association for Children of Alcoholics

The National Association for Children of Alcoholics supports the NAS report recommendations. The reduction of underage drinking is a critical public health imperative. In addition, it can halt the family cycle of addiction, since those who do not drink until age 21 are much less likely to become alcoholics themselves. This is especially relevant to children of alcoholics since they are at great risk of having a genetic vulnerability and being exposed to environmental influences that may make them more susceptible to becoming alcoholics themselves.

One in four children lives in a family with alcohol abuse or alcoholism. This is a critical mass of the nation's children who are at increased risk for alcohol, other drug and mental health problems because of the environment in which they live, and prevention of underage drinking is crucial to their potential for healthy and productive lives.

PREPARED STATEMENT OF JAMES A. O'HARA III, EXECUTIVE DIRECTOR, CENTER ON ALCOHOL MARKETING AND YOUTH

Mr. Chairman, Senator Dodd, distinguished Members of the Subcommittee, your hearing today marks an important recognition of the scope and devastating consequences of underage drinking for our youth and our families. The numbers you are hearing today do indeed tell a story of abuse and risk.

Let me underline a few more of the telling statistics of the abuse and devastating consequences from the recently released National Research Council/Institute of Medicine report, Reducing Underage Drinking: A Collective Responsibility.

- "[A]lmost one-half of the 12-year-olds who reported alcohol use reported having drunk heavily [five or more drinks on same occasion] in the past 30 days."[14]
- "The rate of heavy drinking doubles from age 14 (about 6 percent) to age 15 (about 12 percent) and continues to increase steadily."[15]

---

[14] National Research Council and Institute of Medicine, Reducing Underage Drinking: A Collective Responsibility, Committee on Developing a Strategy to Reduce and Prevent Underage Drinking, Eds. Richard J. Bonnie and Mary Ellen O'Connell, Board on Children, Youth, and Families, Division of Behavioral and Social Sciences and Education (Washington, DC: The National Academies Press, 2003), 41.

[15] Ibid., 41.

- "While only 7 percent of licensed drivers in 2000 were aged 15 to 20, they represented approximately 13 percent of drivers involved in fatal crashes who had been drinking."[16]
- "...29 percent of 15- to 17-year-olds and 37 percent of 18- to 24-year-olds said that alcohol or drugs influenced their decision to do something sexual.[17]

Behind all the numbers and statistics are the shattered lives of our children and families. Let me remind you how a year ago this month we read with shock and disbelief of the 200 or so high school students who arrived drunk to their home-coming dance in Scarsdale, New York.[18] Five of these young people were hospitalized for acute alcohol poisoning. The incident occasioned much debate and concern about parents' responsibilities. It also raises the question of why so many of our teens think the only way to have a good time is with alcohol. In short, it reflects the complicated but devastating reality of underage drinking as described by the NRC/IOM's historic report: "Understanding why adolescents drink is more likely to be found in the confluence of factors."[19]

The Center on Alcohol Marketing and Youth (GAMY) focuses its work on one of those factors—alcohol advertising. In fact, alcohol advertising and its role in underage drinking have been of concern to public health officials and policy makers for many years. Then Surgeon General Antonia Novello requested the Inspector General of the U.S. Department of Health and Human Services to report on alcohol advertising's appeal to underage youth and how effectively the Federal and State Governments, as well as the alcohol industry, were monitoring it. The Inspector General's report, issued in 1991, found that the Federal and State agencies were fragmented in their approaches to alcohol advertising and

---

[16] Ibid., 61.

[17] Ibid., 63.

[18] See, e.g., Jane Gross, "Teenagers' Binge Leads Scarsdale to Painful Self-Reflection," *The New York Times*, Tuesday, 8 October 2002, sec. B, p. 1; "200 students arrive at school dance drunk," *The Times Union*, Friday, 27 September 2002, sec. B, p. 2.

[19] National Research Council and Institute of Medicine, 87.

that the alcohol industry's self-regulatory codes were largely ineffective.[20] At the request of Congress, the Federal Trade Commission has now released two reports on alcohol advertising and underage youth, the first in September 1999 and the second earlier this month. In the 1999 report, the FTC called on the industry to make several reforms in its self-regulation,[21] and in the second report the FTC found that the industry had made significant improvements.[22]

A key point made by each of these reports is that responsibility for alcohol advertising rests with the industry. The industry regulates itself through the codes of the trade associations and of individual companies. In general, these codes address two main topics: content and placement.[23] Over the years, the content of alcohol advertising has generated some of the sharpest controversy in terms of questions of its appeal to underage youth. The Budweiser frogs and Spuds McKenzie may be two of the most well-known and controversial. A 1996 study of children ages nine to 11 found that children were more familiar with Budweiser's television frogs than Kellogg's Tony the Tiger, the Mighty Morphin' Power Rangers, or Smokey the Bear.[24] Even the most recent FTC report that commended the industry for "added attention to the issue of ad content" also remarked, "Still, a visible minority of beer ads feature concepts that risk appealing to those under 21."[25]

---

[20] Office of Inspector General, Department of Health and Human Services, *Youth and Alcohol: Controlling Alcohol Advertising That Appeals to Youth* (Washington, DC: Department of Health and Human Services, 1991), 6, 10-12.

[21] Federal Trade Commission, *Self-Regulation in the Alcohol Industry: A Review of Industry Efforts to Avoid Promoting Alcohol to Underage Consumers* (Washington, DC: Federal Trade Commission, 1999), ii—iii.

[22] Federal Trade Commission, *Alcohol Advertising and Marketing: A Report to Congress* (Washington, DC: Federal Trade Commission, 2003), i.

[23] See, e.g., Beer Institute, "Advertising and Marketing Code," <http://beerinstitute.org/ adcode2.pdf> (Accessed 25 Sept 2003); Distilled Spirits Council of the United States, *Code of Responsible Practices for Beverage Alcohol Advertising and Marketing*, <http://www.discus.org/ industry/code/code.htm> (Accessed 25 Sept 2003); Wine Institute, "Code of Advertising Standards," http://www.wineinstitute.org/communications/statistics/ Code_of_Advertising.htm (Accessed 25 Sept 2003).

[24] L. Leiber, *Commercial and Character Recall by Children Aged 9 to 11 Years: Budweiser Frogs Vs. Bugs Bunny* (Berkeley: Center on Alcohol Advertising, 1996).

[25] Federal Trade Commission, *Alcohol Advertising and Marketing*, ii.

While the FTC did not specify which ads were in this "visible minority," here are examples of ads that have, in fact, generated significant controversy over their content in the past year:

- "Because We Can," a television ad for Coors Light
- "Laundromat," a television ad for Smirnoff Ice
- "Cat Fight," a television ad for Miller Lite

These ads have raised questions in the minds of many in the public health community about the adequacy of alcohol industry self-regulation. On the other hand, the alcohol industry may well point to them as examples of responsiveness. Coors announced on June 2, 2003 that it pulled "Because We Can" as the result of its participation in the Better Business Bureau's Advertising Pledge Program and a ruling by the BBB APP that the ad violated Coors's own advertising code;[26] Diageo, the parent company for Smirnoff Ice announced last spring that it was pulling its ad because of complaints. According to the data available to GAMY from TNS Media Intelligence/CMR, both of these ads were last broadcast several months before either company announced their decisions.[27]

The Center's primary focus, however, has been on the placement of alcohol advertising—where the industry chooses to place its ads, and who is exposed to the advertising and how frequently. We are a public health project based at Georgetown University's Health Policy Institute and funded by grants from The Pew Charitable Trusts and the Robert Wood Johnson Foundation. Since September 2002 we have released a series of reports on the exposure of underage youth—ages 12 to 20—to alcohol advertising in the measured media of magazines, television and radio. Our research has, in effect, been an attempt to conduct public health surveillance of alcohol advertising, using the databases routinely used by advertising agencies and consumer product companies in the planning of

---

[26] "Advertiser's Statement, Submitted: 2 June, 2003," in *Final Decision, Better Business Bureau Advertising Pledge Program*, Case No. 02-02a, Decided May 16, 2003, <http://www.bbb.org/app/case/Case02-02a.pdf> (Accessed 25 Sept. 2003).

[27] TNS Media Intelligence/CMR.

advertising campaigns. To assist us in this effort, we have employed the services of Virtual Media Resources, a media research and planning firm based in Natick, Massachusetts.

We have found widespread and pervasive overexposure of underage youth to alcohol advertising in all three media.

For Magazines

Youth saw more beer and distilled spirits advertising than adults in magazines in 2001—45 percent more for beer brands and 27 percent more for distilled spirits brands.[28]

Marketers of low-alcohol refreshers, the so-called "malternatives" such as Smirnoff Ice, delivered 60 percent more magazine advertising to youth than adults in 2001.[29]

These ads have been placed in magazines like Vibe and Spin that, respectively, had underage audiences of 41 percent and 39 percent in 2001, as well as in magazines like Allure with a 34 percent underage audience and In Style with 25 percent underage readership.[30]

For Television

Almost a quarter of the television alcohol advertising in 2001—51,084 ads—was more likely to be seen by youth than by adults.[31]

---

[28] "More likely to be seen by" (as well as percentage measures of youth overexposure and other comparisons of adult and youth exposure to alcohol advertising in this testimony) is based on "gross rating points," which measure how much an audience segment is exposed to advertising per capita. Another way of measuring advertising exposure is "gross impressions" (the total number of times all the members of a given audience are exposed to advertising). The adult population will almost always receive far more "gross impressions" than youth because there are far more adults in the population than youth. Center on Alcohol Marketing and Youth, *Overexposed: Youth a Target of Alcohol Advertising in Magazines* (Washington, DC: Center on Alcohol Marketing and Youth, 2002), 1.

[29] Ibid., 1.

[30] The beer and distilled spirits industries have now revised their codes to prohibit placement where underage youth are 30 percent or more of the audience. Ibid., 11.

[31] Center on Alcohol Marketing and Youth, *Television: Alcohol's Vast Adland* (Washington, DC: Center on Alcohol Marketing and Youth, 2002), 2.

In 2001, alcohol advertising on television reached 89 percent of young people 12-20, who saw an average of 246 alcohol ads each. The 30 percent of young people ages 12—20 who were most likely to see alcohol advertising on television saw at least 780 alcohol TV ads in 2001.[32]

The alcohol industry's television advertising has been placed on shows like *That '70s Show*, *The Parkers*, and *MADtv*.[33]

For Radio

Youth heard more radio advertising for beer, "malternatives" and distilled spirits in 2001 and 2002 than adults 21 and over. Underage youth, ages 12—20, heard 8 percent more beer and ale advertising and 12 percent more malternative advertising. The exposure was even greater for the distilled spirits category, where youth heard 14 percent more advertising.[34]

The vast majority of radio advertising reaching underage youth was placed on radio stations with four formats: Rhythmic Contemporary Hit, Pop Contemporary Hit, Urban Contemporary and Alternative. The artists featured on these formats are, for example, 50 Cent, Jennifer Lopez, LL Cool J, Nelly, Justin Timberlake, Eminem, Ja Rule, Dru Hill, Snoop Dogg, Red Hot Chili Peppers, Audioslave and Foo Fighters.[35]

Let me explain what we did and what these numbers mean. Standard industry databases provide information on where ads are placed. TNS Media Intelligence/ CMR provides information on where ads are placed in magazines and on television programs, and Media Monitors, Inc. (MMI) provides information on which radio stations broadcast ads and at what time of the day. Other industry-standard databases—such as MRI, Arbitron and Nielsen Media Research—provide information on the audience composition for magazines, for radio stations and for television

---

[32] Ibid., 2.

[33] The beer and distilled spirits industries have now revised their codes to prohibit placement where underage youth are 30 percent or more of the audience. Ibid., 2—3, 7.

[34] Center on Alcohol Marketing and Youth, *Radio Daze: Alcohol Ads Tune in Underage Youth* (Washington, DC: Center on Alcohol Marketing and Youth, 2003), 5.

[35] Ibid., 9, fn 27.

programming. Each of these audience composition databases obviously has certain limitations on how that data is collected, but these are the databases on which the advertising and consumer product industries rely, and are the databases on which the alcohol industry trade associations indicate they will rely to ensure that member companies place their ads appropriately.[36] The ad placement data and audience composition data were analyzed by VMR to calculate the reach (what proportion of a given age group had the opportunity to see an ad) and the frequency (on average, how many times someone in a given age group would be exposed to an ad). We expressed the reach and frequency of alcohol advertising to underage youth—ages 12 to 20—and to legal-age adults—those over age 21—in terms of gross rating points (GRPs), a measure used by media planners to compare the weight of advertising delivered per capita to different age groups or to other demographic segments. By comparing GRPs, which account for the size of the population of a particular age group, we are able to see which age group is more likely to be exposed to, or to see, alcohol advertising. As I mentioned, this is the kind of public health surveillance we already should have in our fight to reduce and prevent underage drinking, but it has been lacking.

The alcohol industry frequently cites gross impressions as a more appropriate way to measure alcohol advertising. For example, the following statement was made by the Distilled Spirits Council of the United States (DISCUS) on June 20, 2003:

"CAMY wants the public to believe more youth hear and see alcohol ads than adults. They are just plain wrong and their own data confirm this fact. If you dig beneath their rhetoric and look at their own data, it shows spirits advertising is clearly directed to adults," said Distilled Spirits Council President Peter Cressy.

The table below—derived from CAMY's own data—shows distilled spirits advertising is directed to adults.

---

[36] Federal Trade Commission, *Appendix D and Appendix E, Alcohol Marketing and Advertising*, D-6-7, E8-10.

Percentage of Impressions Derived from 21+ Audience
Media—Percent
Print—81 percent
Radio—83 percent
TV—76 percent

Source: Derived from CAMY Reports"[37]

Well, there are a lot more adults than there are children. By omitting the fact that 84.2 percent of the age 12+ population are adults (age 21 and over), and 15.8 percent are underage youth (ages 12 to 20), DISCUS tells only part of the story in stating the percentages of gross impressions. Because of the disparity in population size, there are more impressions per person for youth and fewer per person for adults.

To examine this criticism from an advertising perspective, take the case of magazines. In 2001, 19.1 percent of all magazine gross impressions for distilled spirits were for youth ages 12-20, and 80.9 percent were for adults, age 21+. This equates to more GRPs for youth than for adults; that is, more impressions per person for youth than adults. While "only" 19.1 percent of gross impressions were delivered to youth, an even smaller percentage (15.8 percent) of the total population (age 12 and older) is composed of youth. Therefore the number of GRPs for youth is disproportionately large: 12,550 for youth, versus 9,916 for adults. In fact, youth received 26.5 percent more GRPs than adults—or 26.5 percent more impressions per person (See Table 1).

Put in terms of reach and frequency, the GRP analysis shows clearly what is hidden by relying on gross impressions: for distilled spirits advertising in magazines in 2001, 92 percent of youth ages 12-20 (reach) saw on average 136 ads (frequency), while 95 percent of adults age 21+ (reach) saw on average 104 ads (frequency). Simply stated, youth were

[37] Distilled Spirits Council of the United States, *CAMY Releases Another Misleading Report on Underage Drinking*, 20 June 2003 <http://www.discus.org/mediaroom/2003/release.asp?pressid=K)5> (Accessed 25 Sept 2003).

greatly overexposed to the distilled spirits advertising in magazines in 2001.

Our research has utilized the most current data available to provide a reliable and verifiable analysis of underage youth exposure to alcohol advertising. The key public policy question going forward is how we protect underage youth from excessive exposure to alcohol advertising. It should be kept in mind that the alcohol industry has already agreed that there should be some limits to their advertising by the very fact that for years they have had voluntary codes restricting the placement of their own advertising.[38] The IOM report also lays out what we believe is a convincing public policy rationale for limits on the alcohol advertising that reaches underage youth:

"It is sometimes assumed that, in the absence of compelling evidence of causation, there is no legitimate basis for limiting the exposure of young people to alcohol advertising. This assumption is wrong for three reasons. First, the absence of definitive proof may be caused by the methodological complexity of the inquiry rather than the absence of a contributing effect. Second, there is a sound common sense basis for believing, even in the absence of definitive proof, that making alcohol use attractive to young people increases the likelihood that they will become alcohol consumers as young people rather than waiting until they are adults. Third, persistent exposure of young people to messages encouraging drinking by young people (even if they appear to be 21) contradicts and interferes with the implementation of the nation's goal of discouraging underage drinking."[39]

The last point made by IOM deserves underlining: the alcohol industry's advertising of the good times to be had by the consumption of alcohol undercuts and drowns out the messages of responsibility and caution given by parents and other adults. And parents know this and want something done. We commissioned public opinion research by Peter D. Hart Associates and American Viewpoint and found that parents overwhelmingly (81 percent) believe that, due to the potentially harmful

[38] Beer Institute, "Advertising and Marketing Code;" Distilled Spirits Council of the United States, *Code of Responsible Practices for Beverage Alcohol Advertising and Marketing*; Wine Institute, "Code of Advertising Standards."

[39] National Research Council and Institute of Medicine, 136-7.

effects of its products, the alcohol industry has a special responsibility to avoid exposing young people to messages encouraging alcohol consumption.[40]

The beer and distilled spirits industries, as of this month according to the recent FTC report and their own trade associations, have now committed not to place alcohol advertising where the underage audience is 30 percent or more.[41] This is a significant reduction from the previous industry threshold of 50 percent and is to be welcomed. Whether it is sufficiently protective of our children remains the question, however.

The IOM has recommended that industry move toward a 15 percent threshold, and CAMY's own research suggests a 15 percent threshold is the most protective and likely to prevent routine overexposure of underage youth, ages 12 to 20. The reasoning is straightforward. Underage youth represent 15.8 percent of the U.S. population, age 12 and over. Advertising placed in venues where the audience composition is 15 percent or less simply follows the distribution of the population. As I said, the IOM has called for the industry to move toward this threshold. In addition, when a distilled spirits company sought to break the decades-old voluntary ban on distilled spirits advertising on broadcast television, it proposed to limit its advertising to late-night television, and in other dayparts to limit its advertising to programs where the underage audience was 15 percent or less.[42] Also, the company promised to air one of its responsibility ads for every four product ads.[43] Finally, a representative for the leading beer company in the United States—

Anheuser Busch—was recently quoted as saying the "vast majority" of their advertising in the last 10 years has been placed on programs "which

---

[40] Memorandum, *Results of a National Survey of Parents*, from Peter D. Hart Research Associates, Inc./American Viewpoint to All Interested Parties, Washington, DC, June 24, 2003, <http://camy.org/research/files/hartmemo07O3.pdf> (Accessed 25 Sept 2003).

[41] See, e.g., Federal Trade Commission, Alcohol Advertising and Marketing, ii; Beer Institute, "Advertising and Marketing Code;" Distilled Spirits Council of the United States, *Code of Responsible Practices for Beverage Alcohol Advertising and Marketing.*

[42] Stuart Elliot, "NBC, with Conditions, to Accept Ads for Liquor," *The New York Times*, Friday, 14 December 2001, sec. C, p. 1.

[43] Ibid.

traditionally attract audiences that are approximately 80 percent adult."[44] Clearly, what needs to happen is a balancing of the public health goal of limiting underage youth exposure to alcohol advertising and of the rightful economic self-interest of alcohol companies to advertise to their legal audience. With a distilled spirits company indicating that a 15 percent threshold is economically viable and with the country's largest beer company saying that a "vast majority" of its advertising has met a 20 percent threshold for the last 10 years, it would appear that some reduction from the newly announced 30 percent threshold, which allows for placement of alcohol ads where underage youth are twice their number in the general population, is still achievable and would further the public health goal. Let me be clear that there are many devils in the details: Is the threshold computed on a population base of age 2 and over or age 12 and over? Is the threshold applied to each brand of a company since advertising plans are normally developed for a specific brand, or is it company-wide?

But even as we have this policy debate on a reasonable standard that would protect the health and well-being of our children and recognize the economic self-interest of the industry, the IOM pointed to several steps that our Public Health Service and other Federal agencies can take today:

- A national media campaign that educates adults about the real dangers and risks of underage drinking and their important responsibilities in reducing and preventing it.[45]
- A coordinated effort with increased funding commensurate with the problem by the Federal agencies now responsible for underage drinking prevention programs so that they are more effective, better-leveraged and complement one other, and achieve real results so that 10 years from now we aren't seeing the same stalled progress identified by the IOM.[46]

---

[44] Theresa Howard, "Alcohol advertisers agree to raise standards to help keep their messages away from kids," *USA Today*, Wednesday, 10 Sept 2003, sec. B, p. 5.

[45] Recommendation 6-1. National Research Council and Institute of Medicine, 110.

[46] Recommendation 12-1. Ibid., 237.

- An annual report with key indicators of underage drinking. This is basic public health surveillance that should already be done so that we can assess what is working and what isn't.[47]
- The filling of key gaps in our public health surveillance—the monitoring of underage youth exposure to alcohol advertising and the collection of data on our public health surveys on brand use by underage persons just like the data we already annually collect for underage use of cigarette brands.[48]

In closing, let me quote the IOM report: "The problem of underage drinking in the United States is endemic and, in the committee's judgment, is not likely to improve in the absence of a significant new intervention."[49] Let me put the IOM's conclusion another way: Unless we act now, we will have failed to have learned the lessons from Scarsdale, New York and hundreds of other communities around this country where our children and families have suffered the tragic consequences of underage drinking.

Table 1. 2001 Distilled Spirits Magazine Advertising Exposure to Youth and Adults

2001 Distilled Spirits Magazine Advertising Exposure to Youth and Adults Gross Impressions, Population and GRPs

	Gross Impressions		Population		
Demographic	Count	% of Total	Count	% of Total	GRPs
Youth Ages 12-20	4,487,590,000	19.1%	35,757,000	15.8%	12,550
Adults Age 21+	18,966,052,000	80.9%	191,267,000	84.2%	9,916
Total Age 12+	23,453,642,000	100.0%	227,024,000	100.0%	10,331

Sources: TNS Media Intelligence/SMR; Mediamark Research Inc.

[47] Recommendation 12-3. Ibid., 238.

[48] Recommendations 7-4, 12-5, 12-6. Ibid., 145, 240, 241.

[49] Ibid., 103.

PREPARED STATEMENT OF DAVID K. REHR, PH.D., PRESIDENT, NATIONAL BEER WHOLESALERS ASSOCIATION

Introduction

Chairman DeWine, Mr. Kennedy, and Members of the Substance Abuse and Mental Health Services Subcommittee, the members of the National Beer Wholesalers Association (NBWA) appreciate the opportunity to submit this testimony in connection with the subcommittee's hearing on underage drinking and the recently released report by the National Academy of Sciences (National Academies). We also thank the Chairman for convening this forum, and providing the opportunity to share the industry's thoughts on this important topic, draw attention to the many valuable responsibility programs being implemented by the beer industry and express our concern for the underlying National Academies process that preceded the study released on September 10, 2003.

Background on National Academies Study

During the debate on the 2002 Labor, Health and Human Services, and Education Appropriations Bill, NBWA, in conjunction with industry allies, advocated for and supported the House and Senate appropriators' decision to study existing Federal, State, and non-governmental programs designed to reduce and prevent underage drinking. NBWA also supported the decision to appropriate $500,000 to the National Academies to review such programs. Conference Report attached as Appendix A.

Both decisions were supported because NBWA and its members do not condone or support abuse of our products, and we are committed to reducing and combating underage alcohol-related issues. Additionally, the wholesaler industry has many successful, effective underage responsibility programs that it was anxious to share with the National Academies, and NBWA was enthusiastic about participating in a process that was initially perceived to be fair and even-handed.

The study of programs designed to reduce underage drinking was determined as necessary, in part, due to a report that was released in May of 2001 by the Government Accounting Office (GAO) titled "Underage Drinking—Information on Federal Funds Targeted at Prevention," wherein it was concluded that:

- Twenty-three Federal agencies have program efforts that address underage alcohol prevention, and for fiscal year 2000 an estimated $71 million was specifically allocated to efforts designed to reduce underage drinking.
- SAMHSA and approximately 16 other Federal agencies identified about $1 billion of fiscal year 2000 combined funding that addressed alcohol prevention and illegal drug use. A breakdown of how that funding is allocated could not be determined.
- An additional estimated $769 million out of $2.2 billion of block, formula and incentive grant funds may have been used by States to address prevention of drug and alcohol use by youth.
- The Federal Government spends substantial resources on underage prevention, with no real means of accounting for these resources or the effectiveness of these efforts, questioning the way in which Federal agencies are spending taxpayer dollars. Appendix B.

As a first step, the National Academies posted the project scope on July 11, 2002, revealing for the first time publicly its decision to expand the scope of the study to include areas that were not mandated by Congress. Appendix C.

The Labor-HHS report language requested a study of an array of programs designed to prevent and reduce underage drinking and established a very specific list of inquiries to which Congress was seeking a reply. The National Academies went beyond the scope of this charge and chose to delve into areas of legislative authority, thereby overreaching and contradicting Congressional intent. To be specific, the conference report language does not seek input from the National Academies or its advisory committee with regard to tax-related issues. However, the project scope suggests, with some emphasis, the need for an excise tax increase, a decision that is outside the authority and jurisdiction of the National Academies, and should not have been singled out in the study's stated scope as an area of emphasis or extraordinary review by the selected committee.

Simply stated, the scope decided upon by the National Academies and its specific instructions to the committee are material alterations of the Congressional report language. By taking this liberty, the National Academy guided the committee to a predetermined approach and blatantly disregarding Congressional intent.

With regard to the committee selection process, it is important for the subcommittee to know that prior to the National Academies posting the names of the twelve panelists who were ultimately chosen to conduct the study, several members of Congress and the licensed beverage industry wrote the National Academies with recommendations of qualified experts to participate in the study. Congressional letters are on file with the National Academies. Industry letter attached as Appendix D.

However, none of those who were recommended were chosen, in spite of the fact that their professional backgrounds and relative expertise more than adequately qualified them for inclusion on the study committee.

The process underway at the National Academies was beginning to show repeated signs of exclusion of outside stakeholder recommendations and efforts for equal participation and inclusion. After the National Academies posted the twelve proposed panelist's names and brief biographies, concerns for a fair and meaningful approach grew stronger. Not only had the project's scope been expanded, revealing the National Academies' interest in overemphasizing tax increases, the proposed committee panel did not represent an overall balance of professional views and backgrounds. It remains uncertain whether the committee knew that eight of 12 of panelists chosen to serve had conflict of interest issues surrounding their acceptance of funding from one of the nation's largest Neo-Prohibitionist foundations.

Therefore, on August 12, 2002, the licensed beverage industry made a written inquiry regarding general information on the nominees and seeking verification that Federal law was being followed with regard to the selection process. Appendix E.

Additionally, during the brief time that was allowed for comment on the proposed study panelists, follow-up letters making recommendations of alternate experts were again sent by two Members of Congress. Again, those names were rejected by the National Academies.

They provide the subcommittee with an idea of how the National Academies conducted the study, the following is intended to highlight just some of the areas of concern previously expressed to the National Academies.

Federal Advisory Committee Act

Membership in Federal advisory committees, including committees created by the National Academies, is regulated by the Federal Advisory Committee Act (FACA). Pursuant to section 15(a)(2) of FACA, the National Academies is obligated to ensure that individuals appointed to an advisory committee have no conflicts of interest, that the overall membership of the committee is "fairly balanced" and that the final report will reflect the Academy's independent judgment. The FACA requirements, including especially the fair balance requirement, are intended to ensure that advisory committees do not become vehicles by which narrow special interest groups may capture a governmental process to advance their own agendas.

National Academies Secretive Process

In response to NBWA's written request for pertinent information regarding the nominees, their professional backgrounds, potential conflicts of interests and the individual or organization who submitted or sponsored each of the 12, the National Academies, citing internal policies, refused to produce any information, stating that it considered such information to be "privileged" and "not available for public release," revealing that their committee selection process is shrouded in secrecy, protected by its own established policies and insulated from public review, scrutiny and comment.

Without access to relevant information and documentation on those chosen and the process surrounding their selection, which has been restricted from access by the National Academies, the public is unable to demonstrate that reasonable steps were taken to ensure that the committee is fairly balanced.

In a letter to Congress, National Academies President Bruce Alberts provides a typically bureaucratic response to offer assurances that conflicts of interest were reviewed and those panelists who voluntarily took or received financial support would either request to be removed or be passed over. Neither of which was done, casting doubt on the legitimate scientific approach taken by the National Academies.

National Academies Failure to Balance

The National Academies is obligated by a general duty, internal guidelines and Federal law to protect the overall process of the study at issue, with the goal of ensuring its objectivity, fairness and lack of bias. A process that is unfair will render a study that is as well. Without the former, the National Academies cannot ensure—to Congress or the public—the latter. With regard to the study at issue, the advisory committee is not fairly balanced. At least five individuals who strongly support tax increases or restrictive alcohol access laws as effective were chosen.

- Mark Moore published an article entitled "Actually, Prohibition was a Success, "wherein he contends the restrictive alcohol access laws of the Prohibition era effectively lowered the prevalence of drinking.

- Marilyn Aguirre-Molina has made claims that the alcohol industry is "killing" young people and "stealing" society's heroes, holidays, and values. She has asserted in writing that restrictive alcohol access laws most effectively prevent problem drinking.
- Philip Cook's academic articles endorse increased alcohol taxation: "Current [alcohol] excise taxes are too low, both nationally and in every State. The rates are far less than the average social cost of each drink consumed. Raising the excise tax would be in the public interest."
- Judy Cushing supports restrictive alcohol access laws and is currently involved in a lobbying effort aimed at increasing Oregon's beer excise tax.
- Joel W. Grube's academic writings conclude that price and tax increases are among the most effective policies for limiting youth drinking.

In light of the well-established positions of these panelists on restrictive access and tax increases, the other panelists do not fairly balance or provide for an overall balance of views on the committee as a whole. Additionally, Richard Bonnie, Robert Hornik, Bonnie Halpern-Felsher and Janis Jacobs do not appear to have any significant expertise as regards underage drinking.

Other worthy candidates were recommended for inclusion to render a more fairly balanced advisory committee. NBWA, joined by the Beer Institute and the Wine and Spirits Wholesalers of America, Inc., nominated three distinguished academics— Richard Jessor, Robert Pandina and David Anderson. Members of Congress also made independent recommendations.

When considered as a whole, the panel was not and could not reasonably have been regarded by the National Academies as "fairly balanced." The panel was calculated to ensure a final consensus report that would endorse the National Academies' apparently preconceived conclusion that underage drinking is most effectively combated by increased excise taxes and restrictive alcohol access laws.

National Academies Ignored Industry Responsibility Programs

The National Academies and the advisory committee that was selected have both exhibited conduct that suggests a failure to follow Congress's mandate to "review existing Federal, State, and non-governmental programs, including media-based programs, designed to change the attitudes and health behaviors of youth." Many organizations, including the NBWA, submitted documents, articles, videotapes and other materials on a broad range of established responsibility programs designed to address underage issues; however, evidence strongly suggests that National Academies and the committee ignored outright the industry programs submitted.

Through national, State and local efforts, beer wholesalers and the beer industry in general actively participate in a broad array of highly successful prevention programs that effectively address illegal underage concerns. As a result, the beer industry has gained a wealth of knowledge and information on underage issues, including information relevant to many of the areas addressed in the fiscal year 2002 Labor, Health and Human Services, Education and related agencies conference report that called for the study that will be addressed during today's subcommittee hearing.

Additionally, the beer industry has been successful in reducing illegal underage purchase and consumption through a variety of efforts. These efforts are outlined in documentation previously provided to the National Academies committee, and include information on countless programs, such as point-of-sale ID programs, retailer education and server training efforts, public service announcements, supplier partnerships on paid advertising and efforts at the State level for stricter penalties on retailers and consumers engaged in illegal underage purchase and consumption. In fact, illegal drinking among high school seniors has dropped 30 percent over the last two decades, according to a study sponsored by the National

Institute on Drug Abuse. Thanks to the industry's prevention programs, and the efforts of parents, teachers and others, 82 percent of the nation's youth are now making the right decision to not drink alcohol illegally according to research from the U.S. Department of Health and Human Services.

Materials were submitted on approximately 125 beer industry programs being conducted nationwide. These programs were provided in November of 2002 to the National Academies for review. Regrettably, the committee never reviewed these materials and as late as July of 2003, they remained unopened in cellophane shrink-wrapped packaging.

National Academies Workshop Activities

At a workshop conducted on October 10—11, 2002, limited time or attention was paid to the topic of programs or their review. During the 2 days of workshop discussions, minimal time was given to the discussion of existing programs, in particular private-sector programs. However, significant time and discussion was allowed to address discuss vilification of the licensed beverage industry—a legal industry.

The following are examples of comments made:

- "…if the government is willing to demonize a large industry, it can really impress teenagers." Robin Room, Stockholm University
- "So in conclusion, I think, again, governments can use a variety of policies to raise price. Taxation is clearly the easiest…" Frank Chaloupka, University of Illinois at Chicago

The workshop participants that were invited by the National Academies further reveals the intent to push the study efforts in a predetermined direction as opposed to an objective and balanced review by those representing an array of opinions and attitudes toward effectively addressing underage drinking. For example, James O'Hara, with the Center on Alcohol Marketing and Youth (CAMY), was invited to participate.

The work of CAMY and Mr. O'Hara has been described by Robert Lichter, the head of the Statistical Assessment Service, as "tainted by advocacy," "done to influence government action" with findings that "were tilted to require FTC action." The CAMY study at issue looked at alcohol advertising in national magazines in 2001 and concluded that various brands advertised heavily in "youth-oriented" magazines. Magazines such as Sports Illustrated, People and Cosmopolitan were included in the study in spite of the fact that the overwhelming majority of the readership of these publications is beyond—considerably beyond—21-years-old.

Because industry concerns were going unaddressed by the National Academies, on June 2, 2003, approximately 136 members of the United States House of Representatives joined in writing to National Academies President Bruce Alberts asking that he ensure that the study remain on track and within the perimeters of Congressional intent.

On June 18, 2003, I also wrote to Mr. Alberts to reiterate prior concerns over the way the study was being conducted, the secretive nature of the National Academies staff and the fact that information was being unnecessarily guarded. Specifically, an inquiry was made as to why the National Academy file contained a copy of a previous letter from industry, wherein the National Academy had redacted from public viewing, non-controversial text regarding the National Academy's obligations under Federal law. Appendix F.

I have enclosed Mr. Albert's response for the subcommittee's review as well as a copy of the original letter and the redacted version of the letter that was placed in the National Academies public file. Appendix G.

I urge the subcommittee to review Mr. Albert's explanation in his letter dated August 13, 2003, and compare the two letters submitted—both the complete version and the redacted version—and make your own determination as to whether or not the contents that were redacted fit within the category described in paragraph two of Mr. Albert's letter. Possibly you will be enlightened as to the ways of the National Academy.

Additionally, in Mr. Albert's letter, he states that the "extensive programmatic and research information" provided by organizations have been "carefully considered" by the committee. I would ask that the subcommittee inquire as to the degree of consideration the National Academies' committee was able to give to programs that were never removed from shrink-wrapped packaging.

CONCLUSION

While the process underlying the National Academies study is replete with efforts to exclude the industry, silence its voice and disregard its successful efforts on the important issue of reducing and eliminating underage drinking, a more important fact remains—a significant opportunity to offer Congress with a meaningful review has been missed. What was needed, and what Congress requested, was a thorough review of which government and private-sector programs work and which do not. Some of the most effective programs are being conducted in our communities, not necessarily by government agencies. Private sector groups, foundations, non-profit organizations and faith-based groups are avoiding bureaucratic red tape and taking their message directly to homes and schools. Congress needs to know what works.

- The National Academies report failed Congress and America's kids. Rather than serving as a blueprint for all parties—government, community groups, law enforcement and the beer industry—the report lacks scientific back-up to combat illegal underage drinking.

- The report is a result of biased academics, the majority of whom should have been dismissed from the panel for obvious conflicts of interest.
- It is beyond irresponsible that the National Academies chose to disregard Congress's instructions and squandered half-a-million dollars to produce an unreliable study that fails to adequately identify real solutions to successfully combat illegal underage drinking.
- Unfortunately, Congress is no closer today to identifying successful programs to address illegal underage drinking, than it was a year and a half ago, and $500,000 taxpayer dollars ago.

Notwithstanding these misguided efforts, the beer industry remains committed to the fight against illegal underage drinking. Let's focus on real solutions, such as the programs that are working in our communities, and not tax hikes and untested programs. Working together, we can keep alcohol out of the hands of our children, and available for adults of legal drinking age to enjoy safely and responsibly.

APPENDIX A

107th Congress Report; House of Representatives; 1st Session

Making appropriations for the departments of Labor, Health, Human Services, and Education, and related agencies for the fiscal year ending September 30, 2002, and for other purposes

December 19 (legislative day, December 8), 2001.—Ordered to be printed

Mr. Regula, from the committee of conference, submitted the following:

Conference Report

[To accompany H.R. 3061]

The committee of conference on the disagreeing votes of the two Houses on the amendment of the Senate to the bill (H. R. 3061) making appropriations for the Departments of Labor, Health and Human Services, and Education, and related agencies for the fiscal year ending September 30, 2002, and for other purposes," having met, after full and free conference, have agreed to recommend and do recommend to their Respective Houses as follows:

That the House recede from its disagreement to the amendment of the Senate, and agree to the same with an amendment, as follows: I lieu of the matter stricken and inserted by said amendment, insert:

That the following sums are appropriated, out of any money in the Treasury not otherwise appropriated, for the Departments of Labor, Health and Human Services, and Education, and related agencies for the fiscal year ending September 30, 2002, and for other purposes, namely:

Title I - Department of Labor
Employment and Training Administration
Training and Employment Services

For necessary expenses of the Workforce Investment Act, including the purchase and hire of passenger motor vehicles, the construction alteration, and repair of buildings and other faculties, and the purchase of real property for training centers as authorized by the:

General Departmental Management

The conference agreement includes $347,554,000 for general departmental management instead of $338,887,000 as proposed by the House and $422,212,000 as proposed by the Senate. In addition, the agreement provides $21,552,000 in. program evaluation funds as proposed by the House. The Senate did not provide for evaluation funds in this account.

Within the total provided, $4,000,000 is for the United States-Mexico Border Health Commission as proposed by the Senate. The House did not specify an amount for the Commission.

The conference agreement includes $500,000 for the National Academy of Sciences and Institute of Medicine (NAS/IOM) to develop a cost-effective strategy for reducing and preventing underage drinking. The House had included funds for a similar purpose within the appropriation for the Substance Abuse and Mental Health Services Administration, while the Senate bill included funds for this purpose in this account.

To help develop a cost-effective strategy for reducing and preventing underage drinking, the NAS/IOM shall review existing Federal, State and non-governmental programs, including media-based programs, designed to change the attitudes and health behaviors of youth. Based on its review, the NAS/IOM shall produce a strategy designed to prevent and reduce underage drinking including: an outline and implementation strategy, message points that will be effective in changing the attitudes and health behaviors of youth concerning underage drinking, target audience identification, goals and objectives of the campaign, and the estimated costs of development and implementation. The review and recommendations of the NAS/IOM shall be reported to the Committees on Appropriations of the Congress, the Secretary of Health and Human Services, the Secretary of Education, and the U.S. Attorney General no later than nine months after the date of enactment of this Act.

APPENDIX B

United States General Accounting Office

GAO

Report to the Chairman, Subcommittee on Criminal Justice, Drug Policy, and Human Resources, House Committee on Government Reform, and to Representative John L. Mica

May 2001

UNDERAGE DRINKING

Information on Federal Funds Targeted at Prevention

GAO

Accountability * Integrity * Reliability

GAO-01-503

Contents

GAO
Accountability * Integrity * Reliability

United States General Accounting Office
Washington, DC 20548

May 8, 2001

The Honorable Mark E. Souder
Chairman, Subcommittee on Criminal Justice,
Drug Policy, and Human Resources
Committee on Government Reform
House of Representatives

The Honorable John L. Mica
House of Representatives

Multiple surveys indicate substantial alcohol consumption among youth, even though the purchase and public possession of alcohol by persons under the age of 21 are illegal in every state and the District of Columbia.[1] Many federal programs address prevention of alcohol use among underage youth. This letter responds to a request that we identify the nature and extent of federal efforts related to the prevention of underage drinking, to assist Congress in its deliberations on whether additional attention to alcohol use by youth is needed.[2] Specifically, our objectives were to identify (1) the amount of appropriated fiscal year 2000 federal funds that addressed prevention of underage drinking, and (2) fiscal year 2000 funded program activities that included media components to publicize the problem of underage drinking.

Scope and Methodology

To identify fiscal year 2000 appropriated federal funding that addressed prevention of underage drinking, we first identified agencies that had program activities that addressed prevention of alcohol use and then asked agency officials to provide information on their program activities affecting youth under the age of 21. We used the Office of National Drug Control Policy's (ONDCP) fiscal year 2001 budget summary that included fiscal year 2000 funding information to identify federal agencies with

[1]For information regarding the states' adoption of a 21-year minimum age for the purchase and public possession of alcohol, see the "Enforcing the Underage Drinking Laws Discretionary Grants Program," issued by the Justice Department, Office of Juvenile Justice and Delinquency Prevention, at *www.ojjdp.ncjrs.org/grants/UNDERAGE.html.*

[2]We defined prevention to include initiatives such as those associated with information, education, research, screening, and brief intervention or treatment.

program activities related to prevention of underage drinking. We used the ONDCP budget report because it listed agencies with activities that supported one of ONDCP's strategic goals—to educate and enable America's youth to reject illegal drugs as well as the use of alcohol and tobacco. To identify additional federal agencies that might have program activities that addressed prevention of underage drinking, we solicited suggestions from officials of federal agencies identified as having alcohol prevention programs about other federal agencies that would have such program activities. We identified 23 federal agencies as having program activities that to some degree addressed prevention of underage drinking. Appendix I provides more information on these federal agencies.

We asked the agencies we identified to provide information on activities funded in fiscal year 2000 that addressed prevention of underage drinking either specifically or in part. We asked for information on, among other things, the nature of their programs, the type of funding (e.g., discretionary, block, formula, and incentive grants; contracts; cooperative and interagency agreements; and agency program funds), and the amount of the fiscal year 2000 appropriated federal funding for each program. We categorized federal program activities that addressed prevention of underage drinking by drug focus and audience. With respect to drug focus, the categories included (1) activities that targeted alcohol use or (2) activities that targeted both alcohol and other drug use. With respect to audience, the activities were categorized by those that (1) targeted youth or (2) targeted both youth and the broader community.[3]

With respect to media components, we asked federal agency officials with programs that addressed prevention of underage drinking to identify those program activities funded in fiscal year 2000 that had a media component to publicize the problem of underage drinking. We defined media component as radio and television broadcasts. We also asked officials to provide a description of the media component.

We relied on information and records provided by agency officials and did not independently verify the information. We performed our audit work in Washington, D.C., from November 2000 through April 2001 in accordance with generally accepted government auditing standards.

[3]The broader community includes parents, college students over age 21, teachers, and health care professionals.

Results in Brief

An estimated $71 million of fiscal year 2000 appropriated federal funds were specifically addressed to the prevention of underage drinking (i.e., alcohol use by youth). Five federal agencies—(1) the Substance Abuse and Mental Health Services Administration (SAMHSA), (2) the National Institute on Alcohol Abuse and Alcoholism (NIAAA), (3) the Office of Juvenile Justice and Delinquency Prevention (OJJDP), (4) the National Highway Traffic Safety Administration (NHTSA), and (5) the Centers for Disease Control (CDC)—identified about $52 million in fiscal year 2000 appropriated funding that specifically addressed prevention of underage drinking to youth. Additionally, three of these agencies identified about $19 million that addressed prevention of underage drinking but targeted both youth and the broader community. Table 1 summarizes the appropriated fiscal year 2000 federal funding that specifically addressed prevention of underage drinking.

Table 1: Summary of Fiscal Year 2000 Appropriated Federal Funds That Specifically Addressed Prevention of Underage Drinking, by Federal Agency

	Appropriated federal funds (in millions)		
Agency	Targeted to youth	Targeted to youth and the broader community	Total
SAMHSA	$2.1	$1.6	**$3.7**
NIAAA	19.2	17.0	**36.2**
OJJDP	27.8	0	**27.8**
NHTSA	2.9	.3	**3.2**
CDC	.2	0	**.2**
Total	**$52.2**	**$18.9**	**$71.1**

Source: GAO analysis of agency data.

In addition, many federal agencies had program activities that addressed prevention of underage drinking but for which agency officials could not isolate funding specific to alcohol. SAMHSA, OJJDP, CDC, and another 15 federal agencies identified about $1 billion of fiscal year 2000 appropriated federal funding that addressed prevention of alcohol use but also targeted other drug use. These activities addressed prevention of alcohol and other drug use that targeted either youth or both youth and the broader community. However, officials could not tell us what portion of this appropriated federal funding was targeted specifically to alcohol prevention activities. Furthermore, three federal agencies—Office of Elementary and Secondary Education, SAMHSA, and NHTSA—identified an estimated $769 million out of $2.2 billion of block, formula, and incentive grant funds that may have been used by states to address prevention of drug and alcohol use by youth.

Figure 1 shows the amount of fiscal year 2000 appropriated federal funding that specifically addressed prevention of underage drinking versus funding that, in part, may have addressed prevention of underage drinking.

Figure 1: Fiscal Year 2000 Appropriated Federal Funding That Addressed Prevention of Underage Drinking Specifically or Addressed Underage Drinking in Part

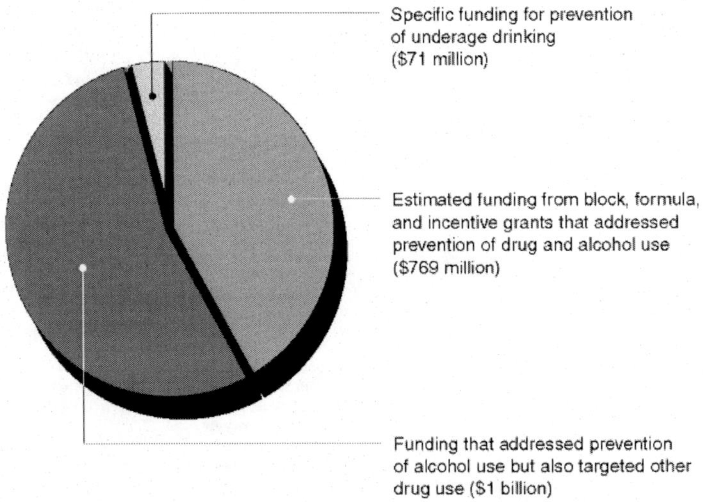

Source: GAO analysis of agency data.

Appendix II provides information on federal agencies' fiscal year 2000 appropriated federal funding that addressed prevention of underage drinking.

Three federal agencies—NIAAA, NHTSA, and SAMHSA—identified seven program activities that included a media component targeting either alcohol use by youth or alcohol use where the audience was both youth and the broader community. The fiscal year 2000 appropriated funding for these seven program activities was approximately $1.5 million. In addition, agencies provided general information regarding the extent to which media components were included in block, formula, or incentive grants and in ONDCP's National Youth Anti-Drug Media Campaign. Appendix III provides more information on federal agency fiscal year 2000 program activities that included a media component.

Agency Comments and Our Evaluation

On March 23, 2001, we provided a draft report for comment to the GAO liaisons for the 23 agencies included in this report. Based on reviews within these agencies by relevant officials, the GAO liaisons provided technical and editorial comments, or indicated no comment, by E-mail or letter. Technical and editorial comments have been incorporated, where appropriate. The Department of Health and Human Services (HHS) expressed concern about the consistency of some information provided on the part of one HHS agency, SAMHSA, that had provided information that focused on alcohol use by youth and had not included activities related to addressing "alcohol and drug use" by youth or by youth and the broader community (i.e., that addressed underage drinking in part). SAMHSA provided additional information that has been included in this report. Through the agency comment process, we provided all agencies an opportunity to correct inconsistencies.

In addition, HHS noted that in some instances GAO performed analysis of agency data and in other instances agency data were reported without analysis. GAO analyzed data for agencies that were able to provide specific information on activities related to prevention of underage drinking. However, many agencies were unable to identify specific funding activities related to prevention of underage drinking. For these agencies, we reported the funding level identified with the general program activity.

As arranged with the Subcommittee, we plan no further distribution of this report until 30 days after the date of this letter. We will then send copies to Representative Elijah Cummings, Ranking Minority Member, Subcommittee on Criminal Justice, Drug Policy, and Human Resources, House Government Reform, and Representative Dan Burton, Chairman, and Representative Henry Waxman, Ranking Minority Member, House Committee on Government Reform. We will also send copies to Senator Fred Thompson, Chairman, and Senator Joseph Lieberman, Ranking Member, Senate Committee on Governmental Affairs. We will also make copies available to others on request. This report will also be available on GAO's home page at http://www.gao.gov.

Please call me on (202) 512-8777 if you or your staff have any questions regarding this report. The information presented in this report was developed by Linda Watson, Assistant Director; Jared Hermalin, Senior Analyst; and Lou Smith, Analyst.

Richard M. Stana
Director, Justice Issues

Appendix I: Federal Agencies That Had Fiscal Year 2000 Program Activities Addressing Prevention of Underage Drinking

This appendix provides information on the 23 agencies identified as having program activities addressing prevention of underage drinking.[1] Included are agency descriptions, the targeted drug and audience for the program activity, and information on agencies' total appropriated fiscal year 2000 federal funding related to prevention of underage drinking, which includes both funding that was specific to prevention of underage drinking and funding that, in part, may have addressed prevention of underage drinking.

The agency description includes mission information for agencies that had a more significant role in addressing prevention of underage drinking. For agencies that had program activities that addressed underage drinking but for whom conducting such activities was not a primary role, we have described the program activities related to the issue of prevention of underage drinking. Focusing on the targeted drug and audience allowed us to differentiate among agencies and program activities that specifically addressed prevention of underage drinking versus those that addressed, in part, prevention of underage drinking (i.e. addressed alcohol and other drug use) and whether the targeted audience was specific to underage youth (i.e., youth under the age of 21) or encompassed a broader community to include parents, college students over age 21, teachers, and health care professionals. The fiscal year 2000 funding provides an explanation of each agency's funding in relation to its program activities related to prevention of underage drinking.

Department of Health and Human Services

Administration for Children and Families

Description: The Administration for Children and Families (ACF) manages state grants and childcare programs, including programs to increase child abuse prevention and treatment activities. It also seeks to develop family preservation and family support services, the Head Start Program, programs that provide services for runaway and homeless youth and their families, child welfare training programs, and child abuse and neglect and research and demonstration programs. At least 10 percent of the funds ACF awards to grantees as part of its Runaway and Homeless Youth Programs are used to support a variety of substance abuse prevention activities, including efforts to prevent underage drinking. These activities include literature, counseling, or a mixture of efforts.

Targeted drug and audience: The program activity targeted drug and alcohol use. The target audience for the program was youth under the age of 21.

Fiscal Year 2000 funding: Commenting on its Runaway and Homeless Youth program, an official of the Administration for Children and Families estimated that approximately $15,000,000 in fiscal year 2000 appropriated funding may have addressed, in part, prevention of underage drinking. However, the official could not tell us what portion of appropriated federal funding may have addressed alcohol prevention activities.

[1] Prevention is defined as activities such as those associated with information, education, research, and early intervention or treatment.

Substance Abuse and Mental Health Services Administration (SAMHSA)

Description: SAMHSA's goal is to strengthen the capacity of the nation's health care system to provide prevention, diagnosis, and treatment services for people at risk of or experiencing substance abuse[2] or mental illnesses. SAMHSA is composed of three centers: (1) the Center for Mental Health Services promotes improved mental health; (2) the Center for Substance Abuse Prevention promotes strategies to prevent substance abuse—whether illicit drug use, misuse of legal medications, use of alcohol and tobacco by youth, or excessive use of alcohol; and (3) the Center for Substance Abuse Treatment promotes efforts to improve the lives of individuals and families affected by alcohol and drug abuse by helping to ensure access to clinically sound, cost-effective addiction treatment to reduce the nation's health and social costs. SAMHSA also conducts the National Household Survey on Drug Abuse and other surveys on alcohol and other drug use and abuse by youth as well as adults. The three centers administer grants, contracts, and interagency agreements for their respective fields of specialty.

Targeted drug and audience: SAMHSA's program activities included those that targeted just alcohol use and others that targeted both drug and alcohol use. The targeted audience also varied, with some program activities addressing youth and others addressing a broader community.

[2]According to the *Diagnostic and Statistical Manual of Mental Disorders*, 4th ed. (DSM-IV), a diagnosis of substance abuse requires that an individual exhibit a pattern of abuse that can be demonstrated by either of the following: continued use despite a persistent social, occupational, psychological, or physical problem that is caused or made worse by substance use, or recurrent use in physically hazardous situations.

Fiscal year 2000 funding: As shown in table 2, SAMHSA's total funding related to prevention of youth alcohol and drug use was $628,180,834.

Table 2: SAMHSA's Fiscal Year 2000 Appropriated Federal Funding That Addressed Prevention of Youth Alcohol and Drug Use, by Program Activity

Program activity	Federal funds appropriated in fiscal year 2000
Block grants	$320,000,000[a]
Discretionary grants (514)	$218,301,163
Contracts (42)	$87,405,081
Interagency agreements (8)	$2,474,590
Total	**$628,180,834**

[a]This amount represents the 20 percent minimum designated by statute for substance abuse prevention activities, including alcohol and drug abuse. (42 U.S.C. 300x-22(a), (b) (1)). It includes not only youth services, but those services for all age groups.

Source: GAO analysis of SAMHSA information.

Centers for Disease Control and Prevention (CDC)

Description: CDC is an operating division within the Public Health Service and is charged with protecting the public health of the nation by providing leadership and direction in the prevention and control of diseases and other preventable conditions as well as by responding to public health emergencies. CDC's National Center for Injury Prevention and Control funded several projects in fiscal year 2000 related to prevention of underage drinking. CDC's National Center for Chronic Disease Prevention and Health Promotion administers the Youth Risk Behavior Survey (YRBS) that is to provide data on health risk behaviors related to unintentional injuries and violence, tobacco use, alcohol and other drug use, sexual behaviors, dietary behaviors, and physical activity. However, an official told us that the survey is conducted biennially and was not done during fiscal year 2000.

Targeted drug and audience: The National Center for Injury Prevention and Control funded one activity that addressed alcohol and youth, two that addressed alcohol and targeted both youth and the broader community, and one activity that addressed drug and alcohol use and the targeted audience was youth.

Fiscal year 2000 funding: As shown in table 3, CDC officials identified $660,697 in fiscal year 2000 appropriated funds as related to youth alcohol and drug use.

Table 3: CDC's Fiscal Year 2000 Appropriated Federal Funding That Addressed Prevention of Youth Alcohol and Drug Use, by Program Activity

Program activity	Federal funds appropriated in fiscal year 2000
Contract (1)	$20,000
Discretionary grants (3)	$640,697
Total	**$660,697**

Source: GAO analysis of CDC information.

Indian Health Service (IHS)

Description: IHS is an operating division within the Public Health Service and provides a comprehensive health services delivery system for American Indians and Alaskan Natives, with opportunity for maximum tribal involvement in developing and managing programs to meet their health needs. It assists Native American tribes in developing their health programs and facilitates and assists tribes in coordinating health planning; obtaining and utilizing health resources available through federal, state, and local programs; operating comprehensive health programs; and evaluating health programs. IHS distributes funds to its 12 area offices, which further distribute funds to tribal programs.

Targeted drug and audience: The IHS program activities addressed drug and alcohol use. According to an IHS official, there are no programs specifically funded for underage drinking prevention, but the issue of adolescent alcohol abuse is addressed in the prevention and treatment programs developed by the tribes. The targeted audience is youth for some program activities and the broader community for others. These programs include Youth Residential Treatment, Community Education and Training, Community Rehabilitation and Aftercare, contract health services, Navajo Rehabilitation Program, urban clinical service, and Wellness Beyond Abstinence. According to IHS officials, each of the over 400 tribal programs is designed to meet the needs of its service area. Each tribal program incorporates local beliefs and practices into its alcohol prevention and treatment programs for adolescents.

Fiscal year 2000 funding: An IHS official identified $41,945,000 in fiscal year 2000 appropriated federal funding that, in part, addressed prevention of underage drinking. However, the official could not tell us what portion of appropriated federal funding may have addressed alcohol prevention activities. According to IHS, reports show that some areas spend from 20 to 34 percent of their budgets on prevention and treatment initiatives for adolescents.

The National Institute on Alcohol Abuse and Alcoholism (NIAAA)

Description: NIAAA, within the National Institutes of Health (NIH), conducts and supports biomedical and behavioral research in order to provide science-based approaches to the prevention and treatment of alcohol abuse and alcoholism. It provides a national focus for the federal effort to increase knowledge and disseminate research findings to the scientific community, the health care system, and the public. NIAAA administers grants and contracts to carry out its program activities.

Targeted drug and audience: NIAAA program activities targeted alcohol use and abuse. Some program activities targeted only youth, and others targeted both youth and the broader community.

Fiscal year 2000 funding: As shown in table 4, NIAAA's fiscal year 2000 appropriated federal funding included $36,208,030 for program activities related to prevention of underage drinking.

Table 4: NIAAA's Fiscal Year 2000 Appropriated Federal Funding That Addressed Prevention of Underage Drinking, by Program Activity

Program activity	Federal funds appropriated in fiscal year 2000
Discretionary grants(90)	$35,478,030
Contracts (2)	$730,000
Total	**$36,208,030**

Source: GAO analysis of NIAAA information.

The National Institute on Drug Abuse (NIDA)

Description: NIDA, within NIH, has as its mission to lead the nation in bringing the power of science to bear on drug abuse and addiction through the strategic support and conduct of research across a broad range of disciplines and the effective dissemination and use of the results of that research to improve drug abuse and addiction prevention, treatment, and policy. One initiative within NIDA, the Monitoring the Future Study, is a drug survey conducted annually. The survey has been administered to 12th graders since 1975 and to 8th and 10th graders since 1991; a follow-up sample of high school seniors is also included. The study serves several purposes, including (1) an assessment of the prevalence and trends in drug use and related attitudes and beliefs, and (2) a determination of the lifestyles and value orientations associated with drug use. The study encompasses the use of illicit drugs as well as alcohol, cigarettes, smokeless tobacco, and steroids.

Targeted drug and audience: The Monitoring the Future Study survey included questions about drugs and alcohol, among other things. The targeted audience is school age children.

Fiscal year 2000 funding: According to a NIDA official, NIDA awarded a grant for $4,634,257 in fiscal year 2000 for the Monitoring the Future Study. The study addressed, in part, prevention of underage drinking.

Department of Justice

Office of Juvenile Justice and Delinquency Prevention (OJJDP)

Description: OJJDP, within the Office of Justice Programs, provides national leadership, coordination, and resources to develop, implement, and support effective methods to prevent and control juvenile delinquency and improve the juvenile justice system. This includes activities to enforce underage drinking laws, educate the public about the problem, and involve the justice system in responding appropriately and effectively to underage drinking. These activities are accomplished through retail compliance initiatives, prevention programs, and fostering a juvenile justice system that, among other things, provides appropriate sanctions, treatment, and rehabilitative services based on the needs of the individual juvenile.

OJJDP administers the Enforcing the Underage Drinking Laws (EUDL) Program, which provides funds to states to support and enhance efforts to prohibit the sale of alcoholic beverages to—or the consumption of alcoholic beverages by—minors (persons under age 21) . Congress appropriated $25,000,000 for the program in fiscal year 2000. The funds are disbursed through block and discretionary grants. The block grant provided $360,000 to each state and the District of Columbia. In addition, $6,640,000 was made available for discretionary grants to support local program activity within states and territories, training and technical assistance to the states, and evaluation of the overall program. EUDL grants to states are awarded to an appropriate state agency designated by each state's governor.

Targeted drug and audience: The EUDL program is designed to reduce the availability of alcoholic beverages to minors and prevent the consumption of alcoholic beverages by minors. Related OJJDP program activities include grants that target drug use by youth, including alcohol.

Fiscal year 2000 funding: As shown in table 5, OJJDP's fiscal year 2000 total appropriated federal funding related to prevention of youth alcohol and drug use was $44,023,796.

Table 5: OJJDP's Fiscal Year 2000 Appropriated Federal Funding That Addressed Prevention of Youth Alcohol and Drug Use, by Program Activity

Program activity	Federal funds appropriated in fiscal year 2000
Block grants (EUDL)	$18,360,000
EUDL discretionary grants (14)	$6,640,000
Tribal Youth discretionary grants (34)	$7,702,019
Other discretionary grants	$11,321,777
Total	**$44,023,796**

Source: GAO analysis of OJJDP information.

Office of Community Oriented Policing Services (COPS)

Description: The mission of COPS is to improve public safety in neighborhoods and communities through partnerships with communities, policing agencies, and other public and private organizations. As part of its mission, the COPS program provides funds for school safety and community crime prevention initiatives. These initiatives include assigning officers to schools to perform a variety of functions, which may encompass activities such as teaching crime prevention and substance abuse classes.

Targeted drug and audience: The COPS initiatives, in part, targeted drug and alcohol use (i.e., substance abuse). The targeted audience included youth and the broader community.

Fiscal year 2000 funding: A COPS budget official identified $180,000,000 in fiscal year 2000 appropriated federal funding for activities that supported law enforcement officers who were directly assigned to schools. Funding, in part, may have addressed prevention of underage drinking, but the official could not tell us what portion of appropriated federal funding may have addressed alcohol prevention activities.

Department of Transportation

National Highway Traffic Safety Administration (NHTSA)

Description: NHTSA funded programs that addressed the problems of drunk and drugged driving and prevention programs targeting zero tolerance for alcohol and drug use among youth. NHTSA administers a formula and incentive grant program, awards discretionary grants and contracts, and enters into cooperative agreements with other entities.

NHTSA reports that, under the Highway Safety Act of 1966 (23 U.S.C. 402), it provides "section 402" formula grant funds to states, territories, and Indian nations to conduct highway safety programs, which may include underage drinking programs. In addition, NHTSA reports that, under 23 U.S.C. 410, it awards "section 410" incentive grants to states for the implementation and enforcement of state programs to reduce traffic safety problems resulting from alcohol-impaired driving, such as underage drinking programs.

Targeted drug and audience: These NHTSA program activities targeted drug and alcohol use. Some program activities targeted youth; others targeted both youth and the broader community.

Fiscal year 2000 funding: As shown in table 6, NHTSA's total fiscal year 2000 appropriated federal funding related to prevention of youth alcohol and drug use was $23,903,000. The fiscal year 2000 funding for the formula and incentive grants represents estimated portions that addressed prevention of underage drinking.

Table 6: NHTSA's Fiscal Year 2000 Appropriated Federal Funding That Addressed Prevention of Youth Alcohol and Drug Use, by Program Activity

Program activity	Federal funds appropriated in fiscal year 2000
Formula grants (section 402)	$15,600,000
Incentive grants (section 410)	$5,100,000
Discretionary grants (7)	$550,000
Contracts (6)	$2,573,000
Cooperative agreements (2)	$80,000
Total	**$23,903,000**

Source: GAO analysis of NHTSA information.

Department of Education

The Office of Elementary and Secondary Education

Description: The Safe and Drug-Free Schools Program, within the Office of Elementary and Secondary Education, is the federal government's primary vehicle for reducing drug, alcohol, and tobacco use, and violence, through education and prevention activities in the nation's schools. This program consists of two major programs: (1) State Grants for Drug and Violence Prevention Programs and (2) National Programs. State Grants is a formula grant program that provides funds to state and local education agencies, as well as governors, for a wide range of school- and community-based education and prevention activities. The National Program carries out a variety of discretionary initiatives that respond to emerging needs. Among these initiatives are direct grants to school districts and communities with severe drug and violence problems, program evaluation, and information development and dissemination.

Targeted drug and audience: The Safe and Drug-Free Schools Program targets drug and alcohol use, among other things. The target audience is school-age children, but program activities can also include the broader community.

Fiscal year 2000 funding: As shown in table 7, the Office of Elementary and Secondary Education's total fiscal year 2000 appropriated federal funding related to prevention of youth drug and alcohol use was $589,350,000.

Table 7: Fiscal Year 2000 Appropriated Federal Funding Identified by the Office of Elementary and Secondary Education as Addressing Prevention of Youth Drug and Alcohol Use, by Program Activity

Program activity	Federal funds appropriated in fiscal year 2000
State Grants	$428,600,000
National Programs	$160,750,000
Total	**$589,350,000**

Source: Office of Elementary and Secondary Education.

Department of Labor

Employment and Training Administration (ETA)

Description: ETA administers the Job Corps Program, which is a national residential training and employment program whose purpose is to assist eligible young people to become more responsible, employable, and productive citizens. Enrollees must be at least 16 but not yet 25 years of age. As part of the Job Corps Program, trainees are to be screened for drug and alcohol problems and to be provided prevention and intervention services.

Targeted drug and audience: The program activity targeted drugs and alcohol use. The target audience includes both youth and adults.

Fiscal year 2000 funding: An ETA official identified $8,272,023 in fiscal year 2000 appropriated federal funding that, in part, may have addressed prevention of alcohol use. However, the official could not tell us what portion of appropriated federal funding may have addressed alcohol prevention activities for youth.

Bureau of Labor Statistics (BLS)

Description: BLS identified three surveys in its National Longitudinal Surveys (NLS) program that provide information on underage drinking. The 1979 NLS of Youth includes a nationally representative sample of nearly 10,000 people who were born in the years 1957 to 1964 and lived in the United States when the sample was selected in 1978. The respondents were 14 to 22 years of age when they were first interviewed in 1979. Individuals were interviewed every year from 1979 to 1994 and biennially since 1994. In 1986, BLS began a new survey of the children born to female respondents of the 1979 NLS. This survey is called the Children of the NLS Youth of 1979 and is funded by the National Institute of Child Health and Human Development (NICHD). In 1997, BLS began another NLS with a nationally representative sample of nearly 9,000 youths who were born in the years 1980 to 1984. These youths were ages 12 to 16 as of December 31, 1996. All three surveys collect information about youth alcohol and drug use, among other things, that could be used by policy makers to help monitor trends and to devise drug and alcohol prevention strategies.

Targeted drug and audience: The NLS program targets drugs and alcohol. The targeted audience includes both youth and adults.

Fiscal year 2000 funding: A BLS official identified $10,200,000 of appropriated fiscal year 2000 federal funding for the NLS Youth of 1979 and NLS Youth of 1997 surveys. In addition, the official identified $3,000,000 in appropriated fiscal year 2000 federal funding for the Children of the NLS Youth of 1979. Thus, a total of $13,200,000 of fiscal year 2000 appropriated federal funding addressed, in part, prevention of underage drinking.

Executive Office of the White House

Office of National Drug Control Policy (ONDCP)

Description: ONDCP is to set goals and objectives for national drug control that include reducing the number of illegal drug users, preventing use of illegal drugs, and reducing the availability of illegal drugs. In this capacity, ONDCP carries out numerous responsibilities, one of which is oversight of the High Intensity Drug Trafficking Areas (HIDTA) Program, whose mission is to reduce drug trafficking activities in the most critical drug trafficking areas. Several HIDTAs integrate drug education and early intervention programs with law enforcement efforts to reduce youthful involvement with illegal drugs and strengthen families and communities. ONDCP also awards funds under the Drug-Free Communities Support Program and provides general oversight of drug abuse prevention programs. The Drug-Free Communities Support Program supports community anti-drug coalitions throughout the United States in developing and implementing comprehensive long-term plans to prevent and treat drug abuse among youth. In addition, ONDCP was required by Congress in 1998 to undertake a National Youth Anti-Drug Media Campaign to reduce and prevent drug use among youth.[3] The campaign supports the first goal of the 2000 National Drug Control Strategy, which is to educate and enable America's youth to reject illegal drugs as well as alcohol and tobacco.

Targeted drug and audience: ONDCP program activities targeted drug and alcohol use. Its targeted audience included both youth and the broader community.

[3] 21 U.S.C. 1801(a) (Supp. IV 1998).

Fiscal year 2000 funding: As shown in table 8, ONDCP officials identified $219,944,000 in fiscal year 2000 appropriated funds as related to youth alcohol and drug use prevention.

Table 8. ONDCP's Fiscal Year 2000 Appropriated Federal Funding That Addressed Prevention of Youth Alcohol and Drug Use, by Program Activity

Program activity	Federal funds appropriated in fiscal year 2000
National Youth Anti-Drug Media Campaign	$184,297,000
Drug-Free Communities Program	$30,000,000
HITDA	$3,124,000
Other prevention activities	$2,523,000
Total	**$219,944,000**

Source: GAO analysis of ONDCP information.

Department of Defense (DOD)

DOD's Office of the Assistant Secretary of Defense (Health Affairs) identified several military branches as having programs that may have addressed, in part, prevention of underage drinking. In addition to these programs, DOD also administers a worldwide survey of health behaviors among military personnel. The survey, which began in 1980, asks active duty service members about various health behaviors, including the use of illegal drugs, alcohol, tobacco, and at-risk sexual behavior. The survey was last administered in 1998 and is to be administered in 2001.

U.S. Marine Corps

Description: The Young Marines Program focuses on illicit substance abuse prevention with children 8 to 17 years of age.

Targeted drug and audience: According to a DOD official, all of the youth outreach programs funded with DOD counterdrug funds were all-encompassing. As such, they may have included an anti-alcohol message but did not specifically target underage drinking. The programs addressed school-age children.

Fiscal year 2000 funding: A DOD official identified $2,000,000 in fiscal year 2000 appropriated funding from its counterdrug program activities for the Young Marines program that, in part, may have addressed prevention of underage drinking. However, the official could not tell us what portion of the funding may have addressed prevention of alcohol use.

National Guard

Description: The National Guard does not disperse its funding directly to its various programs, but rather sends its funding to its state counterdrug coordinator. The states then distribute funding to the programs based upon the governor's and adjutant general's priorities. The National Guard program activities included Drug Abuse Resistance Education (DARE),[4] Drug Education for Youth (DEFY), Adopt a School, and Lunch Buddy.

Targeted drug and audience: According to DOD, all of the youth outreach programs funded with DOD counterdrug funds are all-encompassing. As such, they may include an anti-alcohol message but do not specifically target underage drinking. The programs addressed school-age children under 18 years of age.

Fiscal year 2000 funding: A DOD official identified $25,500,000 in fiscal year 2000 appropriated federal funding from counterdrug activities that was used to fund the National Guard programs. These programs may have, in part, addressed prevention of underage drinking, but the official could not tell us what portion of appropriated federal funding may have addressed alcohol prevention activities.

United States Army

Description: The U.S. Army Center for Substance Abuse Programs (ACSAP) is the Army's lead agency for substance abuse prevention, education, and training. ACSAP provides operational supervision, direction, evaluation, oversight, and policy development for all elements of the Army Drug and Alcohol Prevention and Control Program. This program serves more than 2 million Army personnel and their families assigned to over 150 installations and Reserve commands worldwide on needs as they pertain to alcohol and other drug prevention.

Targeted drug and audience: The program targeted both drug and alcohol use. The targeted audience included both youth and the broader community.

Fiscal year 2000 funding: According to a DOD official, the Army did not have a discrete budgeted program that addressed prevention of alcohol use by youth. Funding is for the Army Center for Substance Abuse Programs, which is inclusive of all drugs and is targeted to a broad audience.

United States Navy

Description: The Navy has a program that provides a means for command- or self-referral, without risk of disciplinary action or career implications, to service members who admit to having purchased, possessed, or consumed alcohol in violation of the minimum age requirements of the military installation, state, country, or local jurisdiction in which the member is located. The program also provides for alcohol counseling and/or treatment.

Targeted drug and audience: The Navy program targeted alcohol use by service members under the minimum drinking age.

Fiscal year 2000 funding: According to a DOD official, the Navy did not have a discrete budgeted program that addressed prevention of alcohol use by youth. Funding for this program is included in the Navy's larger and broader prevention efforts.

Federal Corporation

Corporation for National and Community Service (CNCS)

Description: CNCS is a federal corporation governed by a 15-member bipartisan Board of Directors appointed by the President with the advice and consent of the Senate. The Corporation has three major service activities: AmeriCorps, Learn and Serve America, and the National Senior Service Corps. CNCS awards grants to state commissions, which in turn award sub-grants to local organizations. A small number of these organizations receive grants for activities specifically involving drug prevention (i.e., to include alcohol and other drugs). Other organizations run youth programs, such as after-school programs, which by keeping youth off the streets are considered to have an impact on the drug and alcohol prevention effort.

Targeted drug and audience: The program activities targeted drug and alcohol use, among other things. The targeted audience included both youth and the broader community.

Fiscal year 2000 funding: A CNCS official identified $9,000,000 in fiscal year 2000 appropriated federal funding that was awarded to organizations and that, in part, may have addressed prevention of alcohol use.

[4]DARE is a school-based program that uses trained, uniformed police officers in the classroom to increase students' knowledge about substance abuse and enhance their social skills. Various law enforcement agencies participate in the program, such as the National Guard, the National Park Service, and the U.S. Forest Service.

According to the official, this funding level represents spending defined by CNCS as having an indirect impact on the overall drug prevention effort and it is impossible to separate out what portion of the funding may have specifically addressed alcohol prevention activities for youth.

Department of the Treasury

Bureau of Alcohol, Tobacco and Firearms (ATF)

Description: ATF provides funding to state and local governments, through cooperative agreements, for the Gang Resistance Education and Training (GREAT) program. GREAT is a police-delivered program oriented toward bringing an anti-violence, anti-drug message to the nation's youth.

Targeted drug and audience: The GREAT program addressed drugs and alcohol use, among other things. The targeted audience is youth.

Fiscal year 2000 funding: An ATF official identified $16,000,000 in fiscal year 2000 appropriated federal funding for GREAT.

Department of the Interior

Bureau of Indian Affairs (BIA)

Description: The Office of Alcohol and Substance Abuse Prevention (OASAP) was established in the Office of the Secretary of Indian Affairs in April 2000 to monitor and evaluate the BIA programs that have alcohol and substance abuse prevention-related activities. The Director of OASAP reported that BIA has several programs that may have addressed prevention of underage drinking. These include the OASAP activities focused on the American Indian and Alaskan Native youth populations; the Office of the Indian Education Program, which funds BIA-operated schools; and grant and contract Tribal schools, which provide students with education about drug and alcohol use. BIA also provides a juvenile delinquency prevention program in the Office of Law Enforcement and a child protection program and youth emergency shelters program in the Social Services Program.

Targeted drug and audience: BIA activities targeted drug and alcohol use. The targeted audience is school-age children.

Fiscal year 2000 funding: As of February 2001, OASAP had not completed its evaluation of BIA programs. According to an agency official, reporting on the exact amount of appropriated funding for each of these programs, or the extent to which funding may have addressed prevention of underage drinking, is difficult. OASAP identified about $1,800,000 in fiscal year 2000 appropriated federal funding that may have addressed, in part, prevention of underage drinking (i.e., addressed alcohol and drug use education for its youth population). Of this amount, the agency official estimated that $1,600,000 was spent in BIA-funded schools on prevention of alcohol and drug use education activities in the classrooms.

National Park Service

Description: The National Park Service has programs to help increase public education and awareness of the consequences of illicit drug, alcohol, and tobacco use by underage populations. For example, the National Park Service participates in DARE, a law enforcement officer-led series of classroom lessons that teach children from kindergarten through 12th grade to resist peer pressure and live productive drug- and violence-free lives.

Targeted drug and audience: The National Park Service's education programs target drug and alcohol use, among other things, by school-age children.

Fiscal year 2000 funding: A National Park Service official identified $343,000 in fiscal year 2000 appropriated federal funding that, in part, may have addressed prevention of underage drinking. However, the official could not tell us what portion of federal appropriated funding may have addressed prevention of underage drinking.

Department of Agriculture

Forest Service

Description: The U.S. Forest Service participates in the DARE Program in rural areas within and adjacent to National Forest System lands.

Targeted drug and audience: The DARE program may have addressed drug and alcohol use. The targeted audience is youth.

Fiscal year 2000: A Forest Service official identified $125,000 in fiscal year 2000 appropriated funding that, in part, may have addressed prevention of underage drinking. However, the official could not tell us what portion of appropriated federal funding may have addressed prevention of underage drinking.

Department of Housing and Urban Development (HUD)

Public and Indian Housing

Description: HUD administers the Drug Elimination Grants for Low-Income Housing. Program activities include, among other things, drug prevention, intervention, and treatment.

Targeted drug and audience: HUD program activities may have, in part, addressed prevention of underage drinking as part of drug prevention initiatives. The targeted audience included youth and the broader commuinity.

Fiscal year 2000 funding: According to a HUD official, this program and others within HUD may have addressed prevention of underage drinking through alcohol counseling or job counseling to youth. However, HUD records do not reflect the extent to which this may have occurred.

Appendix II: Information on Fiscal Year 2000 Appropriated Funding to Address Prevention of Underage Drinking

This appendix provides information on funding appropriated in fiscal year 2000 that agencies identified as addressing the prevention of underage drinking (i.e., by youth under the age of 21).[1] The fiscal year 2000 funding was categorized by drug focus and target audience. We categorized drug focus to include two options: (1) alcohol use or (2) alcohol and other drug use. With respect to target audience, we categorized the audience as either (1) youth or (2) youth and the broader community.[2]

Information on fiscal year 2000 funding for activities such as discretionary grants, contracts, interagency agreements, and cooperative agreements is presented in table 9; information on block, formula, and incentive grant programs is presented in table 10. Because block, formula, and incentive grant programs allow recipients substantial discretion in allocating funds and require limited federal administrative reporting, agency officials estimated the portion of these grants that addressed prevention of underage drinking. Therefore, the information is presented separately to distinguish between appropriated funding for particular program activities identified by agencies and estimated block, formula, and incentive grants.

Table 9 provides information on (1) funding for activities that were particular to addressing prevention of alcohol use and that targeted youth (i.e., that addressed prevention of underage drinking specifically); (2) funding for activities that were particular to addressing prevention of alcohol use and that targeted both youth and the broader community (i.e., that also addressed prevention of underage drinking specifically); and (3) funding for activities that addressed prevention of alcohol use and other drug use (i.e., that addressed, in part, prevention of underage drinking) and that targeted either youth or youth and the broader community.

[1]We defined prevention as initiatives such as those associated with information, education, research, and early intervention or treatment.

[2]The broader community includes parents, college students over age 21, teachers, and health care professionals.

Table 9: Fiscal Year 2000 Appropriated Federal Funding That Agencies Identified as Addressing Prevention of Underage Drinking

Agency	Appropriated funding for activities that addressed prevention of underage drinking by targeted drug and audience			
	Drug: Alcohol *Audience*: Youth	*Drug*: Alcohol *Audience*: Youth and the broader community	*Drug*: Alcohol and other drug use *Audience*: Youth or youth and the broader community	Total
Department of Health and Human Services				
Administration for Children and Families (ACF)	0	0	$15,000,000	**$15,000,000**
Substance Abuse and Mental Health Services Administration (SAMHSA)	$2,094,590	$1,601,624	$304,484,620	**$308,180,834**
Centers for Disease Control and Prevention (CDC)	$241,098	0	$419,599	**$660,697**
Indian Health Service (IHS)	0	0	$41,945,000	**$41,945,000**
National Institute on Alcohol Abuse and Alcoholism (NIAAA)	$19,200,270	$17,007,760	0	**36,208,030**
National Institute on Drug Abuse (NIDA)	0	0	$4,634,257	**$4,634,257**
Department of Justice				
Office of Juvenile Justice and Delinquency Prevention (OJJDP)	$27,797,467	0	$16,226,329	**$44,023,796**
Community Oriented Policing Services (COPS)	0	0	$180,000,000	**$180,000,000**
Department of Transportation				
National Highway Traffic Safety Administration (NHTSA)	$2,931,000	$272,000	0	**$3,203,000**
Department of Education				
Office of Elementary and Secondary Education (National Programs)	0	0	$160,750,000	**$160,750,000**
Department of Labor				
Employment and Training Administration (ETA)	0	0	$8,272,023	**$8,272,023**
Bureau of Labor Statistics (BLS)	0	0	$13,200,000	**$13,200,000**
Executive Office of the White House				
Office of National Drug Control Policy (ONDCP)	0	0	$219,944,000	**$219,944,000**
Department of Defense (DOD)				
National Guard	0	0	$25,500,000	**$25,500,000**
U.S. Marine Corps	0	0	$2,000,000	**$2,000,000**
Federal Corporation				
Corporation for National and Community Service (CNCS)	0	0	$9,000,000	**$9,000,000**
Department of the Treasury				
Bureau of Alcohol, Tobacco, and Firearms (ATF)	0	0	$16,000,000	**$16,000,000**
Department of the Interior				
Bureau of Indian Affairs (BIA)	0	0	$1,800,000	**$1,800,000**
National Park Service	0	0	$343,000	**$343,000**
Department of Agriculture				
U.S. Forest Service	0	0	$125,000	**$125,000**
Total	**$52,264,425**	**$18,881,384**	**$1,019,643,828**	**$1,090,789,637**

Source: GAO analysis of agency data.

Table 10 provides information on agency block, formula, and incentive grants that addressed, in part, prevention of underage drinking (i.e., that addressed prevention of youth drug and alcohol use). The agencies provided information on the total fiscal year 2000 appropriated federal funding for these grants and estimated the portion that addressed prevention of youth drug and alcohol use. As can be seen from the table, about one-third of the total block, formula, and incentive grant funding is estimated to address, in part, prevention of underage drinking.

Table 10: Estimated Portion of Fiscal Year 2000 Appropriated Federal Funding for Block, Formula, or Incentive Grants That Addressed Youth Drug and Alcohol Use

Federal agency	Block, formula, or incentive grant program	Total fiscal year 2000 appropriated funding	Estimated portion that addressed, in part, prevention of underage drinking
Department of Education			
Office of Elementary and Secondary Education	Safe and Drug-Free Schools and Community Act–State Grants Program	$439,250,000	$428,600,000
Department of Health and Human Services			
SAMHSA	Substance Abuse Prevention and Treatment Block Grant	$1,600,000,000	$320,000,000[a]
Department of Transportation			
NHTSA	State and Community Highway Safety Grant Program	$152,800,000	$15,600,000
	Alcohol Impaired Driving Countermeasures Grant Program	$36,000,000	$5,100,000
Total		**$2,228,050,000**	**$769,300,000**

[a]This amount represents the 20 percent minimum designated by statute for substance abuse prevention activities, including alcohol and drug abuse. (42 U.S.C. 300x-22(a), (b)(1). It includes not only youth services, but those services for all age groups

Source: Office of Elementary and Secondary Education, SAMHSA, and NHTSA.

Appendix III: Federal Agencies' Fiscal Year 2000 Program Activities Related to Underage Drinking That Included a Media Component

This appendix provides information on federal agency program activities that included a media component to publicize the problem of underage drinking. We defined media component as radio and television broadcasts. Agency officials provided information on particular program activities that had a media component and general information regarding the extent that media components were included in formula or block grants and in the Office of National Drug Control Policy's (ONDCP) National Youth Anti-Drug Media Campaign.

Three agencies identified particular program activities with a media component. As shown in table 11, for these three agencies, agency officials identified 7 program activities with a media component out of 122 program activities funded through discretionary grants, contracts, or interagency agreements.

Table 11: Agency Program Activities That Specifically Addressed Alcohol Use by Youth and Included a Media Component

Agency	Total number of program activities that addressed alcohol use by youth or targeted both youth and the broader community	Activities with a media component that targeted alcohol use by youth	Activities with a media component that targeted alcohol use by youth and for which the audience was both youth and the broader community	Agency fiscal year 2000 appropriated funding for program activities that included a media component
National Institute on Alcohol Abuse and Alcoholism (NIAAA)	90	2	0	$1,054,876
Substance Abuse and Mental Health Services Administration (SAMHSA)	15	0	3	$291,600
National Highway Traffic Safety Administration (NHTSA)	17	2	0	$123,000
Total	**122**	**4**	**3**	**$1,469,476**

Source: GAO analysis of agency data.

Tables 12 provides information on the media components for the program activities for the three agencies listed in table 11, including a description of the media aspects of the program activity and the fiscal year 2000 funding for the total program activity.

Table 12: Program Activities That Included Alcohol-Related Media Components Targeted to Youth

Program activity by agency	Description of media component	Fiscal year 2000 funding for the program activity
NIAAA		
Public Service Announcements	This project proposes to develop and distribute two 30-second television and two 30-second radio public service announcements. The targeted audience for these will be 11- to 13-year-olds. This activity has been funded by NIAAA and SAMHSA in the amounts of $350,000 and $95,000, respectively.	$445,000
Media Intervention to Prevent Youth Alcohol Use	This project includes, among other things, a mass media campaign that is to target young people to reduce their demand for alcohol through positive images of nondrinking lifestyles. The campaign messages will begin in the 4th and 5th grade at eight rural school districts in a particular state and are to continue over a 4-year period. Parents of these young people will also be targeted by a mass media campaign modeling supportive parental behaviors.	$609,876
SAMHSA		
Alcohol Tips for Teens	The tips are a series of 11 brochures. SAMHSA plans to issue a press release that is to be directed toward print and radio media. The Director for the Centers for Substance Abuse Prevention also plans to provide an editorial for the print media on the tips. The program targets 12- to 17-year-olds, schools, counselors, and healthcare professionals.	$40,600
Preventing Underage and Binge Drinking and Alcohol Problems Among Youth and College Students in El Paso and Brownsville, Texas	A subcontractor is scheduled, among other things, to conduct surveys at the Mexican border and to provide technical support in media advocacy of the survey findings, including a local seminar, two media advocacy seminars, and two police workshops. The goals of this project are to increase media recognition of the problem, decrease cross border high-risk activity, and decrease violence associated with binge drinking and alcohol use. The targeted audience is underage youth, especially college students.	$250,000
Addiction Technology Transfer Center	This program activity is for a national broadcast of a seminar entitled "Combating Underage Drinking." The seminar was advertised by flyers and on SAMHSA's Web site. The targeted audience is student service professionals, faculty, and students in postsecondary institutions in a particular state.	$1,000
NHTSA		
Black Entertainment Television Network (BET)	BET conducted a series of forums in selected locations that facilitated teen discussions focusing on the dangers of impaired driving, underage drinking, penalties for violators of zero tolerance laws, and general traffic facts. During the 1999 and 2000 prom and graduation season, BET's national youth talk show "Teen Summit" aired a segment on alcohol-free events for prom attendees and driving tips for teens who planned to drive to the prom. BET cable estimated that more than 6 million youth viewed the special prom and graduation episode.	$63,000
National Zero Tolerance Education	Project funded a 1-hour single site teleconference focusing on youth and law enforcement relationships as they relate to Zero Tolerance enforcement and promotion. The teleconference will be broadcast by satellite and will also be available on the Internet.	$60,000

Source: NIAAA, SAMHSA, and NHTSA

In addition to the particular program activities identified as having media components, agency officials who manage block or formula grant programs said that these programs may also include media components. However, they could not provide detailed information on state program activities under these grants because block and formula grant programs allow recipients substantial discretion to identify problems, design programs, and allocate funds. In addition, federal administrative reporting requirements for these types of grants are limited.

While federal program managers did not have specific information regarding the use of the block or formula grant funds, NHTSA and Office of Elementary and Secondary Education officials provided general information regarding the use of these funds for media campaigns. NHTSA officials said that the State and Community Highway Safety Grant Program permitted states to use funds to pay for media advertising as part of a highway safety program in fiscal year 2000, and that the Alcohol Impaired Driving Countermeasures Grant Program permits states to use funds to pay for the development of materials for free television or radio airings or print advertisements, but does not permit payment for media advertising.

According to an official at the Office of Elementary and Secondary Education, 838 projects—about 40 percent of the projects implemented—in the Safe and Drug-Free School and Communities Act State Grant Program included media activities. About one-third of the 23 projects funded in the National Program authorized in the same act included some type of media advertising component.

Besides the programs mentioned above, ONDCP officials said that some of the match funding from the National Youth Anti-Drug Media Campaign had been used to air anti-alcohol public service announcements to youth. The agency does not routinely track the extent to which this has occurred. However, ONDCP had a one-time value estimate of $25 million on the amount provided to nonprofit groups and government agencies for alcohol-related messages during a 30-month time period ending in December 2000. The targeted audience for these messages included both youth and the broader community.

APPENDIX C

THE NATIONAL ACADEMIES | Current Projects | Publications | Directories | Search | Site Map | Feedback

ABOUT THE NATIONAL ACADEMIES
EMPLOYMENT
FOR CONGRESS
FOR MEMBERS
GIVING TO THE NATIONAL ACADEMIES
PRESIDENTS' CORNER
SUBSCRIBE TO WHAT'S NEW!

View Current Projects
By Last Update
By Subject
By Project Title
By Unit
Provisional Committee Appointments Open for Formal Public Comment

View Completed Projects
By Subject
By Project Title
By Unit

SEARCH PROJECTS

The Current Projects System

- More Project Information and to provide FEEDBACK on the Project

Project Title: Developing a Strategy to Reduce and Prevent Underage Drinking

Project Identification Number: BCYF-I-02-01-A

Responsible Staff Officer: Susan Cummins

Major Unit:
Division of Behavioral and Social Sciences and Education
Institute of Medicine

Sub Unit:
Board on Children Youth and Families

Project Scope:
A. Statement of Task:
The Board on Children, Youth and Families of the National Research Council and the Institute of Medicine will form a new committee to review existing Federal, State and non-governmental programs, including media-based programs, designed to change the attitudes and health behaviors of youth. The review will include programs that focus directly on behavior change as well as those designed to change underage drinking behavior through reduction of adolescent access to alcohol (such as through increased excise taxation, aggressive enforcement of age and identification checks, and restriction of alcohol on college campuses). The committee shall produce a consensus panel report based on this review. The report will provide a cost-effective strategy to prevent and reduce underage drinking, including: an outline and implementation plan, message points that will be effective in changing the attitudes and health behaviors of youth concerning underage drinking, target audience identification, goals and objectives, and th e estimated costs of development and implementation.

The committee will meet several times during the course of this study. It will begin by developing a general approach to conducting this project, including the identification of criteria for selection of appropriate programs for review. The committee will plan and oversee a public forum to obtain input from all relevant stakeholders and will hear presentations from a variety of experts regarding various aspects of substance abuse prevention and youth behavior change. These presentations may be accompanied by additional independent analyses or commissioned work that addresses various components of the overall committee charge.

The committee will produce a consensus report that will be widely disseminated to interested stakeholders.

B. List of Sponsers
U.S. Department of Health and Human Services

C. Starting Date
The approximate starting date is 06/01/2002

D. Reports
A final Report will be issued at the end of the project in approximately 12 months

Project Duration: 12 months

THE NATIONAL ACADEMIES Current Projects Publications Directories Search Site Map Feedback The National Academies Current Projects Publications Directories Search Site Map Feedback

APPENDIX D

Beer Institute,
Wine and Spirits Wholesalers of America, Inc., WSWA,
National Beer Wholesalers Association, NBWA,
Alexandria, VA 22314,
May 20, 2002.

Mary Ellen O'Connell,
Study Director,
Board on Children, Youth and Family,
National Research Council /Institute of Medicine,
2001 Wisconsin Avenue, NW,
Harris-156 Washington, DC 20007.

Dear Ms. O'Connell: In response to the National Academy of Sciences (NAS) notice for public comment, we are writing to recommend several experts for consideration as participants in the NAS study addressing underage purchase and consumption of licensed beverages.

As representatives of various national associations that represent those in the licensed beverage industry, we believe that the below-mentioned experts, who are widely respected in their fields, possess the scientific and clinical background necessary to contribute to the task of analyzing existing underage prevention programs and aiding in the development of a cost-effective strategy to reduce underage abuses.

Pursuant to the Labor, Health and Human Services and Education Appropriations conference report for fiscal year 2002, Congress has requested that NAS and Institute of Medicine (IOM) "develop a cost-effective strategy for reducing and preventing underage drinking." As part of the study, Congress has called for a review of existing Federal, State and non-governmental programs.

In response to this congressional mandate, we believe that these experts can provide valuable assistance in the NAS effort to evaluate those programs sponsored and implemented by Federal and State governments as well as the vast range of privately implemented programs that have so successfully addressed the underage issue through a variety of approaches, including youth behavioral changes and modifications.

While we do not agree with all of their professional conclusions, given their established backgrounds, we believe each would make an excellent choice for the NAS/ IOM study panel. These individuals have previously participated in a broad range of studies sponsored by Federal agencies, have significant experience with youth culture, and possess a vast array of knowledge and information that would be of great benefit and value to the goal that Congress has targeted. Curriculum vitae information has been included for your review on each of the following recommendations:

Richard Jessor, Ph.D., Director of Institute of Behavioral Sciences, Department of Psychology, University of Colorado:

Dr. Jessor has devoted his professional career to the study and research of adolescent and youth development, including the social psychology of risk behavior and socializing problem behavior among youth. He has served for the past 10 years as the director of the MacArthur Foundation Research Network on Successful Adolescent Development Among Youth in High-Risk Settings. He has served on multiple advisory boards and prominent committees empanelled to research and review alcohol-related issues, including serving on numerous boards for the National Institute on

Alcohol Abuse and Alcoholism (NIAAA) as well as for the NAS. Additionally, he has received grant support from NIAAA, the National Institute of Drug Abuse (NIDA), National Institute of Mental Health and Robert Wood Johnson Foundation.

Robert J. Pandina, Ph.D., Director and Professor of Psychology, Center for Alcohol Studies, Rutgers University:

Dr. Pandina serves on the review and editorial board of the American Journal of Drug and Alcohol Abuse and the Journal of Studies on Alcohol. He serves as the Director of the Center's Health and Human Development Laboratory, which is conducting a longitudinal study of alcohol- and drug-using behavior, its etiology, and its consequences. He has received grants from NIAAA, NIDA, and the New Jersey State Department of Health. His research interests include psychopharmacology and neuropsychology; alcohol and drug dependence longitudinal studies; forensic psychology; and sports psychology. Dr. Pandina serves on several advisory and editorial boards and serves as a Scholar in Residence at the National Institute on Drug Abuse.

David Anderson, Ph.D., Associate Professor of Education, George Mason University:

Dr. Anderson is an associate professor and Director of the Center for the Advancement of Public Health at George Mason University. He serves as a project director and researcher on numerous national, State, and local projects and also teaches graduate and undergraduate courses on drug and alcohol issues. He has been involved in developing and implementing drug and alcohol prevention programs, with a targeted emphasis on schools and local communities. Anderson also co-authored two national surveys on college drug and alcohol prevention efforts and is co-director of the Promising Practices: Campus Alcohol Strategies project, which identifies exemplary alcohol abuse prevention strategies. With a shared interest in the success of the pending NAS study, we believe each of these experts to be worthy of serious consideration for inclusion on the study panel. Additionally, we look forward to a conclusion that reveals meaningful ways to further build upon the success of all existing programs, including those implemented within the licensed beverage industry, designed to prevent and reduce underage purchase and consumption. Thank you for your consideration.

Sincerely,
Jeff Becker,
President, The Beer Institute.

David K. Rehr,
President, National Beer Wholesalers of America.

Juanita Duggan, Executive Vice President I CEO,
Wine and Spirits Wholesalers of America.

APPENDIX E

Beer Institute,
Wine and Spirits Wholesalers of America, Inc., (WSWA),
National Beer Wholesalers Association, NBWA,
Alexandria, VA 22314,
August 12, 2002.
Mary Ellen O'Connell,
Study Director,
Board on Children, Youth, and Families,
National Research Council I Institute of Medicine,
500 5th Street, NW,
11th Floor, Washington, DC 20001.

Re: Project #BCYF-I-02-01-A, Developing a Strategy to Reduce and Prevent Underage Drinking

Dear Ms. O'Connell: In response to the National Academy of Sciences (NAS) July 23, 2002, posting of provisional committee nominees for the above-referenced study, we are writing to provide formal comments on the proposed committee as well as the process by which the nominees have been reviewed and selected by NAS.

As representatives of various national associations that represent those in the licensed beverage industry, we advocated for and support the House and Senate appropriators' decision to study existing Federal, State, and non-governmental programs designed to reduce and prevent underage drinking. We also support the decision to involve NAS in the process to review such programs, having previously recommended several experts for inclusion on the NAS advisory committee.

Through national, State and local efforts, our various, associations and their respective members actively participate in hundreds, if not thousands, of highly successful programs that effectively address underage concerns. As a result, the licensed beverage industry has gained a wealth of knowledge and information on underage issues, including many of the areas detailed in the relevant section of the fiscal year 2002 Labor, Health and Human Services, Education and related agencies conference report.

To assist the committee in this important endeavor and to help establish an environment that will contribute to the return of a study that is viewed as fair and credible, NAS is obligated by a general duty, National Research Council (NRC) guidelines, and Federal law to protect the overall process and ensure its objectivity, fairness and lack of bias.

A process that is contaminated or unfairly slanted will yield a study that is as well. Alternatively, a fair process that ensures a balanced committee, void of biases and conflicts of interest, and one that adheres to proper procedure will assist in producing meaningful results. Without the former, NAS cannot ensure—to Congress or the public—the later. Of equal importance is the fact that a great deal of congressional and public attention will undoubtedly be paid to the results of this study, in turn, making strict adherence to and compliance with a process that assures fairness and balance all the more critical.

With a shared interest in the outcome of the study, we are writing to express several concerns that we believe could potentially interfere with the study's goals, as they were carefully contemplated and determined by

Congress, and which could ultimately weaken and undermine the credibility and value of the study at issue.

A. The Overall Composition of the Proposed Committee Lacks Fairness and Balance as Required by Section 15 of the Federal Advisory Committee Act

NAS has not met the requirements of the 1997 Amendments to the Federal Advisory Committee Act (FACA), which State that those with conflicts of interest are to be excluded and that committee panels must be fairly balanced in terms of the points of view represented and the functions to be performed.

Section 15 of FACA states:

> The Academy shall make its best efforts to ensure that (A) no individual appointed to serve on the committee has a conflict of interest that is relevant to the functions to. be performed, unless such conflict is promptly and publicly disclosed and the Academy determines that the conflict is unavoidable, (B) the committee membership is fairly balanced as determined by the Academy to be appropriate for the functions to be performed, and (C) the final report of the Academy will be the result of the Academy's independent judgment. The Academy shall require that individuals that the Academy appoints or intends to appoint to serve on the committee inform the Academy of the individual's conflicts of interest that are relevant to the functions to be performed.

When Congress clarified FACA's application to NAS, NAS readily agreed to a standard intended by all to protect the integrity of NAS research and study efforts, while at the same time ensuring fairness in the process, public access to information, review by a balanced and unbiased advisory committee, and avoidance of conflicts of interests.

The need for balance and avoidance of biases has been further reiterated in the NRC's "Conflicts of Interest Policy" and its "Updated Checklist for Responsible Staff Officers for Compliance with Section 15 of the Federal Advisory Committee Act," wherein NRC internal policy calls for an unbiased committee or, alternatively, the identification of a "balance of potentially biasing backgrounds or professional or organizational perspectives," when an unbiased panel is not selected. NRC procedures also state that "bias" can be determined by a candidate's expression of a particular point of view.[50]

Taken as a whole, the proposed committee does not represent a balance and is comprised of individuals who are biased on the issues. It is unfairly weighted and reflects an unequal distribution of professional backgrounds, points of view and professional affiliations. More importantly, it is dominated by individuals who have taken positions publicly on most every aspect regarding underage drinking, and who share a single view toward the licensed beverage industry, making it difficult for NAS to renounce the claim that the majority of the committee has already taken sides and is predisposed in its joint opinion of the issues that it will be reviewing.

With this in mind, we do not believe that the committee under consideration can or will maintain an objective view on the issues at hand. With the majority of the panelists of a predisposed opinion, the integrity and credibility of the pending study is already called into question.

Having expressed concerns with the proposed committee and the ultimate reliability of the conclusions to be rendered, we would ask the NAS to release the names of the alternate candidates it has slated pursuant to NRC procedure and—practice. A public release of the alternative list would allow for a meaningful review of all names being considered and would provide the public with an opportunity to assist in assuring that a fair and balanced committee is selected.

---

[50] All references to the National Research Council's (NRC) Updated Checklist for Responsible Staff Officers for Compliance with Section 15 of the Federal Advisory Committee Act (FACA) are derived or extracted from the August 10, 1998, update of the policy original drafted and released on December 17, 1997. References to its Conflicts of Interest Policy are from NRC's 1992 publication. A request to the National Academy of Sciences (NAS) for the most recent publications has been made but not yet received.

B. Panel Recommendations Include Those with Stated Biases and Predetermined Positions on the Issues to Be Addressed by the Study

The 20-calendar day timeframe for interested parties to provide comment does not allow for a meaningful and fair review of the proposed committee. In the very short time we have had to review, research and comment on the panelists' backgrounds, we have already determined that at least five or more have made public statements or taken positions publicly on the issues they are to address. The positions of those proposed should be viewed as a strong indication of their prospective biases.

Specifically, positions have been taken by Marilyn Aguirre-Molina, Dr. Philip Cook, Dr. Joel Grube, Dr. Mark Moore, Dr. Denise Herd and others indicating their lack of objectivity on many of the issues surrounding the study and their biases favoring a predisposed and single position.

C. Conflicts of Interest Are to Be Avoided

The Section 15 FAA requirements state that the NAS shall require individuals to inform the Academies of any potential conflicts of interest. NRC policy on "Disclosure of Personal Involvements and Other Matters Potentially Affecting Committee Service" defines "conflict of interest" as "…any financial or other interest or affiliation which conflicts with the service of an individual because it could impair the individual's objectivity or could create an unfair competitive advantage for any person or organization…"

With the brief amount of biographical information that has been posted, it is virtually impossible for an interested party to determine if there is a potential or actual conflict of interest on the proposed committee. In order to raise a conflicts concern, sufficient details must be given. The public is handicapped in its desire to ensure that the committee is free of a conflict.

Additionally, while the actual NRC "Potential Sources of Bias and Conflicts of Interest" forms may be confidential, the fact that a proposed panelist has completed and returned the form should not be. To date, we have been unable to confirm or verify that the NAS has followed this process and that in fact, among those recommended to conduct the study, no conflicts of interest exist. Merely declaring that a policy exists is of little use without a means of determining and guaranteeing its implementation.

D. Inadequate Biographical Information Has Been Posted with Regard to the Provisional Committee Nominees

Section 15 of FACA requires the Academies to provide biographies of those slated to serve on the committee. The NRC has stated that the biographical postings shall include specific information about the backgrounds, qualifications; affiliations, and prior committee service of each proposed committee member. The NRC has also emphasized that responsible staff officers will review with the executive directors the potential sources of conflicts and biases that have been accumulated from various sources, including public feedback.

Again we would argue that without a more complete and meaningful release of information, the public is restricted in its desire to participate in the process and its right to access of information. The information posted and provided by the NRC is overly brief and insufficient. As has been revealed by our independent efforts alone, there is substantially more background information on the suggested panelists that is relevant to the study and should be posted and disclosed.

The clear intent of both Congress and the NRC with regard to the above-referenced requirement was to ensure that interested parties were provided with enough information to allow for a meaningful review of the nominees. Without adequate and detailed information, a review is essentially meaningless.

Interestingly, NRC allows for each nominee to "approve" the text of his biographical information before being posted. While we understand the nominee has a right to protect certain pieces of information and that the NAS has a legal obligation to assist in protecting the nominees' privacy concerns, the fact that a nominee may "approve" the information being released allows for mischief.

We ask that you post additional information on these individuals' backgrounds and their research in order that the public may participate in identifying potential sources of bias and possible conflicts of interest. Congress and Federal agencies cannot conceal information of this nature; therefore, the conclusions of a committee on which Congress is to rely should not be derived from a process that lacks fair and adequate disclosure of information.

Specifically, we are requesting that additional biographical information be posted that discloses all relevant conflicts or bias information, including the number of NAS committees each nominee has served on in the past, any previously stated positions or opinions on the issues and programs to be addressed by the study, any past or current relations the nominees have with NAS, the United States Department of Health and Human Services, or any interested party. We would also like clarification by NRC that either no conflicts of interest or biases exist or that the existence of such has been properly disclosed.

To disclose this information after the close of the 20-day formal comment period is of little or no use.

E. The Scope of the Project as Stated by NAS Does Not Comply with the Intent of Congress and Exceeds the Authority NAS Has Been Granted

The intended scope of the study as stated by NAS differs from the conference report language of the fiscal year 2002 Labor/Health and Human Services appropriations bill. The study's determinations are important to Congress and those engaged in the effort to prevent and reduce underage drinking; therefore, it is important to ensure that the committee refrains from deviating from the scope of Congress's intent.

The conference report language requests a study of an array of programs designed to prevent and reduce underage drinking, and enumerates a very specific list of inquiries to which Congress is seeking a reply. NRC policy states that the "project scope description should be… consistent with the terms of reference in a contract, grant, or cooperative agreement."

For NAS to go beyond the scope of the request set out in the conference report and delve into areas of legislative authority defies its own procedures and is overreaching and contradictory to congressional intent. Nowhere in the report language does Congress seek input from NAS or its advisory committee with regard to tax-related issues. Yet, the scope as stated by NAS suggests, with some emphasis, that the study will be reviewing excise tax measures.

NAS holds itself out as a "private, non-profit, self-perpetuating society of distinguished scholars engaged in scientific and engineering research, dedicated to the furtherance of science and technology and to their use for the general welfare." According to the NAS original charter, Congress signed NAS into being to "…report upon any subject of science or art."

This mandate does not extend to NAS legislative authority in any area, and certainly not in the area of recommending tax increases on the public, an area of sensitivity and one that is specifically reserved for Congress and its congressional committees. Any decision to implement or increase excise taxes, or any other tax, is totally outside the authority and jurisdiction of NAS, and we strongly object to the inclusion of any tax-related matters in this study.

We are also concerned that the stated scope does not provide much detail or information regarding the types of programs that will be studied. The conference report references non-governmental programs for review. We believe private sector programs can contribute a great deal to the value of the project. There are many highly successful and well-received programs that have been implemented by various local and community organizations, parent and civic associations, businesses, schools, non-profits, and the licensed beverage industry. We would urge that these programs also be reviewed and receive equal weight and consideration.

Sincerely,
Jeff Becker, President, Beer Institute. Juanita Duggan, Executive Vice President / CEO, Wine and Spirits Wholesales of America.

David K. Rehr,
President, National Beer Wholesalers Association.

REDACTED VERSION OF APPENDIX E

Beer Institute,
Wine and Spirits Wholesalers of America, Inc., WSWA,
National Beer Wholesalers Association, NBWA,
Alexandria, VA 22314,
August 12, 2002.

Mary Ellen O'Connell,
Study Director,
Board on Children, Youth and Families,
National Research Council /Institute of Medicine,
500 5th Street, NW, 11th Floor,
Washington, DC 20001.

Re: Project# BCYF-1-02-O1-A, Developing a Strategy to Reduce and Prevent Underage Drinking

Dear Ms. O' Connell:

REDACTED
REDACTED
REDACTED

REDACTED
REDACTED
REDACTED
REDACTED

E. The Scope of the Project as Stated by NAS Does Not Comply with the Intent of Congress and Exceeds the Authority Nas Has Been Granted

The intended scope of the study as stated by NAS differs from the conference report language of the fiscal year 2002 Labor/Health and Human Services appropriations bill. The study's determinations are important to Congress and those engaged in the effort to prevent and reduce underage drinking; therefore, it is important to ensure that the committee refrains from deviating from the scope of Congress's intent.

The conference report language requests a study of an array of programs designed to prevent and reduce underage drinking, and enumerates a very specific list of inquires to which Congress is seeking a reply. NRC policy states that the "project scope description should be consistent with the terms of reference in a contract, grant, or cooperative agreement."

For NAS to go beyond the scope of the request set out in the conference report and delve into areas of legislative authority defies its own procedures and is overreaching and contradictory to congressional intent. Nowhere in the report language does Congress seek input from NAS or its advisory committee with regard to tax-related issues. Yet, the scope as stated by NAS suggests, with some emphasis, that the study will be reviewing excise tax measures.

NAS holds itself out as a "private, non-profit, self-perpetuating society of distinguished scholars engaged in scientific and engineering research, dedicated to the furtherance of science and technology and to their use for the general welfare." According to the NAS original charter, Congress signed NAS into being to "…report upon any subject of science or art."

This mandate does not extend to NAS legislative authority in any area, and certainly not in the area of recommending tax increases on the public, an area of sensitivity and one that is specifically reserved for Congress and its congressional committees. Any decision to implement or increase excise taxes, or any other tax, is totally outside the authority and jurisdiction of NAS, and we strongly object to the inclusion of any tax-related matters in this study.

We are also concerned that the stated scope does not provide much detail or information regarding the types of programs that will be studied. The conference report references, non-governmental programs for review. We believe private sector programs can contribute a great deal to the value of the project. There are many highly successful and well-received programs that have been implemented by various local and community organizations, parent and civic associations, businesses, schools, non-profits, and the licensed beverage industry. We would urge that these programs also be reviewed and receive equal weight and consideration.

Sincerely,
Jeff Becker, President, Beer Institute.

Juanita Duggan, Executive Vice President I CEO,
Wine and Spirits Wholesalers of America.

David K. Rehr,
President, National Beer Wholesalers Association.
REDACTED

APPENDIX F

National Beer Wholesalers Association, NBWA,
Alexandria, VA 22314-2044,
June 18, 2003.

Dr. Bruce Alberts,
President,
National Academy of Sciences,
500 Fifth Street, NW,
Washington, DC 20001.

Dear Dr. Alberts: As you know, the National Beer Wholesalers Association (NBWA) strongly advocated that Congress include language in the 2002 Labor-HHS Appropriations Conference Report calling for a comprehensive study of existing underage drinking programs. As a result of that legislation, the National Academy of Sciences (NAS) received $500,000 to conduct a thorough review of existing Federal, State and non-governmental programs to combat underage drinking.

As taxpayers and vigorous opponents of the illegal underage purchase and consumption of licensed beverages, NBWA members are concerned by the steps taken by the panel to date that focus on issues beyond Congress's original intent, and which reflect the anti-industry bias of panelists, agendas and witnesses. This is not the first time we have raised these concerns.

In a letter addressed to Study Director Mary Ellen O'Connell dated August 12, 2002, NBWA expressed concerns that NAS did not meet the requirements of the 1997 Amendments to the Federal Advisory Committee Act (FACA). Those requirements state that individuals with conflicts of interest are to be excluded from committee panels, and that those panels be fairly balanced in terms of the points of view represented and the functions to be performed.

Oddly enough, the contents of the copy of this letter that exists in the NAS public file have been redacted, barring the public and media from its review. We find this highly unusual and request an explanation as to why it was done.

NBWA continues to be concerned about the lack of objectivity of the panel as the study moves forward. As a whole, the committee is not fairly balanced, being comprised of several individuals who must be presumed to be biased based on public positions that have revealed their preconceived opinions regarding many of the issues involved.

Several members of Congress, NBWA and industry allied groups made independent recommendations of various, well-respected experts for inclusion on the panel. However, NAS ignored those suggestions and selected a panel of individuals who do not represent diverse views or opinions on the issues they are tasked with reviewing.

As mentioned before, the scope of the study as stated by NAS differs from the intent of Congress as stated in the conference report language. Specifically, the conference report does not seek input from NAS or its advisory committee with regard to tax-related issues. Excise taxes are totally outside the authority and jurisdiction of NAS.

Additionally, the committee appears to have paid little attention to developing real solutions, such as increasing involvement by parents, peers, teachers and community leaders, enforcing existing laws, influencing the personal choices of minors and weighing the value of successful licensed beverage industry responsibility programs.

We are especially disappointed in the lack of consideration given to already established industry responsibility programs during the study process. The beer industry actively promotes responsible consumption of its products and has made a significant contribution to addressing underage issues. A sample of the vast array of programs include point-of-sale ID programs, public service announcements, retailer and server education and educational materials to help parents talk to their children about illegal underage drinking. Information on more than 125 beer industry programs was provided to the committee for review during the study process.

The beer industry's responsibility efforts, along with those of parents, teachers, community leaders and other organizations, have led to real progress in the fight against underage drinking. Research sponsored by the University of Michigan conducted over the past two decades clearly demonstrates that drinking among our nation's youth has significantly declined. The work of the industry should be recognized by the committee and its multitude of programs should be thoroughly reviewed.

The directive of Congress has thus far been ignored in the committee process. In fact, nearly 140 members of Congress recently wrote to NAS requesting that the study focus on the original intent—existing Federal, State and non-governmental programs—and not on untested theories and policy changes intended to adversely affect the licensed beverage industry. NBWA supports comprehensive solutions to the problems associated with the illegal underage purchase and consumption of licensed beverages.

What was meant to be a thorough review of programs to fight underage drinking has gone astray. The NAS study is apparently focused largely on increasing beer excise taxes, developing a taxpayer-funded anti-beer media campaign and imposing unnecessary advertising limits and restrictions.

All in all, the committee is failing to provide an adequate effort to yield a credible, reliable study that Congress may rely on for unprejudiced results. Over the years, the beer industry has made an enormous contribution to reducing illegal underage purchase and consumption, and I again urge the committee to review private-sector programs and give them equal weight and consideration.

Sincerely, David K. Rehr, Ph.D., President.

APPENDIX G

National Academy of Sciences,
The National Academies,
Washington, DC 20418,
August 13, 2003.
David K. Rehr,
President, National Beer Wholesalers Association,
1101 King Street,
Suite 600,
Alexandria, VA 22314-2944.

Dear Dr. Rehr: I write in response to your June 18, 2003 letter regarding the National Academies study on Developing a Strategy to Reduce and Prevent Underage Drinking. Thank you for your continued interest in this important project.

In accordance with Section 15 of the Federal Advisory Committee Act, the National Academies, through our Public Access Records Office, makes available to the public written information presented to the study committee by individuals who are not officials, agents, or employees of the Academies. The extensive programmatic and research information that you and other organizations and individuals have provided to the committee is included in the project's public access file and has been carefully considered by the committee. The National Academies' leadership carefully considers information provided by the public related to the composition of the committee—including particularly suggestions of individuals as prospective nominees to the committee, or comments about the credentials of specific members who have been provisionally appointed to the committee—but this information is not included in the public access file. This type of information is relevant to our institutional management of the study, but is not germane to deliberations of the study committee. The contents of your August 12, 2002 to Mary Ellen O'Connell that were redacted fit into this latter—category as they were specific to National Academies' procedures and specific committee members.

We of course will ensure that the report of the study addresses the questions posed by Congress, and that it reflects the relevant scientific literature. As is the case with all studies conducted at the National Academies, we have tapped the expertise in several of our boards such as the Board on Children, Youth and Families, and have received input from members of the Institute of Medicine, the National Academy of Sciences, and the National Research Council's Governing Board among others. These extensive consultations enable us to provide an objective and independent response to the Congressional request. The statement of task for the committee directs it to equally consider the full range of approaches to reducing underage drinking. During the course of the study, the committee has taken into account, in the context of its charge, the range of input received in the form of commissioned papers, written and verbal testimony, correspondence, and informational materials provided by multiple interested parties, such as your organization.

As you know, the committee's draft report is subjected to a rigorous external review. As a final check on the quality and objectivity of the study, the Academies appoint additional independent experts with a range of views and perspectives to review and comment on the draft report prepared by the committee. The review process is structured to ensure that the report addresses the approved study charge and does not go beyond it; the findings are supported by the evidence and arguments presented; the exposition and organization are effective; and the report is impartial and objective. Once revisions in response to review are made by the committee to satisfy our rigorous review process, the report is transmitted to the sponsoring agency and released to the public. Names and affiliations of reviewers are made public when the report is released.

The review of the committee's draft report is underway, so it would be inappropriate to respond to the views you share regarding the focus of the report, or what is or is not included in it. I look forward to providing you with the committee's report in the near future and to receiving your comments.

Sincerely, Bruce Alberts, President.

Alcohol and the Brain:
How Drinking in Youth Affects Thinking Skills

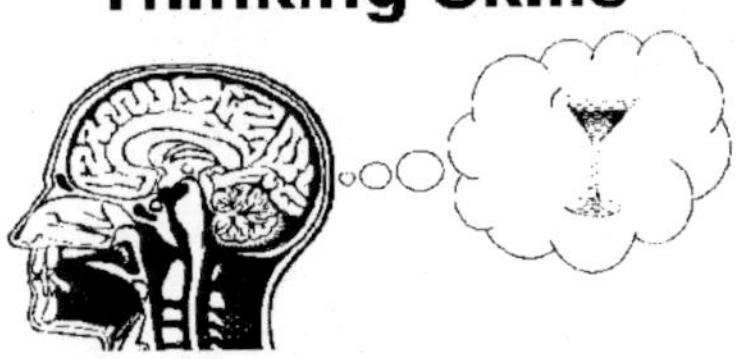

Alecia D. Schweinsburg, B.A.
University of California San Diego, Dept. of Psychology
Veteran's Medical Research Foundation

Alcohol and the Brain:

1. How big a problem is teenage drinking?
2. How are thinking and memory affected?
3. How is the brain affected?
4. How do alcohol ads affect teens?

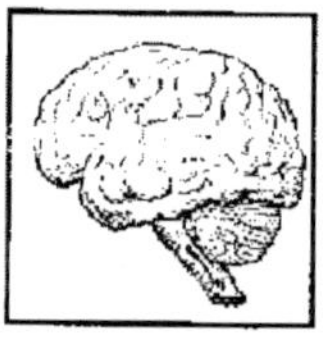

Teenage Drinking

	8th Grade	12th Grade
➢Ever drank	47%	78%
➢Ever been drunk	21%	62%
➢Got drunk last month	7%	30%
➢5+ drinks in a row, last 2 weeks	12%	29%

Source: Johnston et al. (2003). Monitoring the Future Study.

Alcohol Abuse

1 or more of these:

1. Don't meet your obligations
2. Use in hazardous situations (driving)
3. Legal problems
4. Use despite problems

Alcohol-Dependence

3 or more of these:

1. Tolerance

2. Withdrawal

3. Use larger amounts or for more time than intended

4. Can't cut down or control drinking

5. Much time spent getting, using, or recovering

6. Important activities given up or reduced

7. Use despite problems caused or made worse by use

Teen Drinking: Problems

- **Driving:**
  - *Ride with a drunk driver*
  - *Drive drunk*
  - *Arrests*
  - *Motor vehicle accidents*
- **Other problem behaviors:**
  - *Unwanted sex*
  - *Nicotine & other drug use*
- **Health consequences:**
  - *Accidents or injuries*
  - *Overdose*
- **Long-term problems:**
  - *Emotional problems*
  - ***Thinking***

Alcohol and the Brain:

☑ How big a problem is teenage drinking?

☐ **How are thinking and memory affected?**

☐ How is the brain affected?

☐ How do alcohol ads affect teens?

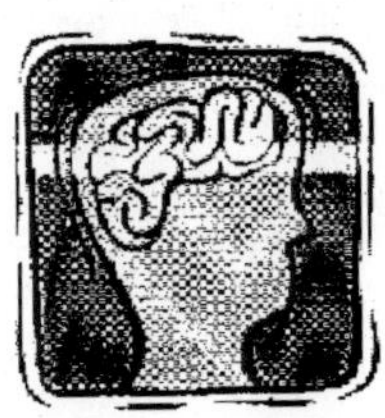

Drinking & Thinking

- Alcoholic <u>adults</u> show thinking & memory abnormalities
- Are these problems also seen in <u>teens</u>???

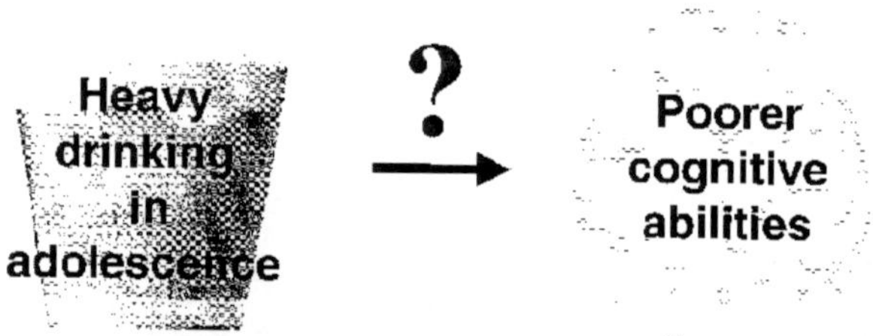

Teens in Recovery

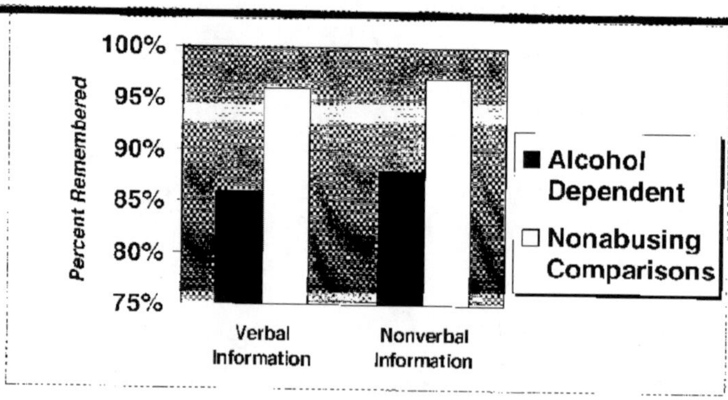

- *The difference between an "A" and a "B"*

Source: Brown, Tapert, Delis & Granholm (2000). <u>Alcohol: Clin & Exp Res</u>.

4 Years After Treatment

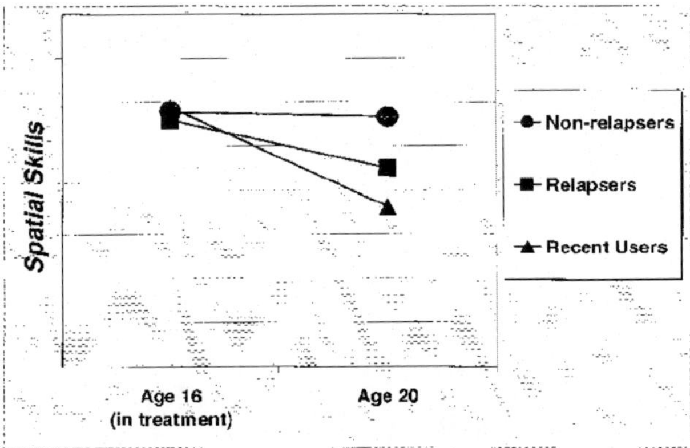

Source: Tapert & Brown (1999). J Int Neuropsych Soc.

Withdrawal Effects

- **Cognitive risk: hangover or withdrawal effects:**
  - *Feeling nauseous or throwing up*
  - *Depressed or irritable*
  - *Feeling dizzy or faint when you stand or sit up*
  - *Shaking of the hands or eyelids*
  - *Aching muscles*
  - *Heart racing*

Gender Differences

- **Females:**
  - *Thinking and memory more affected*
  - *Withdrawal effects implicated*
- **Males:**
  - *Learning new information more affected*
  - *Marijuana use implicated*

Implications

- **Altered brain development**
- **Limited opportunities**
- **More likely to have alcohol problems as adult**

Summary: Drinking & Thinking

1. Alcohol use disordered teens have a cognitive disadvantage
   - ***Memory, spatial skills, attention***
2. Abilities decline with continued drinking
3. Hangover or withdrawal effects
4. Risk for girls
5. Marijuana use
6. Can't say alcohol *caused* problems

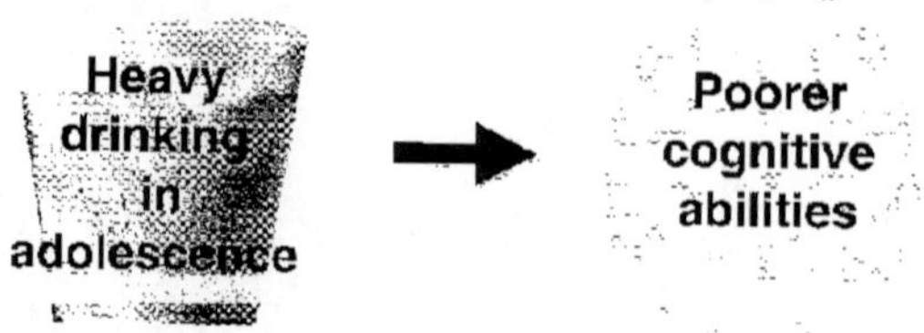

Alcohol and the Brain:

☑ How big a problem is teenage drinking?

☑ How are thinking and memory affected?

☐ **How is the brain affected?**

☐ How do alcohol ads affect teens?

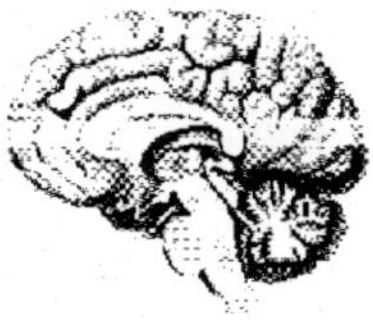

Brain Structure

- **Magnetic Resonance Imaging (MRI)**
  - *Safe for use with children*
  - *Shows small brain parts*

Alcohol & Brain Structure

Non-drinking Youth *Alcohol Use Disordered Youth*

Source: De Bellis et al. (2000). Am J Psychiatry.

Thinking & the Brain

- **Functional magnetic resonance imaging (fMRI)**
  - *Safe for use with children*
  - *Measures brain activity*

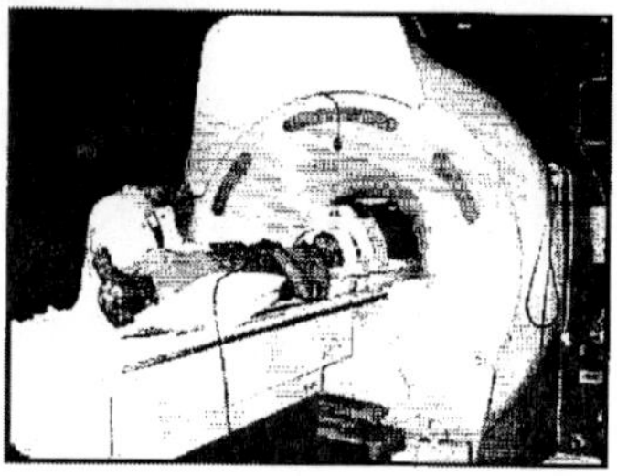

Thinking & the Brain

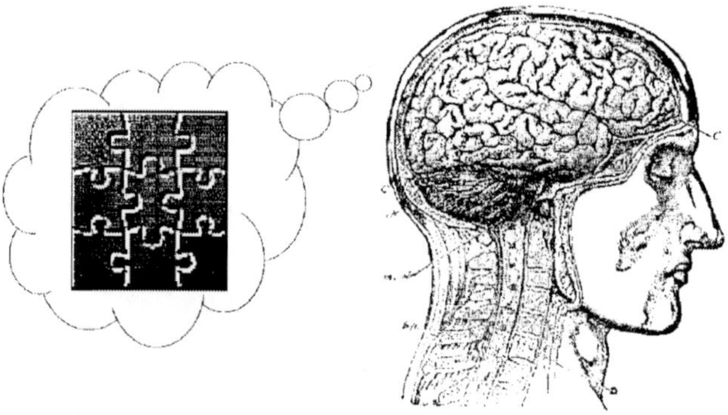

Brain Activation in Teenagers

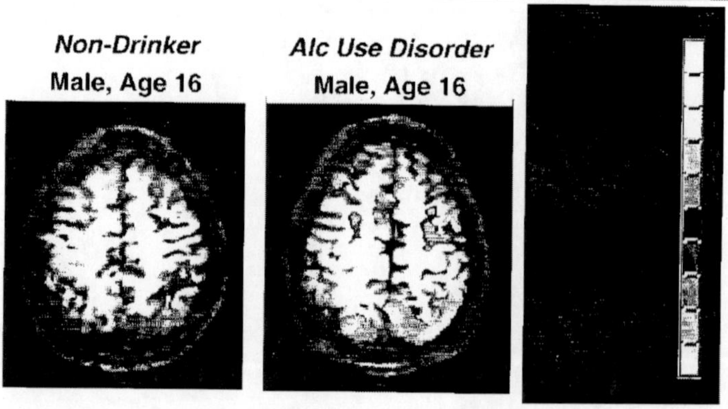

Brain Activation in Young Women

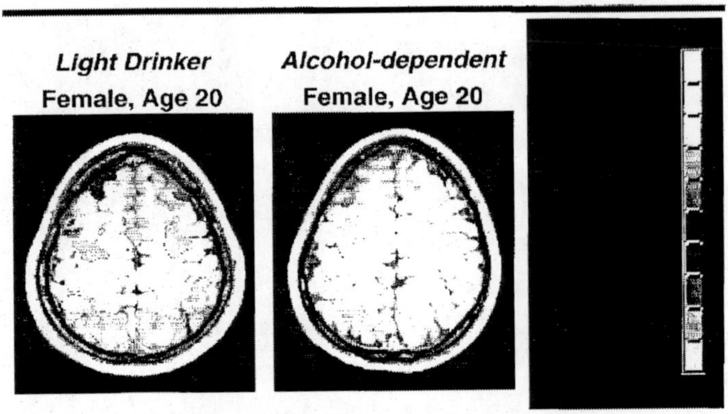

Source: Tapert et al. (2001). Alcohol: Clin & Exp Res.

Withdrawal Effects

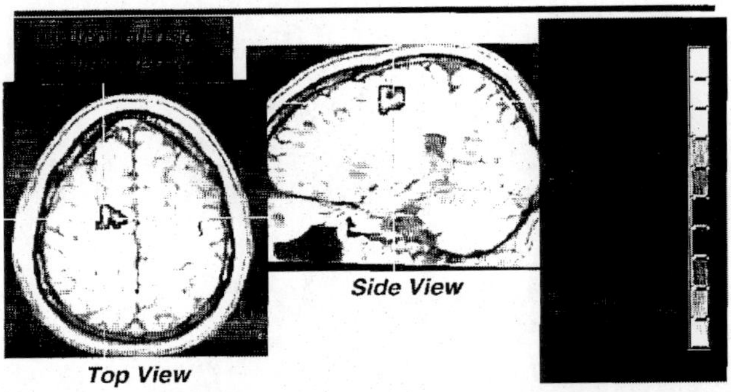

Gender Differences

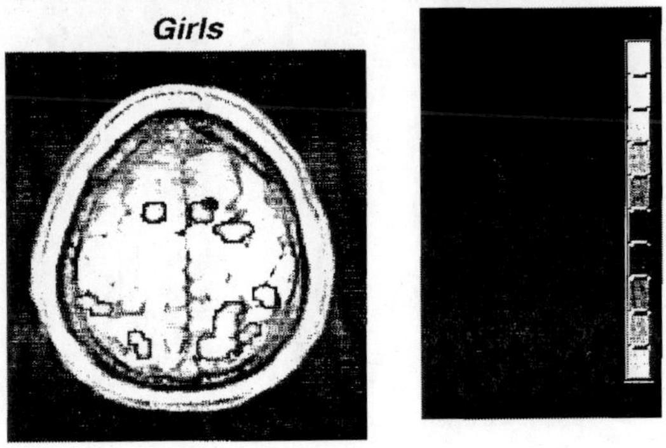

Gender Differences

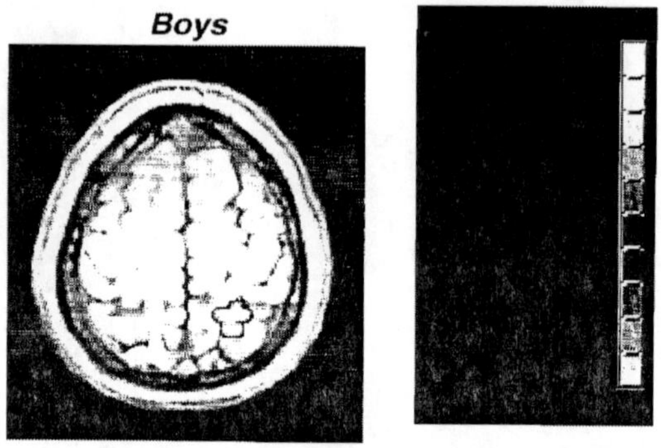

Marijuana Use

- 49% 12th graders have tried marijuana
- 6% 12th graders use marijuana daily
- 58% teenage drinkers also use marijuana

Sources: Johnston et al. (2003); Martin et al., 1996.

Marijuana & Alcohol

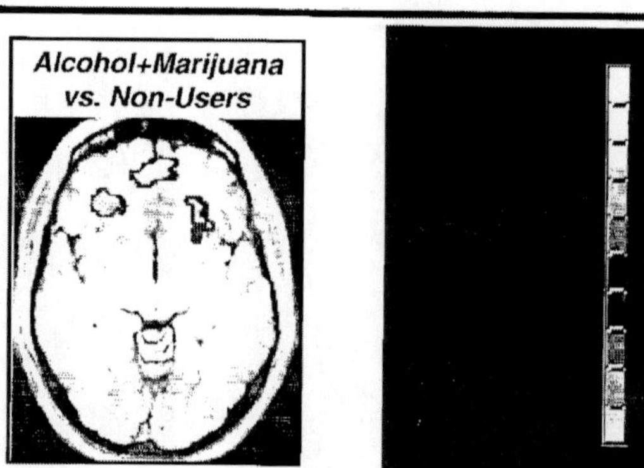

Marijuana & Alcohol

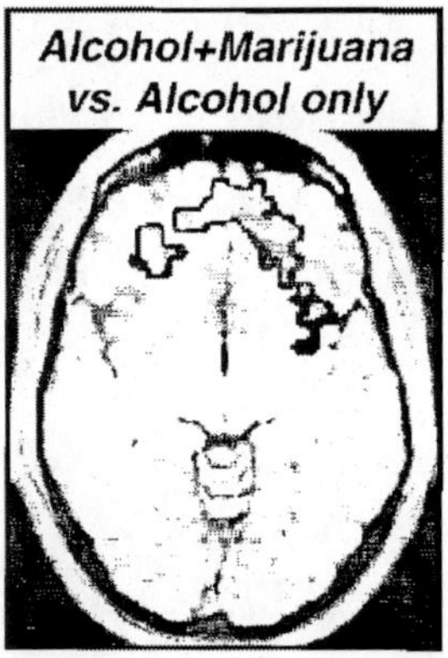

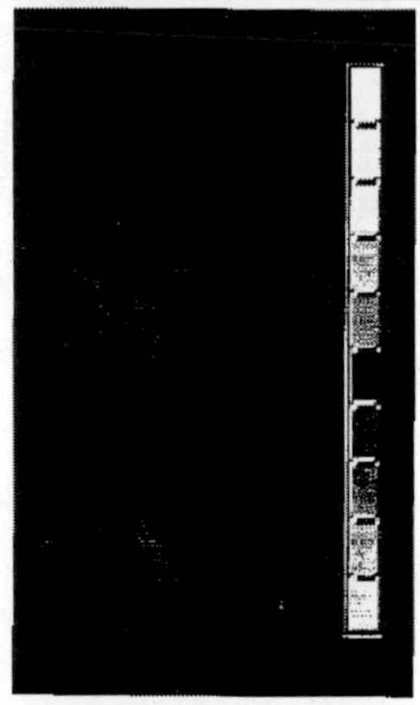

Summary: What About the Brain?

1. Smaller brain parts
2. Disrupted brain activity
3. Decline with continued heavy drinking
4. Risk for females
5. Marijuana use
6. Most alc use disordered youth do <u>not</u> have severe brain damage: *potential for recovery*
7. Can't say alcohol *caused* differences

What We Need to Learn

- More studies are needed:
  - *Larger studies*
  - *Healthy teens*
  - *Non-drinking at-risk teens*
  - *Teens who continue drinking*
  - *Recovery*

What Can We Do About This?

- Inform teens and parents about these effects
- Consider mild thinking & memory problems when working with heavy-drinking teens
- Encourage non-alcoholic social activities

Alcohol and the Brain:

☑ How big a problem is teenage drinking?

☑ How are thinking and memory affected?

☑ How is the brain affected?

☐ **How do alcohol ads affect teens?**

Alcohol Advertisements

How Alcohol Ads Affect Youth

Alcohol Advertisements

Brain Response to Alcohol Ads

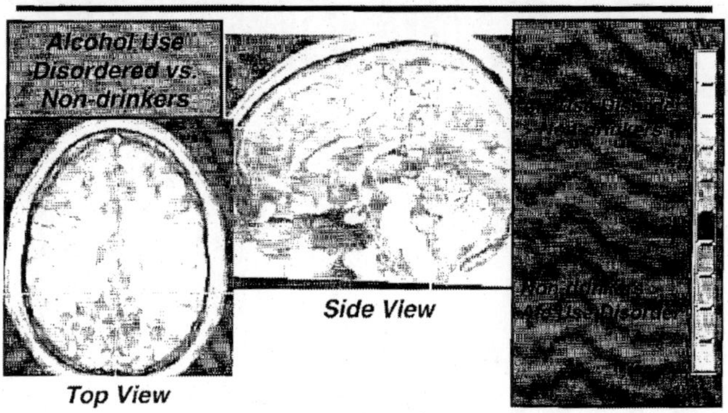

Source: Tapert et al. (2003). Arch Gen Psychiatry.

Implications

- **Alcohol ads elicit activity in brains of teens with alcohol use disorders**
  - *Exacerbate existing problems in drinkers*
- **Influence non-drinkers**
  - *Favorable alcohol beliefs*
  - *Plans to drink in future*
  - *Drinking during youth*

What Can Be Done?

- Change response to ads
- Modify beliefs
- Alcohol ads that don't appeal to youth
- Counter ads:

Alcohol & the Brain: Summary

- **Alcohol use prevalent in youths**
- **Alcohol use disorders affect memory, spatial skills, and attention**
- **Alcohol use disordered teens show altered brain activity to a cognitive task**
- **Alcohol advertisements elicit brain response in teens with alcohol use disorders**

Acknowledgements

- National Institute on Alcohol Abuse and Alcoholism (NIAAA)
  - *Supplemental grant to AA09033 (Sandra Brown)*
  - *R21 AA12519 and R01 AA13419 (Susan Tapert)*
- Susan Tapert, Sandra Brown
- Michael Baratta, Valerie Barlett, Gregory Brown, Lisa Caldwell, Erick Cheung, Alyssa Epstein, Lawrence Frank, Lauren Killeen, Sandra Kindermann, Carmen Pulido, Laura Santerre, Rebecca Theilmann

Thank you!

RESPONSE TO QUESTIONS OF SENATOR REED FROM RICHARD BONNIE

Question 1. Mr. Becker in his written testimony states that the NAS report "ignored the clear direction of Congress to evaluate existing Federal,

State and nongovernmental programs" focusing instead of costly, experimental programs.

As Chair of the NAS Committee that crafted this report, how do you respond to this claim?

Answer 1. The committee reviewed available evidence regarding the effectiveness of a wide variety of government and private programs for the purpose of developing a comprehensive national strategy to reduce underage drinking. We relied on the available scientific literature, commissioned papers, testimony and submissions from the public, and the committee's expertise in areas such as public policy, public health, youth development and substance abuse prevention. The committee's charge was to provide science-based recommendations about how best to reduce and prevent underage drinking, and we believe we fulfilled that charge.

Question 2. I was particularly struck by the number of recommendations in the NAS report geared toward limiting access to alcohol at the State and local level.

What can we do at the Federal level to encourage States and localities to adopt some of these thoughtful recommendations?

Answer 2. To help monitor and increase compliance with access restrictions, the committee recommends that a provision similar to the Synar Amendment's requirement for youth tobacco sales be established for alcohol sales. As a condition of receiving block grant funds, States could be required to achieve designated rates of retailer compliance with youth access prohibitions. Relevant block grants include the OJJDP block grant mentioned above as well as the prevention set-aside of the substance abuse prevention and treatment block grant in SAMHSA. Although not specifically discussed in the report, an incentive for States to increase compliance could also be established by providing bonus funding to States that achieve a particularly high level of compliance.

Both the Federal Government and States should improve coordination of the multiple agencies (e.g., substance abuse, education, transportation, justice) involved in addressing underage drinking. As part of establishing the recommended Federal interagency task force, the Federal Government might direct States to identify a lead State agency contact as a liaison to the Federal Government.

The committee also recommends that funding be provided directly to communities to enable them to develop and implement initiatives specifically aimed at reducing underage drinking. The committee believes that such funding could be modeled after the Drug Free Communities Act which provides funding to communities to develop drug use prevention efforts generally. If such a funding stream is established, communities should be required to implement evidence-based approaches, including limiting access to alcohol.

The Department of Justice, through the Office of Juvenile Justice and Delinquency Prevention (OJDDP), operates the largest Federal program, the Enforcing the Underage Drinking Laws program, specifically targeted at underage drinking. This program provides block grant resources to States and discretionary grants to States and communities. States and localities who receive these funds could be encouraged to adopt the committee's recommendations. The technical assistance center operated by this program is one potential source for such guidance.

Although not discussed in the report, a federally-funded multi-State demonstration effort might serve as a useful first step to mobilize State and local activity to reduce underage drinking.

Question 3. The report also references an initiative between the National Institute on Alcohol Abuse and Alcoholism (NIAAA) and a consortium of college Presidents that presented its findings on strategies to reduce binge drinking on college campuses. The President of the University of Rhode Island was one of the members of this task force.

What role does the NIAAA ("N-I-triple A") initiative play in terms of the comprehensive strategy being advocated in the NAS report?

Answer 3. NIAAA is the Federal agency with lead responsibility for research related to underage drinking. NIAAA should continue and expand its portfolio of research to enable continuous refinement of the national strategy proposed in the committee's report and to increase our knowledge about the effectiveness of particular approaches. For example, information about how the strategy might need to differ for various age groups, and how to reach groups that have not traditionally been reflected in research such as youth in the workplace, needs to be developed. NIAAA could also facilitate State and local action by funding research on State and local-level interventions focused on underage drinking.

Many of the recommendations specific to college campuses made in A Call to Action are similar to those recommended by the committee. Undoubtedly this is because the NIAAA effort involved a similar synthesis of scientific evidence. NIAAA's continued involvement in this initiative, particularly if it is coupled with ongoing research to allow further tailoring of approaches to specific types of campuses, should advance the approach outlined in the committee's report.

Response to Questions of Senator Reed from Jeff Becker

Question 1. One of the recommendations of the NAS report is for the alcohol industry to partner with public entities in the formation of an independent non-profit foundation with the sole mission of designing, implementing and evaluating evidence based programs for preventing underage drinking. Are you and the individual companies willing to discuss such a partnership with other potential partners?

Answer 1. The beer industry agrees with the NAS that partnerships with independent, non-profit and public entities that are leaders in the fight against underage drinking are an important component in the fight against underage drinking. That is why for decades, brewers have financially supported independent groups like BACCHUS/GAMMA, the TEAM Coalition, the National Conference of State Liquor Administrators, local chapters of Mothers Against Drunk Driving, several college and university social norms and anti-alcohol abuse programs, and many others who are experts in their respective fields. The Subcommittee has a comprehensive package of materials on our existing efforts, and we would be pleased to spend some time with members and/or staff to review these initiatives in greater detail.

This packet of material was also supplied to the NAS to use in fulfilling the Congressional request for an examination of existing programs to fight underage drinking. One of the shortcomings in the National Academies report was its failure to evaluate these programs. We respectfully refer the Subcommittee to three recent Federal surveys and reports that do include inventories of existing programs sponsored by brewers, many of which have been independently evaluated. One of the most comprehensive surveys was performed for the Department of Justice Office of Juvenile Justice and Delinquency Prevention (OJJDP). A report that focused on college drinking was released in 2003 by the National Institute on Alcohol Abuse and Alcoholism and a third report and evaluation was released earlier this year by the Substance Abuse and Mental Health Services Administration. The same organization that performed the survey for the OJJDP actually delivered a commissioned paper to the National Academies panel and never mentioned the work that his organization performed with Federal funds.

Brewers have long come to the realization that we are far more effective in the fight against underage drinking when we are able to team with people and organizations that are open to our involvement and treat us as sincere partners in the process. Toward that end, Beer Institute members are not prepared to commit to funding or participating in a non-profit organization dedicated to the design, evaluation, and implementation of underage drinking programs. At this point in time, we do not even understand the expectations for such an organization or its mission and structure. Members of the brewing industry have ongoing and significant commitments to existing non-profit organizations whose missions include programs or research activities to address various aspects of underage drinking. Any significant new commitment would take resources away from those programs.

Please keep in mind that I represent the Beer Institute and its members. I do not speak on behalf of the entire "alcohol industry." In fact, the repeated characterizations of "the alcohol industry" as one unit demonstrates a lack of understanding that the "alcohol industry" is made up of independent businesses operating in a regulated, three-tier system that was designed by Congress and adopted by the States after the repeal of Prohibition to ensure accountability, integrity, and efficient tax administration. As mandated in Federal and State law, production, distribution, and retail sale of alcohol beverages are conducted by over 600,000 separate licensed entities operating throughout the United States. Within that universe, beer, wine, and hard liquor are regulated separately in view of the distinct differences among the products. We briefly referenced this point in our testimony, and we attempted to communicate information about the organization of the industry to the National Academies during the deliberations of the underage drinking panel.

Congress has certainly recognized the need for multiple approaches by authorizing several Federal agencies to address aspects of underage drinking. Those agencies in turn fund hundreds of grantees including research institutions and agencies of State and local government, non-profit community organizations and others. Federal agencies have funded or conducted basic behavioral and biomedical research, a variety of prevention initiatives, grants to State and local law enforcement, educational efforts designed for specific age groups, and drunk driving prevention programs. The work to be done is far beyond the reach of one non-profit group.

Question 2. Setting aside the issue of excise taxes, the NAS report made many other recommendations embracing approaches that the industry supports—such as focusing on parents and also increasing compliance with the underage drinking laws. What parts of the strategy do you agree with?

Answer 2. Without going through an exhaustive point by point review of the National Academies document, brewers and beer wholesalers are already heavily involved in nine of the ten strategy components in the National Academies report. If you consider the fact that brewers already pay billions of dollars in Federal and State excise taxes with virtually no compliance costs to government agencies, beer industry members are involved in all ten areas.

In the September 2003 Federal Trade Commission Report on Alcohol Marketing and Advertising, the Commission found that a focus on two key issues is needed to make further progress in the battle against illegal underage drinking: Educating adults who directly or indirectly supply youth with alcohol, and enforcing the laws against sales to underage people.

In many respects, the FTC's and the National Academies' findings were remarkably simple and poignant. Neither, however, surprised brewers who have devoted tremendous resources to developing programs for parents and educators to use in talking with kids about underage drinking, and developing programs in multiple languages for retailers on the front lines to help them spot fake identification and train them on tactics used by underage people to purchase alcohol. We wholeheartedly endorse and support efforts in these two areas.

RESPONSE TO QUESTIONS OF SENATOR REED FROM WENDY HAMILTON

Question 1. You point out in your written testimony that there have been dramatic declines in the number of drunk driving fatalities involving underage drinkers since the 1980's. However, over the past decade, we have made little progress in further reducing the number of these fatalities. Why has this stagnation occurred?

Answer 1. Our nation accepts underage drinking as a mere "rite of passage," so it is no surprise that underage drinking rates—and associated consequences such as youth alcohol-related traffic crashes—have not improved for the past decade. Progress to reduce youth alcohol use was made in the 1980's in large part due to the increase of the minimum drinking age (MDA) to 21. As the National Academy of Sciences reports:

Limiting youth access to alcohol has been shown to be effective in reducing underage drinking and drinking-related problems. Since 21 became the nationwide legal drinking age, there have been significant decreases in drinking, fatal traffic crashes, alcohol-related crashes, and arrests for "driving under the influence" (DUI) among young people.

Increasing the minimum drinking age to 21 has been one of the most effective public health policies in history, resulting in a significant decrease in fatal traffic crashes, DWI arrests, and self-reported drinking by young people. However, the law alone does not preclude youth from gaining access to alcohol. The National Academy of Sciences also reports:

Given the widespread availability and easy access by underage drinkers, minimum drinking age laws must be enforced more effectively, along with social sanctions. The effectiveness of underage drinking laws could be enhanced through such approaches as compliance checks, server training, zero tolerance laws, and graduated driver licensing laws.

While the effectiveness of the 21 MDA law is undeniable, there is much more that the nation must do to reduce and prevent underage drinking. General deterrence through sanctions, improved enforcement, and public awareness of enforcement is needed in order to effectively implement restrictions on youth alcohol use. It is critical that funding be made available to enforce existing laws and to implement scientifically-proven community prevention programs.

Enforcement of State and local laws has proven to be a highly effective tool in underage drinking prevention. Tougher enforcement of laws aimed at reducing underage drinking is greatly needed, and Congress can provide the impetus for action by enacting a law based on NAS Recommendation 9-3:

> 9-3: The Federal Government should require States to achieve designated rates of retailer compliance with youth access prohibitions as a condition of receiving block grant funding, similar to the Synar Amendment's requirements for youth tobacco sales.

The nation also needs to execute a coordinated effort at the national, State and local level to combat this public health problem. MADD urges Congress to implement NAS Recommendations 12-1 through 12-6, which demonstrate a clear need for better "Government Assistance and Coordination" at the national level in order to reduce underage drinking:

> 12-1: A Federal interagency coordinating committee on prevention of underage drinking should be established, chaired by the secretary of the U.S. Department of Health and Human Services.
>
> 12-2: A National Training and Research Center on Underage Drinking should be established in the U.S. Department of Health and Human Services. This body would provide technical assistance, training, and evaluation support and would monitor progress in implementing national goals.
>
> 12-3: The secretary of the U.S. Department of Health and Human Services should issue and annual report on underage drinking to Congress summarizing all Federal agency activities, progress in reducing underage drinking, and key surveillance data.
>
> 12-4: Each State should designate a lead agency to coordinate and spearhead its activities and programs to reduce and prevent underage drinking.
>
> 12-5: The annual report of the secretary of the U.S. Department of Health and Human Services on underage drinking should include key indicators of underage drinking.
>
> 12-6: The Monitoring the Future Survey and the National Survey on Drug Use and Health should be revised to elicit more precise information on the quantity if alcohol consumed and to ascertain brand preferences of underage drinkers.

The decade-long plateau in underage drinking rates demands attention. The NAS report provides a science-based roadmap to reduce underage drinking, and MADD hopes to work with this Committee to implement this strategy.

Question 2. A central focus of the NAS report is the importance of an adult-oriented strategy to foster the development of a societal commitment to reduce underage drinking. Why do you think parents are accepting of underage drinking?

Answer. Unlike marijuana, ecstasy or cocaine, alcohol is a legal product for people 21 and older. MADD does not take issue with the responsible, legal use of alcohol. However, because alcohol is a legal product for the adult population, and is widely accepted as a "rite of passage," youth prevention is especially difficult. One never hears, "thank goodness my kid is just smoking weed" or "thank goodness my kid is only doing ecstasy;" but parents often do say "thank goodness my kid is only drinking alcohol." Adults and society at large incorrectly view youth alcohol use as a harmless part of growing up, even though alcohol kills 6.5 more youth than all other illicit drugs combined. Clearly there is a gaping hole in messages that go out to parents and communities (and in school curriculum) about the dangers of youth alcohol use.

Adults often facilitate youth access to alcohol—from the store clerk who doesn't check IDs, to the police officer who pours out the beer and send teens home without punishment for breaking the law, to adults who don't mind buying beer for a kid who slips him an extra $10.

In addition, the alcohol industry continues to be the sole continuous source of messages to the nation on alcohol use, and through its targeted advertising practices and slick marketing campaigns portrays alcohol use as fun, sexy and cool. Ads often air during programs that are overwhelmingly viewed by teens.

The need for a comprehensive public education campaign aimed at underage drinking prevention is undeniable as most parents and youth are unaware of the dangers associated with youth alcohol use. Many parents do not recognize the prevalence of, or the risks associated with, drinking for their own children. Parents have not been educated about alcohol's effects on the development of the adolescent brain, and often contribute (whether knowingly or not) to their underage children's drinking by giving kids access to alcohol, by not responding to children's drinking, and by not adequately monitoring their children's behavior. Kids receive mixed messages on a daily basis from their parents, other adults, the media and society at large.

MADD commends the NAS for calling for a national advertising campaign to prevent underage drinking and strongly supports NAS Recommendation 6-1:

6-1: The Federal Government should fund and actively support the development of a national media effort, as a major component of an adult-oriented campaign to reduce underage drinking.

The goals of the national media campaign, as presented by NAS, would be to instill a broad societal commitment to reduce underage drinking, to increase specific actions by adults that are meant to discourage underage drinking, and to decrease adult conduct that facilitates underage drinking.

Question 3. In your experience, how do parental attitudes towards alcohol compare to their attitudes toward tobacco use?

Answer 3. Underage drinking and smoking is illegal, and yet millions of kids continue to engage in these high-risk behaviors every day. While not involved in tobacco policy, we surmise that the "kids will be kids" attitude that parents take towards underage drinking is similar with underage tobacco use.

Youth tobacco use prevention efforts, including media campaigns designed to reduce youth smoking, have been shown to be effective. As more and more parents and kids learn about the dangers associated with smoking, societal attitudes have started to change. MADD will continue to push for the implementation of scientifically-based youth alcohol use prevention efforts, and the implementation of a nationally coordinated strategy—based on the NAS report—to prevent use alcohol use.

[Whereupon, at 11:55 a.m., the subcommittee was adjourned.]

INDEX

A

B

C

D

E

F

G

H

I

J

K

L

M

N

O

P

R

S

T

U

V

W

Y